Major Robert Farmar of Mobile

Major Robert Farmar
(Miniature in the Alabama Department of Archives and History.)

Major Robert Farmar of Mobile

Robert R. Rea

The University of Alabama Press
Tuscaloosa

The paper on which this book is printed meets the minimum requirements of American National Standard for Information Science-Permanence of Paper for Printed Library Materials, ANSI A39.48–1984.

Library of Congress Cataloging-in-Publication Data

Rea, Robert Right, 1922–
Major Robert Farmar of Mobile / Robert R. Rea.
p. cm.
Includes bibliographical references.
ISBN 0-8173-5242-2 (pbk. : alk. paper)
1. Farmar, Robert, 1717–1778. 2. British—Alabama—Mobile—Biography. 3. Soldiers—Alabama—Mobile—Biography. 4. Great Britain. Army—Biography. 5. Mobile (Ala.)—Biography. 6. West Florida—History. I. Title.
F334.M6R33 1990
976.1'2203'092—dc20
[B] 90-32562
CIP

British Library Cataloguing-in-Publication Data available

I suppose every man is shocked when he hears how frequently soldiers are wishing for war. The wish is not always sincere, the greater part are content with sleep and lace, and counterfeit an ardour which they do not feel; but those who desire it most, are neither prompted by malevolence or patriotism; they neither pant for laurels, nor delight in blood; but long to be delivered from the tyranny of idleness, and restored to the dignity of active human beings.

—*Samuel Johnson* (1758)

Contents

Illustrations

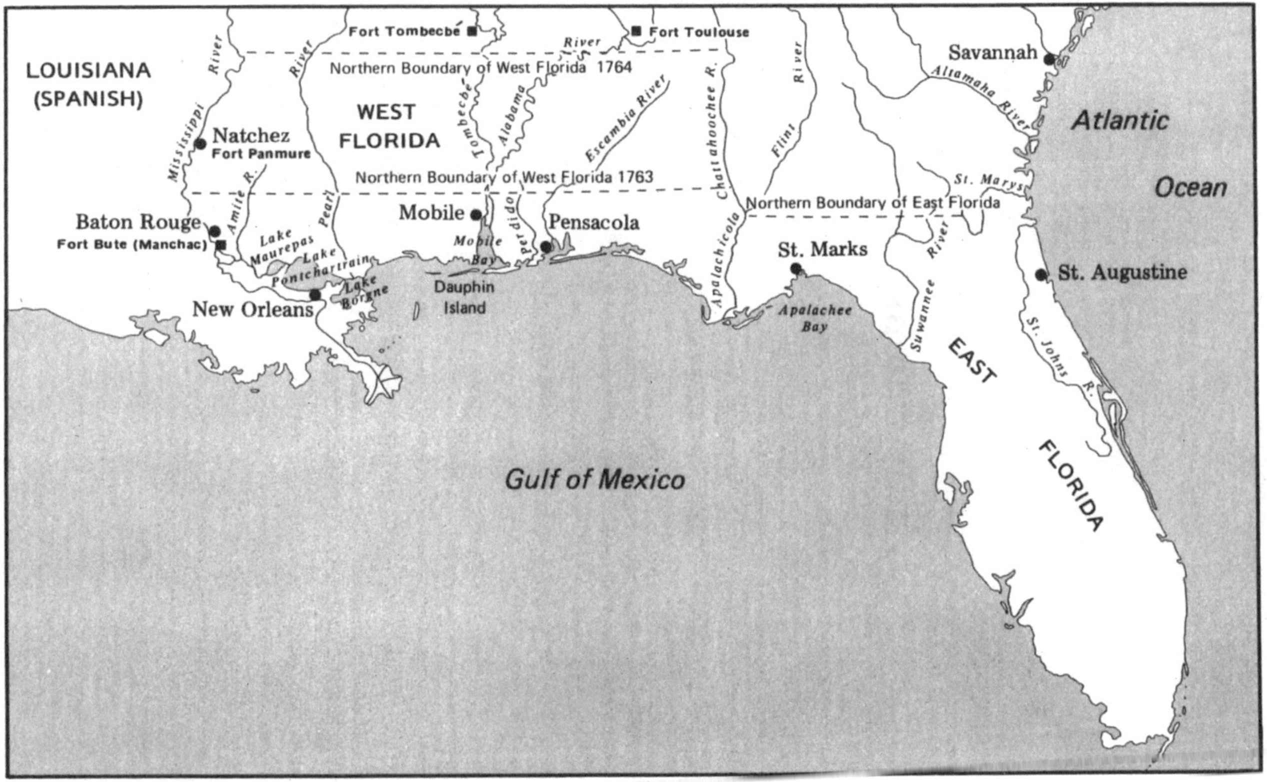

The British Floridas 1763–1783

Acknowledgments

As it has been many years since I initially encountered Major Robert Farmar at the William L. Clements Library, University of Michigan, my obligations for kindness, encouragement, and assistance are legion. Like all scholars who visited the Clements in those days, I remember most fondly its director, Howard Peckham, whom I first met in a fascinating course he taught at Indiana University when I was a graduate student; his successors have been no less hospitable and helpful, and my debt to them is manifest on virtually every page I have ever written about British West Florida.

At the Public Record Office (both at Chancery Lane and Kew) and at the National Army Museum (Chelsea), the kind attention of the staff still overshadows the cold efficiency of computers. British army officers in the regimental quarters at Carlisle Castle and Richmond Castle (Yorkshire) were most gracious toward an inquisitive Alabamian pursuing their few surviving records from the eighteenth century.

Colleagues in the History Department at Auburn University have long suffered my infatuation with British West Florida. I was introduced to Mobile by Malcolm McMillan, accompanied up the Tensaw by Tom Belser. With Robin Fabel I have delighted in and profited from those daily exchanges which link two friends with a common professional interest; that he wrote about George Johnstone and I about Robert Farmar is a bit ironic, but it makes the bond all the stronger.

Mrs. Davida Hastie of Stockton, Alabama, gave Major Farmar a place on earth when she arranged our cruise up the Tensaw River to Farmar's Bluff. I hope this book will justify her patience with me. I am similarly indebted to my son-in-law and grandson, Paul and Bob Machemer, who guided me to the Billopp mansion on Staten Island, where the ghosts of Farmars competed for attention with the skeletons of hermit crabs stranded on the beach.

I am personally obliged to remember two absent historian friends: Robert A. Lindemann, with whom I first visited the Clements Library, and Milo B. Howard, Jr., who introduced me to the Farmar materials in the Alabama State Archives long before he became director of the archives. I would also take this opportunity to express my appreciation to James A. Servies, formerly director of the John C. Pace Library, University of West Florida, for his invaluable support of West Florida studies over many years.

Auburn University has provided financial assistance and released time which was necessary for the completion of my research; I am also grateful for the support of the Auburn Humanities Fund.

Auburn University ROBERT R. REA

Major Robert Farmar of Mobile

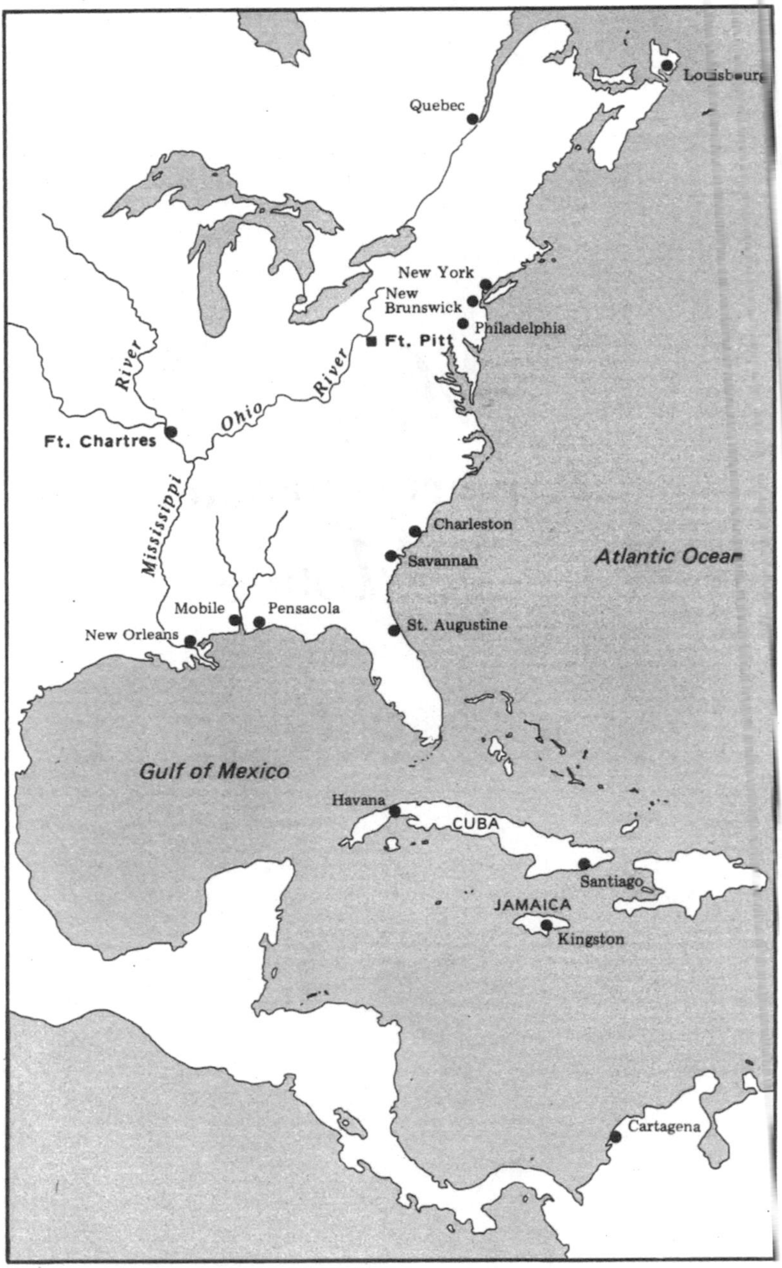

The American Theater of Operations

Introduction

Major Robert Farmar was the British army officer who accepted the transfer of sovereignty from the French at Mobile in 1763 and whose command occupied what is now known as Fort Condé. He subsequently led the successful British military expedition up the Mississippi River from New Orleans to Fort Chartres in the Illinois country and represented British authority in that region until he was relieved. Returned to the Gulf Coast, Farmar settled in the Mobile district and became a prominent figure in British West Florida. For this he has been vaguely—often inaccurately—remembered by historians of Mobile and the Gulf Coast. When the whole of his life and career is displayed, when it is placed in its proper context of the eighteenth-century British army, a far more striking figure emerges, one that links colonies old and new, America and the broader British empire of his time, provincial and imperial interests. It also unveils the man within the uniform.

The British soldier has not fared well in the historiography of colonial North America. His detractors have held the field ever since Braddock's humiliation in 1755. For much of the rest of what Americans prefer to call the French and Indian War, the British army won little luster and many sneers. Few would deny that the redcoat's competence in forest warfare against his native American opponents (particularly when they were led by gallant Frenchmen) left something to be desired.[1] But who ever asked how a regiment of mid-eighteenth-century colonials might have performed on the bloody fields of Fontenoy or Rocoux?

True enough, British generalship between Marlborough and Wellington was less than brilliant; the portly figure of the duke of Cumberland shrinks between such giants, and Cumberland was painfully (and ungraciously) conscious of his own technical inferiority and professional dependence upon that Anglicized Frenchman Lord Ligonier. The rest of the generals are all but—or better—forgotten save by specialists in British military history. Had Wolfe not died at the moment of glory, would even his name be much revered? Who now remembers the names of his brigadiers? Amherst had the good fortune to have his name adopted by a New England college, and a scattering of place-names still reflects the British presence in former colonies, but, typically, the name of General Thomas Gage raises only visions of defiant patriots manning the defenses on Bunker Hill. Best forget what followed. After all, we won the war.

From 1775 to 1783, Americans (at least some of them) knew the redcoat as the enemy, and the force of national mythology is not to be gainsaid. That epoch is now two centuries past, but only in recent years have historians dared to look behind the acrid smoke of Revolutionary battles to find the British soldier as he was.[2] To place him in that distant time and vanished place comes hard in a country now checkered by superhighways, in a society accustomed to instant and visual communication, fast food, and the ubiquitous shopping center. The term *wilderness* has little meaning for modern Americans, but it was there that British redcoats marched and fought in the eighteenth century.

We are also the happy victims of our Anglo-American past. Since the seventeenth century, most memorably since the days of Oliver Cromwell, the English-speaking peoples have had a low regard for the professional soldier. Armies were the tools of tyrants, a lesson Englishmen learned well. "No standing army" was a principle of Liberty as dear to eighteenth-century Englishmen as freedom of speech and press or religious toleration, and from England their love of Liberty crossed the Atlantic to these shores.

It is easy, even convenient, to forget that there was, toward the middle of the eighteenth century, a very real sense of imperial unity between men on both sides of the ocean. It was fostered in part by fear of other European nations and their representatives in North America. It was maintained by the recognition of mutual advantages, both narrowly political and broadly economic. It even had its religious aspects. Nor had it altogether disappeared when that devoted Anglo-American imperialist Benjamin Franklin regretfully took ship from England, turning his back upon the old country in order to help build a new.

The subtleties of language do not always help to bridge the gap of time and space. Truth and justice, like honor and courage, may be eternal, but they are not always the same from generation to generation. *Empire* was a term connoting pride and progress not so long ago; today it sounds as brass to sensitive ears. *Savage* was a word used to describe the American Indian by men who met him in the woods and found his practice of lifting scalps something less than a pardonable folk custom. But who is without his barbarisms? History requires that the values as well as the material circumstances of the past be recognized.

For these reasons, biography may be an historian's most useful tool, even though it be the old-fashioned sort that some would term "life and times." After all, lives are lived in particular times. When Robert Farmar lived, New Brunswick, New Jersey, was a raw new town that his father helped to build; when he died, not all of the few dozen decaying houses of Mobile, Alabama, were habitable. The wilderness separated these scenes of Farmar's life, and the fastest, safest route between them was by sea. It took six weeks for mail to reach New York from London, and twice as long again to find its way to the Gulf Coast. Suffering from heat and cold was the norm, therefore acceptable; hunger was a commonplace for many; sickness and disease were universal. Some people were "gentle," some were not. Social status was intimately related to the possession of land, and for younger sons who would not inherit, there were few options but the church, the law, the king's commission.

It was in this world that Robert Farmar lived and died. He was an American who wore the red coat proudly. His profession took him from New Jersey to the Caribbean, to Great Britain, Europe, Cuba, and back to America, to Mobile. There he settled, brought up a family, and died. Farmar's Bluff is still known to folk in Stockton, although the commemorative plaque has disappeared from Government Street, Mobile.[3] If Farmar is a part of local history, he was part of a world-encompassing imperial history. His life as a British army officer reflects the nature of his profession and its contributions to the making of America. That, too, deserves to be remembered.

I.

The Making of an American Family and a British Army Officer

To say that Robert Farmar was an American is to say much and little. The circumstance of birth in a small and distant colony was of no advantage in an army in which wealth and connection largely determined the course of an officer's career. An American colonial was not an Englishman; the most skilled and devoted service could not change the fact. At the outset as at the end of his long military experience, Farmar would encounter that bitter truth. It mattered not that he was a gentleman voluntarily donning a uniform, that his father was well-to-do and a distinguished figure in his own country, nor, at first, whether Robert performed with distinction. He was still an American, and to many officers of the British army that was a worse blot on the escutcheon than a bar sinister might have been. That Robert Farmar overcame this native disability says much for his grit and determination, a strength of character that might well be described as stubbornness. He had also some reason to take pride in his name and background, for the Farmars were an old and respectable family, and not merely in American terms; if he wished, he could claim—distantly—sufficiently noble connections to support his honor in any regimental mess.

The Farmar family traced its antecedents back to—indeed, beyond—the sixteenth-century Richard Fermor (d. 1552), a merchant of the staple of Calais, who married the daughter of a lord mayor of London and accumulated extensive landed properties, including Easton Neston, near Towcester, in Northamptonshire. Richard's devotion to the old faith cost him dearly when Henry VIII broke with Rome, but his son John was rewarded in the reign of Mary Tudor by knighthood, a seat in parliament, and appointment as sheriff of Northamptonshire. Sir John Fermor's son George (who evidently conformed to Anglicanism) went campaigning in the Low Countries, where he was knighted by Elizabeth's favorite, the earl of Leicester. His star rose higher in 1603, when he entertained the new king, James I, and his oldest son was in turn made a knight. Sir George's third boy, Robert, followed the path blazed by his father; he joined the army fighting in Ireland. He acquired some properties in Cork and Tipperary, but ultimately he was killed in action. From this Anglo-Irish soldier stemmed the line of Major Robert Farmar of Mobile.[1]

The seventeenth century was a troubled and dangerous time in both England and Ireland. Religious strife and civil war bloodied both islands. At mid-century the Fermors of Northamptonshire were staunch Cavaliers, and the Farmars of County Cork are said by the family chronicler to have been royalists; but modern scholarship identifies Major Jasper Farmar (c. 1623–85) as "a Cromwellian soldier." Jasper proudly bore the rank of major, but by what authority or in whose army is uncertain.[2] Suffice it to say that after the Restoration the Farmars retained the property of Garron Kenny Fange, near Youghall in County Cork, and Major Jasper Farmar was a member of the common council of the town. He also became the friend of young William Penn, sent over from England in 1669, to manage the estates of his father, Admiral Sir William Penn, at nearby Shanagarry.[3] On the death of the old admiral in 1671, William became a man of considerable property and possessed a claim against the crown that was finally met in 1681 by the grant of lands in North America, lands destined to become the colony of Pennsylvania.

Matters of religion were of the utmost importance in Stuart England and Ireland, and the affiliation of William Penn with the folk known as Friends or Quakers was of considerable importance in the history of England, America, and the Farmar family. Major Jasper Farmar and his descendants were members of the Church of England, perhaps inclined toward its puritanical side as were many contemporaries.

In addition to his local distinctions, Major Jasper Farmar presided at the head of a very numerous clan. He was a veritable patriarch whose eldest son, Jasper, had his own household. The Farmars appear to have been firmly seated in the Anglo-Irish establishment when William Penn visited his new American proprietary in 1682, yet Jasper Farmar, Jr., followed Penn to Philadelphia, clearly prepared to invest the family's fortunes in the New World. He was evidently pleased with what he saw. As early as September 1683, a property on the banks of the Schuylkill River was described as "Major Farmer's Land," and some of Farmar's servants were involved in marking its boundaries, although the five-thousand-acre estate that Major Farmar purchased was not surveyed and patented until 1684. The rapidity with which the property was made productive indicates that Jasper left it tenanted when he returned to

Ireland, early in 1684, to prepare the family for their transatlantic migration.[4]

William Penn also returned to England to recruit settlers for his "holy Experiment," and when apprised of the Farmars' plans, he wrote to his agents in Philadelphia, urging them to show the "utmost friendship and courtesy" to "Major Farmer, Jasper (whom you know) & their company; he has been an old acquaintance, & deserves in his affections to & preference of Pennsylvania, the kindness of it." Penn also directed that the Farmars were to be provided with any house or other convenience in the proprietor's disposition until they were established "in condition at Farmerstown."[5]

Major Jasper Farmar's will was dated September 25, 1685; the Farmar family arrived in Philadelphia on November 10, aboard the *Bristol Merchant*. The dates must span the westward voyage on which he had embarked with high hopes and with all his family about him. Aboard the ship were Farmar; his wife, Mary Batsford Farmar; and their children, Edward, Sarah, John, Robert, Katherine, Charles, and Edward Batsford. With the major's eldest son, Jasper, were his wife, Katherine, and their children, Thomas, Elizabeth, and Katherine. Several families of servants, nineteen or twenty persons in all, completed the party. Their voyage was no doubt arduous as well as tragically fatal: both Mary and Katherine Farmar were widows when they landed at Philadelphia.[6]

Although the ostensible head of the family was now ten-year-old Thomas, son of Jasper, Jr., it is likely that his uncle Edward directed the families' affairs at first—if indeed the widows Farmar required any guidance. Mary Farmar owned one of the largest and most valuable properties on the Schuylkill River, and Katherine held property in Philadelphia. As early as 1686 it was reported that the younger widow Farmar was building a brick house in town and that the elder "Madame Farmar," whose crops were ready for sale, was constructing a residence of limestone.[7] Their association with Penn served them well. Edward, who took up the family tract on his mother's death in November 1686, was a solid citizen who served as a justice of the peace for forty years (being willing to take and administer oaths), sat as a member of the general assembly for Philadelphia, and lived out his life as a respected landowner in Whitemarsh township.[8] His brother John secured appointment from Penn, in 1692, to search for and assay all sorts of minerals and mines in Pennsylvania.[9]

Fate soon thinned the family ranks, however. The death of the widowed Mary Farmar followed upon the deaths of her three youngest children, suggesting that one of the several communicable diseases so common to the age swept through "Farmerstown" in the fall of 1686. Katherine, the younger Farmar widow, soon took as her second husband Christopher Billop of

Bentley Manor, Staten Island, New York. The Billops were early and prominent settlers on the island, and Katherine must be considered fortunate in her marriage. She took her daughters with her to the big stone house on the southern tip of Staten Island, but it seems likely that young Thomas remained in Pennsylvania with his uncle Edward.

When he came of age, Thomas Farmar's rise to prominence in the affairs of Pennsylvania was surprisingly rapid but readily explained by his family's wealth and the proprietor's friendship. At the age of twenty-five, Thomas was high sheriff of Philadelphia County, and on June 20, 1700, he was also designated water bailiff by Penn. He was named sheriff again in 1701, when Penn issued a new charter for Philadelphia.[10] Such honors were not undeserved. The Farmars were trusty supporters of the proprietary interest, and Penn found Thomas, although a Church of England man, more reliable than many of his good Quaker associates.[11] Farmar did not remain long at his post, however. In August 1703, "having a design to transport himself to England," he sought permission to lay down his office, and a new sheriff was named "on the resignation of Thomas Farmer."[12]

Thomas's sojourn in England was brief. Within two years he had returned to America, to his late mother's home on Staten Island, having strengthened the Farmar-Billop connection by marriage to Anne, the daughter of Christopher Billop's first wife, and the marriage of his sister to Billop's heir and namesake.

It was but a short step, both geographically and politically, from Bentley Manor on Staten Island across the straits to Perth Amboy, New Jersey, and there Thomas Farmar established himself, becoming collector for the port and colonel of the Middlesex County militia. In 1707 he secured election to the New Jersey Assembly and began a long career in the complex and fiery politics of the colony. In 1708, Farmar supported Lewis Morris's attack upon Governor Cornbury, only to be disqualified for nonresidence the next year. Under Governor Robert Hunter, Farmar's career blossomed. Having worked diligently in the assembly in 1710 to secure the new governor his salary, Thomas Farmar became one of Hunter's close associates and was appointed a justice of the supreme court in 1711. In 1716 Farmar again came under attack in the assembly and was threatened with expulsion. Hunter defended his political ally, and when the governor's supporters regained control of the assembly, Farmar was found duly qualified to hold his seat. Hunter's successor, Governor William Burnet, named Thomas Farmar chief justice of the supreme court in 1727, and he served in that capacity until the arrival of a new governor in 1729. At that point Thomas Farmar sought a new base of operations.

In 1730 he was one of the signers of a petition for a charter for the town of

New Brunswick, a dozen miles up the Raritan River from Perth Amboy, where he already had business and property interests. The charter granted, Thomas Farmar became the first mayor of New Brunswick and held the office until 1747. Thomas's sons and sons-in-law were beneficiaries of his prominence and themselves played leading roles in the life of the town.

During those years his political importance in the colony was recognized by his appointment to the council by Governor William Cosby in 1735. He resigned in order to run for a seat in the assembly in 1738, when Lewis Morris returned to New Jersey as governor. Because of his most recent political affiliations, Thomas could not expect to enjoy the favor of the new governor, but he was himself a force to reckon with in the business of the colony, and there were many other Farmars.[13]

Thomas and Anne Farmar were the parents of twelve children, nine boys and then three girls. The eldest, Jasper, went to New York and married into the Miller family. He is said to have been an army officer; his son Jasper (1734–93) certainly was, becoming a captain in the 21st Regiment of Foot and, like his uncle Robert, serving in West Florida. The Millers would also become important in the life of Major Robert Farmar and of West Florida. Thomas's second son, Christopher, died young. The third, Thomas (1711–50), married his cousin Eugenia Billop, the heiress of Bentley Manor and took the name of Billop; their son Christopher became a prominent figure in New York, a grand squire, and a member of the legislature until his Tory proclivities and the American Revolution drove him out. The fourth Farmar son, Brooke, lived in New Brunswick, kept the Red Lion tavern, and served as postmaster; nothing is known of his younger brother Edward. Robert Farmar, the subject of this book and the sixth son of Thomas and Anne, was born in 1717. He was followed by Samuel, who became a New York merchant; William and John, army officers; and Mary, Elizabeth, and Ann.[14]

Out of this numerous progeny Robert Farmar emerges as a younger son, greatly dependent upon his parents and good fortune for his prospects. Both seem to have favored him. He is said to have been sent to England as a youth to be schooled. If so, he might have discovered that the senior branch of the Fermor family had done well for itself. In 1692 William Fermor was created baron of Leominster. As his third wife he took Sophia, daughter of Thomas Osborne, earl of Danby and duke of Leeds. Their son Thomas (1698–1753), a successful courtier, was elevated to the earldom of Pomfret in 1721. A daughter, Juliana, became the wife of Thomas, eldest son of William Penn; a son, George (1722–85), succeeded to the earldom, became a lord of the bedchamber to King George III, and was named to the Privy Council.[15] There is no evidence of a personal relationship between the Farmars of New Brunswick and the Fermors of Easton Neston, but the family connection would not have been embarrassing to a young American in England. By 1740 Robert Farmar was back home in New Jersey, and his father, Thomas, was deeply involved in the assembly—the raising of troops to support Great Britain's war with Spain.

It was in keeping with his times and condition in life that Robert Farmar should first don a uniform as an American officer in an American regiment in an American war. In 1739 the British colonies in North America were a firmly established segment of an expanding empire, populous and prosperous, ready and willing to support the commercial interests and territorial ambitions of an Atlantic system of which they knew themselves to be a part. Young men of good family, recently returned from schooling in England, men like Lawrence Washington of Virginia and Robert Farmar of New Jersey, had experienced the excitement of London, the hub of empire, where merchants trading with the Americas fretted at Spanish efforts to restrain their commercial aggression and Captain Robert Jenkins displayed the famous ear so brutally lopped off by a Spanish *guarda costa.* If the political system of Sir Robert Walpole had produced peace and prosperity for England, it had also bred pugnacity. Politicians sensed the opportunity to embarrass a minister they envied and hated, and a boisterous mob cried in the streets for war with Spain—it promised to be cheap, easy, and profitable. Rejecting Walpole's diplomatic solution to long-standing differences with Spain, parliament demanded war and church bells rang in celebration. Soon enough, Sir Robert observed, they would be wringing their hands instead.

Anglo-Spanish hostilities began in the summer of 1739, and Governor Lewis Morris of New Jersey advised his council of the first preparatory stages on August 17.[16] During the ensuing months, the government in London laid plans for an expedition against Spanish possessions in the Caribbean, in which North American colonial troops would be employed. and Admiral Edward Vernon demonstrated the ease with which victory might be achieved by capturing Porto Bello with a fleet of only six ships.[17]

Joint command of the proposed assault on the West Indies was initially given to Admiral Edward Vernon and General Lord Cathcart. Eight English regiments were assigned to the operation, and the colonists were asked to raise a volunteer force of three thousand men organized in thirty companies. The leadership of the American regiment was entrusted to sixty-four-year-old Alexander Spotswood, seconded by William Gooch, lieutenant governor of Virginia, who succeeded to command on Spotswood's death in April 1740. Colonel William Blakeney, adjutant general for the American regiment, was dispatched to New York to forward colonial preparations with arms, uniforms, and blank commissions. This news was presented to the New Jersey Council by Governor Morris on April 16, 1740, and two days later a proclamation was issued urging the enlistment of men and promising them arms, clothing, and "their Share of any Booty." Recruiters were appointed, gentlemen were invited to form companies, and Governor Morris announced that he would fill in blank commissions for the officers of the two companies of one hundred men New Jersey was asked to raise.[18]

Something more than patriotism was involved in the recruiting process. For those who sought officers' commissions there was pride and prestige, both intimately involved in the local politics of New Jersey. For enlisted men there was better pay than was enjoyed by regular soldiers in the British army. Additional incentives might also be offered. In Pennsylvania, all too many indentured servants saw in the drive for recruits an opportunity to escape their bondage and were inclined to do so in companies being raised in New Jersey and New York.[19]

There were, in fact, more volunteers than anyone expected, but there were insufficient company commissions to meet the demands of those who would be officers as well as gentlemen. To satisfy ardent Americans and take advantage of their welcome manpower, Adjutant General Blakeney advised that colonial governors might give certificates to gentlemen who raised companies but for whom no commissions were available, entitling them to commissions from Lord Cathcart when the expeditionary force reached Jamaica. Blakeney promised to remit funds for the subsistence of such supernumerary companies, but it was clearly preferable to be on the authorized list. Such circumstances added a touch of competition to the recruiting in New Jersey.

The mayor of New Brunswick, Assemblyman Thomas Farmar, saw in the raising of the American regiment an opportunity to advance both his own standing in provincial affairs and the interests of his fifth surviving son, Robert, for whom some provision must be made. In his twenty-third year in good health and high temper, Robert was proper officer material, and a numerous family rallied to his assistance. To beat of drum—and doubtless clink of silver—the Farmars began to recruit a company in and around New Brunswick.

Wars are not fought with men alone; money had also to be raised, and for that Governor Morris turned to the provincial assembly. There he found little enthusiasm: the assembly "would fain have shuffled it off, under pretence of waiting to see what their neighbors of Pensilvania & New York would do." Instead of taking action to meet military expenses, the lower house proposed to adjourn for a fortnight. Lewis Morris prodded and pleaded, but not until June 30 did the assembly appoint a committee, of which Thomas Farmar was the chairman, to draw up a bill for provisioning and transporting troops destined for the West Indies. Colonel Farmar returned with the committee's bill the next day; it was passed on July 2 and delivered to the upper house on July

3. It provided that two thousand pounds, already assessed for other purposes, might be applied to the needs of the Jersey troops; expenditure of this money, however, should remain in the hands of the assembly. The governor would have preferred another source of funds and personal control of them, but by the end of the month Morris concluded that he must take what he could get. The governor later professed great indebtedness to Thomas Farmar for his support in the assembly and declared that he had been "very instrumentall in procuring the £2,000," but Morris may also have held Colonel Farmar responsible for the humiliating terms of the grant and decided to teach him and his son a lesson.[20]

So popular was the Anglo-Spanish war in 1740 that three companies were raised in New Jersey, not just the two requested and provided for. The first was that of Captain James Hooper, who, as sheriff of Middlesex County and Governor Morris's kinsman, was well situated to complete recruiting and receive his commission on August 1, 1740. Governor Morris had also granted warrants to raise men to George Thomas and Robert Farmar. As of August 2, young Farmar had submitted evidence of having filled his company, but if, as was thought to be the case, Thomas had also raised his quota, the requisite certification had not reached the governor. Morris therefore put it to the council whether Farmar should receive the one remaining commission or further time be granted to Thomas. The council agreed to allow Thomas until August 8 to produce proof of his activity; the governor should then commission him whose company had first been filled. This proposal brought both Farmar and Thomas posthaste to the council chamber on August 4.

Inquiry elicited the information that Robert Farmar's company was not, in fact, complete. A dozen men properly belonging to another company were included in his return, thanks to certification by a justice of the peace who was young Farmar's brother-in-law. Another nine men, recruited in New York by one of Robert's older brothers, had not and never did appear. On the other hand, Thomas had marched seventy-seven men to Perth Amboy and claimed to have enlisted many more. In order to resolve the issue, the council directed that Farmar should muster his company at New Brunswick, in the presence of an independent justice of the peace and a British army officer on recruiting service in New Jersey, to be reviewed and certified fit and present by them. Thomas should do the same at Perth Amboy, and Governor Morris agreed to commission whichever gentleman actually produced a full company. Should both companies be properly filled, the governor would deliver commissions to the one that appeared best suited for His Majesty's service. The loser in this competition would receive a certificate entitling him to commissioning at a later date by the appropriate military authorities.

On August 8 both Farmar's and Thomas's certificates were presented to the governor and council, and both were found to have filled their companies. On the council's unanimous advice, Governor Morris commissioned Captain George Thomas and his junior officers, "Thomas having behav'd with much modesty, & being a man of more age and Experience, & having seen more of the world than the other." This was not exactly the basis upon which a decision was to have been made, and it left Robert Farmar, along with Thomas Davis and Edward Seymour, his lieutenant and ensign, with no more than a promise of commissioning.

The two Farmars certainly "thought themselves not well us'd," and young Robert was visibly "much disgusted for not having the Commission." He demanded time, until August 24, to consider whether he would accept the governor's promissory note. Lewis Morris, suspicious of Farmar's motives and perhaps aware that his own vindictive behavior was all too apparent, refused Robert's request and ordered him to keep his company together. The governor explained privately to Adjutant General Blakeney that August 24 was payday for the recruits; once they were paid, he feared that Farmar might "perhaps be weak enough to encourage or wink at desertion," and his company would then scatter. The danger may be doubted. Morris's self-exculpation is evident in his grudging portrayal of Robert Farmar: "He is a vain young man but to do him Justice, has been very diligent in getting his Company together; which I take to be his only merit."

As it turned out, none of the Jersey companies received their pay in late August, and all were considerably out of sorts as a result. Nevertheless, all three were busy learning the rudiments of warfare in daily exercises, two companies at Perth Amboy, "the other within 12 miles of it"—probably Farmar's company at New Brunswick.[21]

Reporting his success in raising both men and money, Governor Lewis Morris boasted that New Jersey might have raised five companies had commissions for their officers been available, and he was proud to observe that out of some three hundred men, there were "not above three servants amongst them." Finding money and shipping took time, however. Not until the morning of September 30 did Farmar's company, together with Captain Thomas and some of his men, board the two small vessels, a snow and a brigantine, that would take them south. They mustered ninety-seven privates fit for service—three sick, a full complement: "Compleat and rather more so," reported Governor Morris, in a better mood now that the troops were departing. Of Robert he could write, "He and his officers have been very diligent and careful, especially one Seymore, his ensign." Two more weeks passed, however, before the ships sailed, and by then the governor was mightily displeased with both commanding officers: Captain Thomas was leaving with certain debts unpaid, and Robert Farmar owed more than a hundred pounds for quarters his men had occupied, whereby "the Landlords complain much." They got under way on October 14, in company with transports carrying New York and New England troops under Adjutant General Blakeney, and arrived at Port Royal, Jamaica, in mid-November.[22] There they found that the English regiments had yet to appear; when they did, in January 1741, they learned that command had passed to General Thomas Wentworth, Lord Cathcart having died during the passage to Jamaica.

If Robert Farmar and his fellows imagined they had come to a tropical paradise, they were quickly disillusioned. Farmar's warrant from Governor Morris was honored promptly enough by General Wentworth, and he received a captain's commission dated January 10, 1741,[23] but all else was disappointment and portended disaster. Funds were short and prices high, even on a captain's pay of ten shillings a day. The fevers of the West Indies immediately began to take their toll, and hospital space was insufficient. The Americans were welcome in the grog shops, whose keepers found them overly susceptible to Jamaican rum, but not in the eyes of British officers, who came to recognize Gooch's regiment by its red coats, brown linen waistcoats, and canvas trousers. "From the first Sight of the *American* Troops they were despised" and held to be "many Degrees worse" than the raw British regiments that joined them in Jamaica.[24] Scorned by General Wentworth, the Americans were suborned by Admiral Vernon to fill the crews of his ships. Valuable time passed before the commanders of the expedition finally selected the port of Cartagena as their target, and then naval considerations persuaded Admiral Vernon to delay their departure for the coast of New Granada (modern Colombia). Once arrived, March 4, it was General Wentworth whose caution stood in the way of prompt action which might have produced victory.

The records do not disclose the disposition of Captain Farmar's company through the long month the British spent before Cartagena. It may be assumed that he and they fared no better nor worse than most of the Americans. The expedition's initial task was to force its way past a series of impressive fortifications guarding the harbors and city of Cartagena, and this was begun on March 9. The first American troops were landed the next day, after British grenadiers had established a beachhead, but the rest remained aboard ship. Ten days later, two hundred more Americans, under Captain Lawrence Washington, were sent into action ashore. The mouth of the outer harbor was secured on March 25, and without opposition the ships and men moved to the inner harbor and landed a force containing two hundred Americans and fourteen hundred British regulars. A successful clash with a Spanish field force on April 5 might have opened the door to the city, but Wentworth failed to pursue a fleeing enemy, and the army spent the next few days bringing up men and equipment for a formal assault on the formidable ditches and walls of Fort San Lazar, Cartagena's last defense.

"By this time," observed an unhappy naval medic named Tobias Smollett,

> the rainy season had begun with such violence, that it was hardly practicable to keep the field, for it poured down in a deluge incessantly, from the rising to the setting of the sun. . . . Such a change of the atmosphere is always attended with an epidemical distemper, in consequence of which the men dropped down so fast that there was scarce a sufficiency to relieve the proper guards of the camp, much less to cut down the wood and raise a battery, so as to attack San Lazaro in form.[25]

Heat and rain began to decimate the British forces, and Wentworth disembarked about fifteen hundred more Americans in order to maintain his manpower: "as Sickness increased among the others (and hourly Attacks expected from the Enemy) it was thought expedient to have them ashore."[26]

The general's low opinion of the Americans' usefulness was apparent when plans were drawn, on April 8, to assault San Lazar. The Americans were assigned the menial task of carrying woolpacks, scaling ladders, and hand grenades for the assault troops. On the morning of the ninth, the British advanced to the attack in two columns, one of which was virtually wiped out on the steep slope before the fort; the other hung on grimly for a few hours before it was withdrawn.

The men of Gooch's regiment, laden with ladders and other equipment intended to enable the British to scale the fort's walls, had advanced behind the regulars into the fire zone. Halted on that murderous ground, "the Americans . . . seeing the troops falling by whole platoons, refused to advance with their burdens; but though they would not advance as pioneers, many of them took up the firelocks which they found on the field, and, mixing among the troops, behaved very bravely."[27] Less kindly, it was said that "finding they were knock'd down without any Arms to defend themselves, [they] threw down their Ladders, &c. and retired to their Camp."[28] Another observer was probably most precise when he wrote, "The *American* Soldiers (not withstanding the utmost Endeavors of their Officers to prevent it) cast [the ladders] down, and either took up Firelocks, or put themselves under Cover from the Shot of the Enemy."[29] It was exactly the response to be expected of raw recruits, briefly trained, long suffering from boredom and lack of exercise before being brought into action, and facing an enemy whom they could not see. It was beside the point to denigrate them as Irish papists or fugitive Englishmen, their officers as "Blacksmiths, Taylors, Shoemakers, and all the

Banditti that Country affords." Theirs was the typically American reaction. If shot at, they would shoot back—or take cover.[30]

One British commentator, at least, responded to the "Heap of Billingsgate" poured out "to vilify the *American* Regiment." "The Companies," he noted, "were chiefly raised by the Interest, and at the Charge of their respective Captains; of whom some were Members of the Assemblies in the Provinces where they resided; others lived upon their own Plantations, and had Commands in the Militia." The officers, "recommended by the Governors, and by the Gentlemen of the first Rank," were "younger Sons of the principal Families." The private soldiers may indeed have been Irishmen or necessitous Englishmen, but "as the Levy was made in Haste, there was neither Time for strictly examining into their respective Circumstances, nor for their being well-disciplin'd before they joined the Army." Observing that they did, in fact, participate in the action before San Lazar, this writer felt obligated, "in Justice to the *American* Soldiers, who were commended with Arms on that Occasion," to declare that "they were in no wise wanting to their Duty."[31]

The unsuccessful attack on Fort San Lazar effectively marked the end of the British effort at Cartagena. Within a week the troops were back aboard their transports, where they suffered the agues and fevers of the tropics three more weeks before sailing north. "They were destitute of surgeons, nurses, cooks, and proper provision; they were pent up between decks in small vessels, where they had not room to sit upright; they wallowed in filth; myriads of maggots were hatched in the putrefaction of their sores . . . and nothing was heard but groans, lamentations, and the language of despair." From the deck of Dr. Smollett's ship "they beheld the naked bodies of their fellow-soldiers and comrades floating up and down the harbour, affording prey to the carrion crows and sharks, which tore them in pieces without interruption, and contributed by their stench to the mortality that prevailed."[32]

The survivors returned to Jamaica at the end of May, the American regiment having suffered the loss of some nine hundred men, largely to disease; another thousand were found to be unfit for duty.[33] A ship carrying news of the raising of the siege of Cartagena arrived in Boston, June 20, with word that Captains Farmar and Thomas of New Jersey were well, and that "the officers and soldiers from North America behaved themselves with much bravery, but many of them are dead."[34]

The leaders of the expedition had not lost hope, however. On June 30, the fleet sailed for Cuba and landed the much-diminished British and American regiments at Guantanamo Bay. Their camp was safe from enemy attack, being more than sixty miles distant from their objective, Santiago, but it was exposed to the worst that heat, rain, and disease could do. When they were finally pulled out in November and returned to Jamaica, only 300 men out of the 2,158 surviving British and Americans were found fit for duty.[35]

A third strike was launched, but not landed, at Panama in March 1742 and a forlorn hope was dispatched to the island of Roatán, off the coast of Honduras, later in the year, with little effect save to raise the number of casualties. The utter failure of the West Indian expedition was evident to all, and the American regiment was officially reduced on October 24, 1742. The few pitiable survivors were transported back to their homes in November.[36]

Robert Farmar had escaped the West Indian death trap earlier that year. Desperate for replacements, General Wentworth detached four officers from Gooch's regiment to return to North America in search of fresh recruits. On February 2, 1742, Wentworth addressed an appeal to Governor Morris, asking that he assist Captain Robert Farmar in finding men in New Jersey, and on February 8, the Rhode Island sloop *Tartar* sailed from Port Royal with Farmar aboard.[37]

Farmar had returned to New Jersey by the first week of April; he presented General Wentworth's plea to Morris and was promised the governor's support. If Farmar had little heart for the task, the provincial council had even less; it advised Morris that no help could be expected from the assembly, and it might have pointed out that Morris's treatment of Thomas and Robert Farmar in 1740 had turned the New Brunswick assemblyman into an opponent of gubernatorial policy.[38] Morris was forced to advise Wentworth that military failure and reports of tropical mortality made recruiting for the American regiment "a very difficult task & . . . obtaining any money from the Assembly . . . altogether so." Farmar's fellow recruiting officer, Lieutenant Anthony Palmer, who had earlier raised a company in Pennsylvania, secured a few Jersey men to fill the rapidly emptying ranks of the regiment, and Farmar succeeded in finding twenty-two men who were shipped off to the West Indies—for which Governor Morris allowed him eighty-eight pounds sterling. In that work Robert was assisted by his youngest brother John, a lad who had been "bred a surgeon" and accompanied the new recruits as a volunteer. Recommended by Governor Morris, who pointed out that he was the second Farmar son to offer his services to the Crown in this war, John was commissioned an ensign in Gooch's regiment by Wentworth on August 27, 1742, after he reached Jamaica.[39] In all probability, Robert allowed himself a well-deserved rest at home in New Brunswick while the West Indian campaign wound down to its miserable conclusion.

The "late American regiment" was consigned to oblivion, but its officers held the king's commission, and that was, or should be, worth something more tangible than the painful memories they carried home. In January 1743 six of the reduced American officers, including New Jersey Captain George

Thomas, visited London and began to press the government for half-pay. Their desires were met by a ministry concerned to maintain good relations with the colonies, but each officer's case was considered separately, and when the first applications for half-pay were heard by a board of general officers at the Horse Guards in May, it was noted that "Capt. Farmer—[was] still abroad in North America." And there he seems to have remained for some time, weighing his prospects and finally determining to go to England himself. On May 1, 1744, he appeared before the board, which included General Wentworth and General Blakeney, to plead his case. He had "raised his Company at his own expense, was in every Expedition," and General Wentworth "gave him a very good character." He was therefore recommended for half-pay, as was his brother, Ensign John Farmar, of whom Wentworth said, "He behav'd well."[40]

Robert Farmar would not, however, retire to New Jersey to live "upon his ffortune." Neither his experience in the American regiment nor the prospects of seven shillings sixpence per diem for the rest of his life had cooled his martial ardor. By the middle of the year 1744, Britain was formally at war with France and greatly in need of junior officers for regiments destined for service in Europe. For a young American without other ties—indeed, for many of the reduced officers of Gooch's regiment—the expansion of the war to the continent of Europe provided an opportunity to advance a military career with little difficulty or cost. Farmar's application for half-pay was no more than insurance against a future he was already pursuing in the regular army. At Kensington Palace, June 15, 1744, royal approval was given to the appointment of "Robert Farmar Esqr to be Captain of a Company in Major Genl Charles Howard's Regt of Foot"—the 19th or Green Howards.[41] At the same time, Robert's brother John Farmar secured appointment as an ensign in Bragg's regiment, the 28th Foot. Although the 28th was in Flanders in 1744, it saw no action and was stationed in Ireland from 1746 to 1758. John Farmar was commissioned lieutenant on May 2, 1751, and secured a company as captain lieutenant on October 3, 1760. By then the 28th had seen its share of action at Louisbourg in 1758 and with Wolfe at Quebec in 1759, along with the 22nd Regiment, to which John Farmar transferred as captain at Havana, July 2, 1762. There the brothers would meet again.[42]

II.

King George's Wars

Captain Robert Farmar held rank in the army of George II from August 6, 1740, when his regimental commissioning at Port Royal was officially recognized at the War Office in London.[1] The American regiment in which he first wore the red coat of the British army had been hastily raised for a particular campaign, rapidly expended, and promptly disbanded. The regiment that Farmar joined in the summer of 1744 was made of very different stuff. Like most of the line regiments of the day, its lineage went back to 1689 and the wars of William III. Under the duke of Marlborough the regiment won its first battle honors at Malplaquet, and the reorganizations of neither the nineteenth nor the twentieth century would dim its pride in being known as the Green Howards.

Until 1751 British regiments usually carried the name of the colonel commanding, but Major General the Honourable Charles Howard was not the only officer of that noble family to lead a regiment. It was merely convenient to distinguish his regiment by the color of their uniform facings—a yellowish green embellishing the red of the coat and lace-trimmed waistcoat—but the name stuck. The men of Howard's regiment also wore a black tricorn hat, trimmed in white, and white trousers with gaiters wrapped above the knee. It was not a uniform designed for comfort or convenience, but rather it was intended to identify the wearer amidst the smoke of battle as he rallied on the shot-torn regimental colors.[2] Robert Farmar would wear that uniform for seventeen long years, and soon enough he would know that red was also the color of blood.

The Anglo-Spanish war of 1739 merged gradually into the European conflict known as the War of the Austrian Succession. In 1740 Frederick II of

Prussia took the field against the Austrian Habsburg heiress Maria Theresa. He wrested the province of Silesia from her grasp and won the sobriquet of Frederick the Great. His success frightened lesser German princes, among whom was George, elector of Hanover and king of England. At the same time, Louis XV of France, with an eye on the Austrian Netherlands, expanded the war to western Europe, and the advance of his armies involved the Dutch Republic, England's ally since the Glorious Revolution and the days of William III. The threat to the king's beloved Hanover led to the dispatch of British regiments to Germany, and in 1743 a French army and a British-Hanoverian force clashed at Dettingen, even though the two Atlantic nations were not yet officially at war with one another. In 1744 that omission was corrected, and further British troops were sent to the Continent to check the French invasion of the Austrian Netherlands. Among these were the Green Howards and Captain Robert Farmar.

Flanders was the cockpit of Europe, and there the British army faced superior numbers of French troops commanded by the great Marshal Saxe. In spite of increasing strength, reaching twenty-five thousand men in 1745, the British could do little except react to French feints and maneuvers unless they were supported by their allies, the Austrians and the Dutch. The former were content to let the western allies defend the Netherlands for them; the latter, weak and disinclined to take the slightest risk, were content that nothing much should happen—and nothing did in 1744. The next year, however, the British army came under the command of an ambitious twenty-four-year-old general, William, duke of Cumberland, the king's younger son, who was most ably advised by the elderly but highly competent French expatriate General John Ligonier. At the beginning of May 1745, Cumberland's allied army took the field, and by the tenth it faced Saxe's French legions entrenched about the village of Fontenoy, some four miles from Tournai. There, on May 11, 1745 (N.S.), Captain Robert Farmar learned about warfare, European style.

The battle of Fontenoy was a classic eighteenth-century engagement, a set-piece wherein the British foot advanced against prepared positions that were supported by artillery to the front and by guns and infantry securely lodged in the fortified village of Fontenoy on their left flank and in a thick wood on their right. Cumberland's outnumbered regiments faced the flower of the French army, and they had to cross a half-mile of open ground before they could come to grips with their enemy. Although Dutch and Austrian troops occupied the center and left of the allied line, the key to the French position lay before the British. There the battle would be decided.

The redcoats began moving out of their camp at two o'clock in the morning, and by six o'clock they were formed in two long lines of regiments, each six men deep, confronting the French defenses. Major General Howard's regiment, posted on the extreme left of the first line, was in closest proximity to the French field works around Fontenoy. Captain Robert Farmar would doubtless recall in later years that behind them, in the second line, stood the 34th Regiment of Foot, with whom he would end his military career. French artillery began to play on them at their first appearance, and the fire was murderous. "The foot were very sadly cut to Pieces, for ye french put grape shot into their cannon & cut them down just as if they were sheering corn."[3]

His brigades dressed as on a parade ground, Cumberland placed himself at their head, and "the two lines moved off with the slow measured step for which they were famous in Europe." Through a hail of shot they advanced in thinning ranks until, at thirty yards, the French infantry opened fire—and only then did the British begin that steady rolling fire that made them feared on every battlefield. Deep into the heart of the French position they drove, forming square in the middle of the French camp. Two regiments, including the Green Howards, were detached to help the Dutch attacking Fontenoy, but finding that they could not penetrate the village and that the Dutch would not support them, Howard's men returned to the British front, only to be met by the order to retire. It took Ligonier's personal intervention to turn them back, and he posted them, along with the 42nd Highlanders (Black Watch) to guard against any pursuit. There was none. Although the British left more than four thousand dead on the field, roughly a third of their number engaged, the French had suffered worse. Howard's regiment had paid a price: its colonel wounded in four places, eight other officers wounded and two killed, a hundred casualties among the rank and file. But if defeated, they left the field unbroken. "As an example of the prowess of British infantry, Fontenoy stands almost without a parallel in its history."[4]

After Fontenoy the British army could do little more than cover Brussels and Antwerp against the advancing French. By August 1745, regiments were being recalled to meet the challenge posed in Scotland by the rising of the clans led by Bonny Prince Charlie. On September 20 the Green Howards had orders to embark for England with General Ligonier, and they landed on the twenty-fifth. They played no combat role in the campaign against the Scottish Jacobite invaders of England. In December they were camped on Dartford Heath, east of London, and on January 5, 1746, they were still at or near that city. While the duke of Cumberland pursued the Scots northward, destroying Stuart dreams at Culloden in April, Major General Howard's regiment recouped its strength in the south of England. On June 7, 1746, they were ordered back to the Continent, where more bloody work awaited them.[5]

Contrary winds delayed their return until July, and in the Low Countries the British faced a desperate situation. The French had captured Brussels and

Antwerp and threatened to invade the United Provinces. The allied army, short of food and forage, could only respond to Saxe's deliberate maneuvers. On October 11 (N.S.) he brought them to battle at Rocoux, near Liège, with their backs to the Meuse River and in a position much disliked by General Ligonier. The allies, at eighty thousand men, were but two-thirds the strength of the French, and Saxe concentrated his force so that the English in Rocoux were outnumbered four to one. Howard's regiment was in reserve when the action began, but they were quickly brought up to contest the very walls and houses of the tiny hamlet. Ligonier then posted them in a sunken road, where they hung on with bloody determination, enabling Ligonier to withdraw his troops from an impossible situation. By all reports, the Green Howards took a beating, losing one officer killed, one taken prisoner, and four wounded. Ligonier observed that the Green Howards "suffered extremely but maintained to the last a hollow way where I had posted them." Of his redcoats in general, Ligonier proudly declared, "The King's troops . . . under all those discouraging circumstances kept their order as if they had been on a review before His Majesty, at every halt facing where the enemy appeared: and let me tell you, My Lord, they must be good troops that will do that." Liège was occupied by the French, and after the battle the armies went into winter quarters.[6]

The campaigning season of 1747 found the duke of Cumberland once more at the head of the British army on the Continent and his old opponent Saxe systematically reducing the defenses of the Dutch Republic. The French drew Cumberland toward Maestricht in June, and on July 2 (N.S.) he rather unexpectedly found himself facing Saxe's army near that city. As at Rocoux, the allies held a line of little straggling villages; the British regiments were stationed on the left around Laffeldt. The battle began about nine o'clock, when Saxe threw his massed infantry against them. Four times in as many hours French attacks swept over the village, only to be thrown back by British counterattacks. "It was," wrote a British officer, "a very warm action for both sides, and great slaughter made in the orchards and in all the hedges round."[7] Again the Green Howards were in reserve when the French first attacked, but they were moved forward at once and remained in the thick of the fighting. Numbers prevailed, however, and the fifth French assault forced the exhausted redcoats back and broke the allied line. Disaster was barely staved off by a sacrificial cavalry charge led by sixty-seven-year-old Ligonier, who was captured by the French. The Green Howards lost their lieutenant colonel, another officer, and a quarter of their strength at Laffeldt; eight other officers were wounded, but the regiment won praise for their stubborn performance.[8]

Cumberland saved Maestricht, as it turned out, but even the generals were talking peace, and there would be no further major engagements. Farmar's regiment was, nevertheless, involved in a bloody action at Wouw at the end of July and suffered considerable losses. Weakened and discouraged, they were marched back to quarters at Gertrudenberg in October, their spirits a little raised, perhaps, by the sound of fife as well as drum, for they were the first line regiment to adopt the tuneful pipe. The Dutch burghers charged dearly that winter for their hospitality; neither fire nor light was available to the exhausted men of Howard's regiment unless they could pay for it out of their own pockets.[9] Happily, there would be no campaigning for them in 1748; the preliminaries of peace were signed that May.

As quiet descended on Europe in 1748, Captain Robert Farmar and the Green Howards fell into the routine of peacetime service, and as the only regiment in the British army to have fought through each of the bloody battles of Fontenoy, Rocoux, and Laffeldt, they deserved a rest. A parsimonious government promptly reduced them to the Irish establishment—which meant that the regiment's ranks were thinned in numbers and that a captain's pay, with servant's allowance, was cut to nine shillings sixpence per day.[10] The regiment also received a new colonel, Major General Lord George Beauclerk, sixth son of the duke of St. Albans and grandson of Charles II and Nell Gwyn. In mid-November 1748 they were ordered to relieve the regiments garrisoning Gibraltar, and there they and their new colonel remained through the next three years. Many years later Robert Farmar would recall the few virtues of garrison duty on the Rock: the weather was much less oppressive than at Mobile, and a captain was allowed two rooms for his quarters. In 1751 Beauclerk's regiment was officially designated the 19th Regiment of Foot, and in 1752 it was brought home to England.[11] There being no barracks or depots for their maintenance, the regiment was scattered about the north of England and the southern part of Scotland, Newcastle-on-Tyne serving as headquarters. Lord George Beauclerk was appointed commander in chief in North Britain (Scotland), and took up residence in Edinburgh in November 1756. Early the next year he found it necessary to replace the major of brigade on his staff, but not until May 2 did the War Office authorize him to fill the vacancy. He promptly responded, "I really think that Captain Robert Farmar of my Regiment is very capable for that post, and he is extreamly well acquainted with Scotland, as my Regiment has been so long here, and he has been a long time in the service and a very sober honest man and one I am sure I can depend on." His lordship's recommendation was accepted, and Robert Farmar joined the Scottish commandant's staff.[12]

For four years Farmar served in Scotland and enjoyed the perquisites of a staff officer, which included four rations per day in addition to his regular pay. The appointment speaks well for his performance on the field of battle but more for his decorum in both military and social circles; Farmar could not have secured such a plum without the commander in chief's approval. At the same time, Beauclerk's family, his connections at court, and his seat in the House of Commons offered Farmar some hope of future advancement if he pleased his colonel. Approaching his fortieth year, he had achieved seniority in the regiment, and his future depended upon connection, influence, and (to some degree) money.

On the other hand, Edinburgh was far from the Horse Guards in London and not the happiest place for an ambitious British army officer. Farmar's duties as brigade major entailed the keeping of records (never his strongest point), reviewing of troops scattered throughout the country, and at least occasionally finding recruits for the 19th Regiment. And he would be expected to share in Lord George's concerns and activities.

A formal review of Beauclerk's 19th Regiment of Foot, held August 14, 1759, provides a detailed description of the peacetime establishment. The regiment mustered 943 men in nine companies; of these 447 were Englishmen, 454 Scots, 41 Irishmen, and 1 foreigner. The men's average age was thirty, their average years of service but three—a reflection of the drafting of veterans to other regiments assigned to active service—and 101 had been enlisted in the past year. Although the men's average height was five feet six and a half inches, the reviewing officer, Major General George Howard, remarked that they were "a very low Body of Men—Of an indifferent Make—Well dressed. Hatts wore well—but indifferently cocked." The drummers and fifers, however, looked and presumably sounded good and marched well. In sum, Howard gave the 19th credit for being "a good Regiment, well disciplined, and fit for Service."[13]

War between France and England was renewed by 1756, and Scottish Highlanders were prime recruits, toughened by their rugged mountain life and susceptible, because of their poverty, to the king's shilling. Getting them into the ranks of a British regiment was not easy, however. "This recruiting," wrote a young officer on that service, "is Both Expensive & mighty troublesome." His dignity would not allow him to travel afoot, and "being a stranger every where I go I am obliged to run into Expences. . . . If I was to settle in any particular place & fall upon some frugal scheme of living I should then be looked upon as a Negligent officer. . . . I am now convinced By Experience, that this is the most Expensive & disagreeable duty an officer can be sent upon."[14]

Scottish recruits were quick to volunteer but difficult to find when a contingent was ready for transportation by sea to England. Clansmen's names were confusingly similar, and their relatives strangely uncooperative when it came to rounding them up. It was easy enough to attribute such unpatriotic conduct to Jacobite sympathies. The Forty-five was well-remembered, and at

Major General Beauclerk's headquarters there was a natural concern that, with French encouragement, the Highlanders might rise again.[15]

The commander in chief in North Britain and his staff were, of course, responsible for the conditioning and training of all troops stationed in Scotland. Each April the regiments were assembled at their respective headquarters for exercises and review before being dispersed to various parts of the country for the summer. In August 1760 Beauclerk reported that he and his staff had just returned to Edinburgh from an inspection tour of four hundred miles—no small undertaking given the state of Scottish roads.[16]

The staff itself was small enough. Beauclerk, now a lieutenant general, had a secretary and two aides-de-camp. He was seconded by Major General Pole and an aide at Fort George, Inverness. The deputy quartermaster general, Captain William Rickson, had one assistant; Major of Brigade Farmar had none. A commissary of stores completed the staff.[17] Beauclerk was greatly disturbed when Ligonier, now commander in chief of all British forces, issued a general order that captains absent from their regiments must return to duty. Assuming that Ligonier did not intend to strip his staff of experienced officers, he remonstrated that "the Duty of Major of Brigade & Deputy Qr Mr Genl in Scotland are different from what they are in most other places, having a great variety & a multiplicity of Circumstances attending them, which do not occur elsewhere."[18]

Edinburgh might suit a lieutenant general, but his staff officers of the 19th Regiment were anxious to find advancement. It was very much a matter of service politics. Deputy Quartermaster General William Rickson, a close friend of James Wolfe, had been assigned his position by Cumberland in 1756, but he was still awaiting formal commissioning a year and a half later.[19] Major Robert Douglas was busy pursuing the lieutenant colonelcy of the second battalion of the Green Howards, and movement at the top might open other ranks. In anticipation, Captain Robert Farmar memorialized Lieutenant General Beauclerk, and his superior forwarded his request for consideration to the War Office, together with his own recommendation: "His long and Faithfull service pleads much in his behalf, to which I can with great justice add that he is a very Carefull diligent Officer, and a deserving good Man, which will I hope weigh with your Lordship to move H. Majesty in his behalf."[20] Nothing came of this approach.

Almost a year and a half later, Beauclerk again sent to London a memorial from Robert Farmar asking that he might succeed to the vacant governorship of Dumbarton Castle:

> Major Farmar has served long, and I can with great Justice assure your Lordship, that he has both as Capt. in my Regimt for several years past and as Major of

> Brigade to the fforces in N. Britain done his duty with the greatest Care & exactness; I therefore beg leave to recommend him to your Lordship as duly qualified for that Employment, and to desire your Lordship would be pleas'd to use Your good Offices with His Majesty towards the obtaining that Government & independent Company for him.[21]

In a short while Farmar came up with another proposition. Major Charles Lumisden of the 19th had decided to retire (if the financial terms were right), having "grown old and incapable of the fatigue a Major must necessarily undergo in the course of his Duty." He offered to withdraw if he could secure a royal warrant guaranteeing him an income of five shillings a day for the rest of his life and have leave to sell his company for fifteen hundred guineas. Apparently this was Lumisden's rock-bottom price, for Farmar had rejected earlier "more extravagant" proposals. The American would accept this offer if Lumisden's five shillings per diem might be withheld from the pay Farmar would receive as a major. It was a bit irregular, but Farmar hoped that that would "not prove a bar to my taking the Majority upon Captain's pay." He pointed out that he was the eldest captain in the regiment, claimed twenty years in rank in the army, and trusted that Beauclerk would "not prefer a younger Captain."[22]

The general only objected to Lumisden selling his company for more than he had paid for it and transmitted Farmar's request to the War Office, noting that he was

> the Senior Captain in the Regiment and one whom I do assure your Lordship my only motive for recommending proceeds from a knowledge I have several years had of his attention to the service, in particular for three years and upward last past that he has been appointed Major of Brigade which duty he has discharg'd with great Assiduity and exactness, and from a persuasion that he will make as good a Field Officer as any in the Army.

Unfortunately for Robert Farmar, Secretary at War William Barrington was "so averse to suffering officers to retire upon any part of their pay" that he refused to bring the matter before the king.[23] Lumisden, who was in London at the time and was trying to close the same deal with Captain Paterson, was no doubt as disappointed as anyone and did not retire until November 1761.[24]

The Seven Years' War finally offered Robert Farmar an escape from the Scottish doldrums. As a part of the British strategy of keeping the French off balance, a series of hit-and-run operations was launched against the Atlantic coast of France. In January 1761 the 19th Regiment was alerted for participation in a secret mission, and at the end of March it sailed for Belle Isle, off the southern coast of Brittany. Word of the impending expedition reached Edinburgh belatedly, but at the first opportunity Captain Farmar sought Lord George's permission to join the regiment. Beauclerk passed Farmar's request to the War Office, once again recommending him for the regimental majority. He described his brigade major as "a faithful and good officer" who had shown "great diligence and exactness" and assured Secretary Charles Townshend, "It would have been very agreeable to me to have him continue in the same Station if his Employment cou'd have procur'd him any Rank, but as that is not the case, I the readier consented to his quitting that Post, in order to his being in a fairer way of obtaining that end. . . . His services entitle him to Preferment."[25] Beauclerk's sincerity need not be doubted; Farmar's advancement cost the Scottish commander in chief his major of brigade, for in June, after Farmar's departure, the position was abolished.[26]

Robert Farmar was granted permission to quit his post at Edinburgh and went to London. What transpired there is obscure, but on May 28, 1761, Charles Townshend advised him:

> I have the satisfaction to inform you that His Majesty has this Day been pleased to promote you to the rank of Major in the 34th Regt of Foot commanded by Lord Frederick Cavendish; And I beg leave to add on my own part, that both from my temper and my publick situation, I take the sincerest pleasure in every such instance & testimony of His Majesty's approbation conferred upon officers of your distinguished Merit & Rank.[27]

What arrangement Farmar made with his predecessor does not appear. A few months later, Townshend observed that fifteen hundred pounds was "the usual price of a Company in the 34th Regt."[28]

The 34th Regiment of Foot was junior to the Green Howards but no less proud of its past. Formed in 1702, in the reign of Queen Anne, the castle at Carlisle became its headquarters in 1703 and remains in its hands today. The 34th stormed Barcelona under Peterborough and took Bouchain under Marlborough. They won honors at Fontenoy, fought at Culloden, and gallantly, though unsuccessfully, defended Minorca in 1756 under General Blakeney. Repeatedly assigned to the amphibious operations against the French coast in the following years, they were, along with the 19th, part of the strike force that sailed for Belle Isle in 1761.[29]

Farmar's new regiment belonged to Lord Frederick Cavendish, a younger son of the duke of Devonshire, who was serving as a brigadier with the army in Germany. Lieutenant Colonel John Reed nominally commanded the regiment in the field, but his repeated appointments to commanding generals' staffs left the 34th in the hands of its major. Robert Farmar would find that his administrative experience in Scotland was as valuable as his field experience in Flanders. Change of regiment meant change of uniform; Farmar would replace his Howard green facings with bright yellow, wear a broad sash of scarlet silk over his right shoulder or around his waist, and hang a silver gorget about his neck. His majority provided a rather handsome income of fifteen shillings a day or £273.15.0 per year and an annual subsistence allowance of £209.17.6—allowing for deductions, better than £400 per year.[30]

When Major General Edward Cornwallis reviewed the 34th Regiment in September 1759, it was a predominantly English regiment of nearly 800 men. The average soldier was five feet seven and a half inches tall and had been in the service for six years. Although 116 men were recent recruits, the average age in the ranks was thirty years. Cornwallis noted that the veterans were "of a Large Size," and that the recruits were "Low but Strong and Serviceable." It was and would prove to be "a good Regiment & very fit for Service."[31]

When Farmar was promoted to the 34th Regiment, the British conquest of Belle Isle had been accomplished. On April 22 the grenadier company of the 19th Regiment stormed ashore and effected a foothold that was rapidly expanded. The month of May passed in the siege of the fortress of Palais, and its citadel capitulated on June 7.[32] The muster rolls of the 34th, drawn up at Sendheath Camp in Surrey, indicate that as of July 1 Major Farmar was at Belle Isle. Assuming that he crossed over as soon as he received his appointment to the regiment, he could have done little but meet his new comrades and take the opportunity to visit the 19th Regiment and commiserate with Captain Paterson, for the hero of the landing operation had lost an arm and the Green Howards had 153 other casualties. Major Farmar returned to England in August. As the 34th was settled into quarters at Hilsea Barracks, Portsmouth, he was able to secure extended leaves of absence during December and January 1762, by permission of Lieutenant General the Earl of Albemarle, under whom he and the 34th would soon go into action.[33]

The years of Robert Farmar's quiet Scottish exile were, in other parts of the world, filled with great and stirring events. The war that began in 1756 matched Great Britain and Prussia against France, Austria, and Russia. Although former allies were now enemies, the interests of the combatants had changed little. War in Germany brought British troops to the Continent in defense of Hanover and in support of Frederick of Prussia. Their ultimate success against the French enabled Frederick to survive the crushing blows of repeated Austrian and Russian attacks. Western Europe was relatively peaceful, for a change, as the Dutch refused to involve themselves and France honored their neutrality; but British amphibious assaults on the French coast, of which that against Belle Isle was the last and most successful, pinned down thousands of French troops along the coast. In India and North America, war was waged by small bodies of European troops and their native allies, with varying results until British seapower began to starve the French of men and supplies. The year 1759 marked a turning point. Decisive victory was won at sea; General James Wolfe broke the heart of French Canada at Quebec, and Robert Clive won dominance for British interests in India. The government at London, directed by William Pitt, took the offensive in what would be known to modern historians as the Great War for the Empire. As in 1739, Britain looked to the West Indies for further conquests, and as her rich sugar islands fell, one after another, France turned to Spain for succor.

At the center of affairs in England, a new king, George III, came to the throne in 1760, and with him new politicians. Anticipating war with Spain, Pitt demanded a pre-emptive strike in 1761; failing to persuade his cabinet colleagues, he resigned. The earl of Bute became the chief minister as well as the favorite of George III; like his master, he was determined to have peace—but Spain would first have war. Britain's plans were already drawn, thanks to Pitt. Havana was to the Indies as Quebec to Canada; from Cuba the Gulf of Mexico opened upon the southern littoral of Louisiana and Florida. Take New Orleans, Mobile, and Pensacola, and with Canada in British hands, a continent would be won. Toward that end George Keppel, Earl of Albemarle, was named to head an expedition against Havana.

The 34th Regiment was formally paraded and embarked at Portsmouth on February 26, 1762, and sailed from England on March 5. As Lieutenant Colonel Reed was assigned to the staff of the 3rd Brigade, the nine companies and 976 men of the 34th were under the direct command of Major Robert Farmar.[34] The expedition enjoyed an easy Atlantic crossing, was joined by other troops at Martinique, and appeared before Havana on June 6.

The harbor and city of Havana were dominated by the great stone fortress of El Morro, and against it Albemarle directed his operations. Troops were landed to the east of El Morro on June 7, the 34th Regiment in the reserve of the first landing, under Colonel Guy Carleton. The beachhead was quickly expanded, and by June 10 General William Keppel's infantry had occupied the commanding heights of La Cabana and the investment of the brooding Spanish stronghold had begun. Camps were laid out, and the troops were employed in the exhausting task of raising batteries and digging entrenchments in the dry, rocky soil. From the outset, disease, heat, and shortage of water began to weaken the besiegers.

The first British batteries opened on July 1, but a fire that destroyed the Grand Battery blunted the effectiveness of the bombardment for some days. Not until the seventeenth were the guns in El Morro sufficiently silenced to allow work to begin on the approaches to the fort and the mining of its walls. Within a few days the Spanish were forced to recognize their imminent danger.

As the city of Havana was open and free from any direct threat, and the great harbor was available to their use, the Spanish were in an excellent position to counterattack the besieging British at any time. At three o'clock on the morning of July 22, a series of attacks was launched across the harbor from Havana and directly from El Morro by at least two thousand Spanish soldiers and seamen with the intent of spiking or destroying the British guns.

Elements of the 34th Regiment under Major Robert Farmar's command guarded two of the batteries that came under attack. They were not caught napping. Farmar "had his men under arms" before the general alarm was sounded, and he rushed 150 redcoats to the defense of the threatened posts. A confused firefight in semidarkness ensued, but in ten or fifteen minutes the Spaniards began to fall back to the beaches, and Colonel Guy Carleton brought up support for the beleaguered batteries. Not content with saving their guns, a body of 230 British soldiers, including the men of the 34th, charged down on the Spaniards as they took to their boats, "but being inferior in number and subject to fire from Spanish ships and forts," they were reluctantly withdrawn, and Farmar satisfied himself by directing their fire at the defeated mass on the water's edge below. Another Spanish party now appeared on the scene, and, Carleton being wounded, Farmar took command of troops that were hurrying up from the camp, attacked, and drove off this second wave of the Spanish assault.[35] Engineer Archibald Robertson remarked that the Spaniards were "everywhere Repuls'd and Pursued into the very water where Numbers of them were Kill'd and Drown'd." In an action that was over in an hour, some five to six hundred Spaniards were killed, at a cost of two British officers and 120 men.[36] The batteries and mining operations were saved, and the Spaniards, who had been prepared to support their surprise attack with a considerable force from Havana, could do no more than await events.

On July 30 the British mines were exploded, and an assault force fought its way into El Morro. The fall of the fortress was inevitably followed, on August 14, by the surrender of the city, for its walls could not withstand bombardment.[37] The return of the triumphant 34th Regiment on August 16, 1762, showed its strength at 29 officers, 313 rank and file fit for duty, and 451 sick.[38]

The Havana campaign cost the British only 560 battle casualties, but sickness and disease took the frightful toll of 4,708. Captain Delacherois vividly described the conditions the troops faced: "The difficulties we meet with are many: sickness, the troops frequently a great want of water & w[ha]t we get but Indifferent. The heat of the Climate & many other difficulties & disasters retards us much in the opperations of the Siege." Although wild cattle were numerous when they landed, the redcoats were soon reduced to "Salt Beef, Pork & Bisquit; as for herbage, we have found very little Except the Cabbage tree & no roots. Wild turkeys, Parrots & Pidgeons are in great abundance but we can't Expect to have 'em 'till our Works is over." He had not enjoyed "the convenience of table, Chair or Bed since I landed: only the ground to serve for all."[39]

General Albemarle was painfully aware of the debility and mortality of his troops. While he was inclined to blame the natural weakness of the British soldier for rum—"that diabolical liquor is the cause of all our sickness"—he could do nothing about the fevers that drove his men to drink. He and they also learned that a red coat made a handsome target for a Cuban guerrilla's gun or knife. The cost could be measured in the 34th Regiment, whose return for October 11 showed only 24 officers and 106 men fit for duty, 281 sick. In less than a month Farmar's command had lost 5 officers, 30 noncommissioned officers, and 177 rank and file, and 170 of the sick had died. Albemarle figured that he had buried three thousand men since the capitulation and at times had no more than six hundred fit for duty.[40] Happily, the burden of the occupation was undemanding; for Major Robert Farmar it meant routine orders from headquarters that he "takes Lord Albemarle's Guard tomorrow."[41] It was some consolation that the Havana prize money surpassed the dreams of all who survived to collect it. Major Robert Farmar's share amounted to £564.14.6., and each private of the 34th pocketed £4.1.8½.[42]

The losses of the army in Cuba put an end to any thought of seizing Florida or Louisiana, but the capture of Havana accomplished a part of the grand strategy. Negotiations for peace moved rapidly in the fall of 1762; Spain agreed to forfeit Florida in exchange for Havana. At the same time, France, ceding her claims east of the Mississippi to Great Britain, graciously offered all west of that river to her ally Spain. In haste to conclude the Treaty of Paris, the ministry in London agreed to the exclusion of the city of New Orleans and the adjacent area referred to as the Isle of Orleans from the British acquisition, although free passage from the sea and up the Mississippi River was secured. The definitive terms of peace were signed at Paris in February 1763, and all around the world British soldiers dreamed of returning home, their work well done.

III.

Mobile, 1763–1765

By the Treaty of Paris in 1763, Great Britain became the possessor of half the North American continent. To her Atlantic coastal colonies were added French Canada, Louisiana east of the Mississippi, and Spanish Florida. In these newly acquired lands lived a foreign and recently hostile population of European origins and a native and still hostile Indian population. The former would be dealt with more easily than the latter.

French Canadians soon found British rule sufficiently mild and tolerant that they accepted and supported it for the next century. The Spanish inhabitants of Florida, concentrated in the towns of St. Augustine and Pensacola, adhered to their Bourbon monarch and left for other parts of his vast realms. On the western frontiers of what was now British North America, at Mobile and in the Illinois country, some French settlers remained in their little towns and villages while others migrated sorrowfully across the Mississippi, intransigent in their enmity toward the British and unwilling to believe that, at the whim of Louis le Bien-aimée, they had been made subjects of the king of Spain.

For the Indian tribes of the interior, many of them active allies of the French during the recent war, the triumph of Great Britain raised serious questions regarding the future. The land hunger of the English was well known, and if their fur traders and frontier diplomats were better supplied with European trade goods than were French *coureurs-du-bois,* their greed was great and their rum was often bad. At the same time, the Indians had become accustomed to the white man's trade and dependent upon his guns. That posed a dilemma that each tribe must resolve within and for itself. North of the Ohio River, the decision for war was taken by the Ottawa chief Pontiac, and his warriors swept the British back to Fort Pitt before the wave of bloodshed was broken by Colonel Henry Bouquet at Bushy Run. Fear that Pontiac's rising might infect the southern tribes hung like a thunderhead over the Carolinas and Georgia; its base lay among the Creeks, Choctaws, and Chickasaws to the west. For the future of British North America, the establishment of British authority on the Gulf Coast was as important as its restoration on the banks of the Ohio.

Throughout the spring and summer of 1763, the government in London considered how best to meet the new problems of empire. Military occupation of the ceded territories was clearly the first step. As early as March, the 34th Regiment, still at Havana, was told off for the occupation of French Louisiana, but not until May was it transferred to the North American command of General Jeffrey Amherst and orders to that effect directed to General William Keppel at Havana.[1] Communication between London, Havana, and New York was agonizingly slow; before word of its new assignment reached Farmar's enfeebled regiment, it had embarked, the second week of July, with the rest of the British forces evacuating Cuba and was happily headed home. On July 18 the fleet was overtaken by a sloop carrying orders for the 34th and 22nd regiments to go to Louisiana, the 35th Regiment to Pensacola. The receipt of the new orders by these regiments on the nineteenth "occasion'd much hurry and was a great disappointment to many," remarked one of the more fortunate officers as he watched the shifting of men and baggage necessitated by this unexpected turn of events. By July 21 the regiments bound for Mobile and Pensacola parted company from the rest of the fleet and set course for Jamaica, en route to the Gulf Coast.[2]

After a voyage protracted by foul winds and calms, Major Farmar and the 34th Regiment reached Port Royal, Jamaica, on August 23. There he found Major Arthur Loftus and the 22nd, who had arrived two weeks earlier, and a useful supply of material gathered by local authorities preparatory to sending another body of troops, recently arrived from Martinique, to occupy Mobile. As Farmar's orders from London took precedence over such local arrangements, he was able to utilize the stores and shipping already gathered, but he found it necessary to draw upon the Treasury for £1,200 in order to provide for all of his requirements. His largest purchase consisted of £52.6.0 worth of medicines, for the regiment was deficient in some and others had been ruined while being transferred from ship to ship when he left the fleet. While at Kingston, Farmar also drew up and printed a manifesto in French to be distributed to the inhabitants of Mobile. On September 1 a convoy of six transports, guarded by H.M.S. *Stag,* Captain William Bayne, sailed from Port Royal for Mobile.[3]

The little English fleet made its way first to Pensacola, which had been occupied on August 6 by the third battalion of the 60th Regiment under Lieutenant Colonel Augustin Prevost. Arriving at the western end of Santa Rosa Island on September 20, Captain Bayne dispatched a schooner to investigate the bar off Mobile Bay and secure a French pilot. Farmar ordered Captain John Lind to Mobile with the official French authorization for its surrender to the British. If, as proved to be the case, the French commandant at Mobile had inadequate instructions for that process, Lind was to proceed to New Orleans, where he arrived September 30, and to secure the necessary directions from the governor of Louisiana, Louis de Kerlérec. On September 26 Bayne and his convoy moved up the bay to the little town of Pensacola. There Farmar would hear from Prevost that several Mobilians had recently visited Pensacola and expressed their impatience to see the British established at Mobile.[4]

Bayne's reconnaissance ship returned on the twenty-eighth with encouraging word regarding the Mobile bar, and on October 3 Major Farmar sent off his brother, Captain John Farmar of the 22nd Regiment, with two of the smallest vessels of the convoy as an advance party, trusting that they might first unload the powder they carried and then be of use in disembarking troops from the larger transports that could not negotiate the shallow bar. The importance of Captain Farmar's mission was emphasized on October 4, when two French pilots appeared at Pensacola and expressed grave doubts that the British vessels would be able to gain entrance to Mobile Bay. Captain Bayne was optimistic, however, and the convoy sailed from Pensacola on October 8 and stood off Mobile Point the next day. Several days were then spent sounding the bar, setting out buoys, and waiting for the ships forwarded with Captain Farmar to appear.[5]

Outside the bar of Mobile Bay, October 14, Major Robert Farmar found that he faced other than navigational problems. From John, whose ships now came down from the town, he learned that Commandant Pierre-Annibal DeVelle, by quibbling over the unloading of their cargo, had been responsible for delaying the return of the powder ships and thereby the further progress of the British troops toward Mobile. Captain Lind, returning from New Orleans, brought a pedantic letter from Governor Kerlérec announcing that gentleman's imminent retirement to France and advising Farmar that the French, having scheduled an Indian congress for November 1, wished to complete it without British interference. As Jean Jacques-Blaise D'Abbadie, Kerlérec's recently arrived successor, and Charles Philippe Aubry, an experienced French military representative, might be expected to appear at Mobile between the fifteenth and twentieth of October, Farmar was asked to delay his landing until they had completed their task. A note to the same purpose from M. DeVelle added to Farmar's wrath at French delaying tactics. While H.M.S. *Stag* and the largest of the transports sailed west to find a safe anchorage at Ship Island, Farmar and Bayne took steps to push the expedition toward Mobile.

On the sixteenth, the three smallest vessels got across the bar; men and supplies were transferred to Captain Farmar's powder ships, and the British flotilla began moving cautiously up the bay—only to be halted by mud flats some two or three leagues below the town on October 18. At that point Major Farmar, Captain Bayne, Major Loftus, and Captain Lind, accepting DeVelle's invitation, rowed on to Fort Condé for a conference. The Frenchman again pressed Farmar to keep his troops in their transports until after the Indian congress, but the major, concerned for the welfare of his scurvy-ridden men, now three months aboard ship, and miffed by DeVelle's failure to provide his guests with quarters, insisted on landing at the earliest possible moment. DeVelle—whom Governor Kerlérec described as "a good officer, a zealous servant of his king, a slave of regulations"—finally agreed to withdraw from Fort Condé in forty-eight hours, and on Thursday, October 20, 1763, the grenadier companies of the 34th and 22nd regiments were landed at Mobile and the Union Jack was raised. Two days later, the French troops departed. It was quite some time before all of Farmar's force was ashore. Everything had to be moved by small boat from ships anchored six miles down the bay; troops aboard the transport at Ship Island were not disembarked until November 25, and supplies were still being off-loaded there a month later.[6]

The place that now came under Robert Farmar's authority offered little comfort or satisfaction to its new masters. It might boast of having once been the principal city of French Louisiana, but in 1763 it had only 350 inhabitants, some 90 families, and a scattering of one-story houses that barely adhered to any street plan and impinged upon the approaches to the fort. The brick exterior of Fort Condé belied its grave deterioration. Constructed in 1717 and renamed Fort Charlotte by Major Farmar, in honor of George III's queen, it had been allowed to go to ruin in recent years. Square, with bastions at each corner, about ninety yards of wall on each side, its parapet rose to a height of twenty feet. The brick work was crumbling; the untended ramparts were covered with bushes and weeds. There were barracks for over two hundred men, but they were in such bad repair as to require rebuilding by the British as well as enlargement. As there was only one officers' room in the fort, Farmar chose to live outside in a private residence. There was no storage for provisions within the walls, and the bakehouse was useless. The wooden palisades on the glacis were rotten and the gates "very bad," the main gate practically off its hinges. The officers' quarters a hundred yards outside the fort were ruinous, floors rotten and window panes broken. Two bake ovens and a storehouse some distance away completed the military complex.[7]

Farmar's first task was to secure the buildings and property belonging to the king of France, all of which were to be handed over, according to the terms of the peace treaty. Governor Kerlérec, however, had already taken care to remove the serviceable cannon from Fort Condé—an action which Farmar vociferously but vainly protested—and French soldiers burned the remaining gun carriages the evening of their departure. Little of value remained beyond the dilapidated furnishings and broken equipment. Outlying buildings erected at public expense were claimed by private persons who could show little or no right to them beyond current occupancy. Wishing to avoid antagonizing the French Mobilians, Farmar accepted their claims for the moment, but he warned English merchants who were already on the spot that, if they purchased property from departing Frenchmen and it proved to be government property, they would be ousted and charged rent for its use.[8]

Having put what men he could under cover in the fort, and billeting the rest in private houses, Major Farmar could leave the routine of military business to his administrative staff, which included as fort major and ordnance storekeeper his brother Captain John Farmar, and Captain John Lind as fort adjutant and surveyor of the works. Upon these men Farmar relied while he attended to more pressing concerns.[9]

Within days of Farmar's arrival at Mobile, he was joined by several notable guests. From New Orleans came the new governor, D'Abbadie, an aristocratic French administrator who would prove something of a thorn in the side of the British, and Aubry, a calm, efficient, and cooperative gentleman who undoubtedly helped to patch up Anglo-French differences and eventually succeeded to D'Abbadie's position.[10] Of more immediate importance to the affairs of British Mobile was Lieutenant Colonel James Robertson, the personal representative of Sir Jeffrey Amherst, commander in chief of all British forces in North America. Dispatched from headquarters in New York, Robertson carried instructions to inspect the garrisons of St. Augustine, Pensacola, and Mobile and to ascend the Mississippi to the Illinois country if possible. He was generously supplied with funds and with complete authority over all troops in Florida and Louisiana. With him came a young engineer-surveyor, Lieutenant Philip Pittman, who was under orders to map and chart the new territories through which Robertson might pass. Robertson and his party reached Mobile on November 9. He found Major Robert Farmar and his French visitors immersed in Indian diplomacy, which meant the daily entertainment of between three and five thousand Choctaw and Alabama tribesmen who were encamped within gunshot of the town, some of whose chiefs were so ill disposed toward the British that they refused to drink Farmar's rum.[11]

During the later stages of the Seven Years' War, French Louisiana had been isolated by the British navy's dominance on the high seas. Because of the interdiction of shipping to New Orleans, it had been impossible for Governor Kerlérec to supply his Indian allies with the presents upon which their lives and their loyalty depended. As the war ended and French hegemony passed to Britain, Kerlérec recognized the desirability of meeting with the Chickasaws, Choctaws, and lesser tribes, and, with generous gifts, securing a peaceful withdrawal and the prospect of their friendship in the future. It was good policy for the French, no less so for the British, whose failure to satisfy the redskins in the north had helped stir up Pontiac's rebellion. Kerlérec and D'Abbadie sent out word that they would meet with the Indians at Mobile on November 1, 1763, and their efforts to delay Farmar's occupation of Fort Condé until after that date were aimed at avoiding complications at the Indian congress.[12] Farmar, trusting no Frenchman and having no experience of Indians, rejected D'Abbadie's request, landed, and found himself surrounded by Indians. He was considerably disturbed by the French assumption of leadership in dealing with them and disdainful of that "most disagreeable custom the French have introduced amongst the Indians . . . of giving them victuals and drink." Nonetheless, Farmar found it expedient to provide some kind of food and quantities of watered rum for as many as five hundred every day during the congress.[13]

To the complications of Indian diplomacy was added the development of a sharp personal antagonism between D'Abbadie and Farmar, both jealous of the authority the one had formerly and the other now possessed. On the day of Robertson's arrival, Farmar delivered a stinging rebuke to D'Abbadie for daring to give "directions to the Inhabitants of this Government, contrary to my express orders" and for having sold certain boats that were formerly French Crown property. For his part, D'Abbadie found that the English gave him more trouble than the Indians and described Farmar as "tough and difficult to deal with." The English were "men drunk with their success, and who regard themselves as masters of the world." Happily, Robertson, who gained a better impression of the Frenchman than did Farmar, was able to mediate their quarrel, and a satisfactory meeting with Choctaw and Alabama tribesmen culminated on November 14, when Farmar, D'Abbadie, Aubry, and DeVelle signed a formal statement addressed to the Choctaw. The Indians were assured of the friendly intent of the new masters of Mobile, urged to maintain the peace, and assured that they would be well supplied with trade goods by the English. D'Abbadie and Farmar harangued the Indians "hand in hand"

and, with utmost solemnity, impressed their seals in red wax on the document.[14]

If Robert Farmar imagined that the sealing of a document concluded his dealings with the Indians encamped around Mobile, he was sadly mistaken. The Choctaw made a long holiday of their visit. There was trading to be done and strangely clad soldiers to be observed and occasionally used as targets; the British major had promised to be generous—let him fulfill his words. From great chiefs like Wolf King down to the youngest warrior, they demanded Farmar's attention; every day he faced twenty to thirty in his quarters, clamoring to be fed and given corn to take back to their squaws and children. His embarrassment was compounded by a shortage of presents and of money with which to procure more. Not until December 27 did Farmar's unwelcome guests return to their villages, leaving him to worry about the Creeks, whose jealousy was bound to raise the price of their friendship.[15]

In order to support their influence with the Indians, the French had maintained small military outposts at Fort Choiseul on the Tombecbé River and Fort Toulouse on the Coosa River, north of Mobile. Farmar moved quickly to bring them within his orbit. Early in November he sent Lieutenant Thomas Ford and thirty men of the 34th Regiment up the Tombecbé, and on the twenty-second of the month they occupied the little stockade that was christened Fort York.[16] Had Lieutenant Colonel Robertson reached Mobile a few days earlier, he would have vetoed Farmar's decision to occupy the fort on the Tombecbé, for he considered "a small garrison out of the reach of succor . . . as so many hostages" in the hands of the Indians. His view, reinforced by the advice of D'Abbadie and the Creek chief Wolf King, prevailed with regard to Fort Toulouse. No troops were sent to the Alabama fort; in fact, Farmar had none to spare. In January 1764 Farmar gave James Germany, an Indian trader, permission to live at Fort Toulouse and instructed him to report to Mobile on the activities of the Creeks in the area.[17]

There were yet other posts to man and consider. A corporal and six men were stationed on Dauphin Island to assist the pilot, there being no other inhabitants on the island. It seemed desirable to Farmar to establish posts at Biloxi and on the route, by way of Lake Pontchartrain and the Iberville River, to the Mississippi, but he would never have the manpower to do so. Robertson thought well of occupying the abandoned French fort at Natchez, and Captain Lieutenant James Campbell was assigned to that post, but more pressing business delayed its occupation for two years.[18]

The pacification of the Indians and the occupation of Fort York were steps toward a more distant goal, the establishment of British authority at Fort Chartres in the Illinois country. Situated some nine hundred miles up the Mississippi River, south of modern St. Louis, Fort Chartres appeared to be the key to controlling the Indians and the fur trade of the old Northwest. Farmar's orders directed him to see to its occupation, and when Lind visited New Orleans in October 1763, he sought the advice and assistance of Governor Kerlérec regarding the ascent of the great river. Lieutenant Colonel Robertson was also instructed to push the project as rapidly as possible, and Amherst had even imagined that Robertson might sail up the Mississippi in the ships that carried him south from New York. In mid-November after the Indian congress at Mobile, Robertson, William Bayne, and Aubry made their way to New Orleans, evidently by way of the Mississippi Sound and Lake Pontchartrain, in order to investigate the shorter inland water route to the Mississippi that was completed (at least on contemporary maps) by the Amite and Iberville rivers. At New Orleans, Robertson consulted with D'Abbadie and secured promises of French cooperation. Assured that seagoing vessels would not serve, he contracted with Pierre Maxent and others to have suitable boats ready for use by mid-January 1764, the appropriate time, he was told, to ascend the river. Returning to Mobile, Robertson left the final preparations in Farmar's hands and departed for New York.

The assault on the Mississippi was assigned to the 22nd Regiment under the command of Major Arthur Loftus, and the supplies of Fort Charlotte were ransacked to provide him and his party of nearly 350 men with sufficient food and equipment for the three months they expected to be on the river. A detachment of the 60th Regiment was brought over from Pensacola to strengthen Loftus's force. Captain Lieutenant Campbell would accompany Loftus as far as Natchez, and engineer Philip Pittman would take the first opportunity to map the course of the Mississippi. Loftus got the 22nd aboard two small transports at Mobile and was ready to sail by January 7, 1764, but problems in transferring men and supplies to another vessel delayed their departure, and Farmar decided to withdraw the men of the 60th Regiment before the expedition finally got under way on January 12.[19]

After Loftus's departure, Major Robert Farmar had time to take stock of his situation at Mobile. He had completed the transfer of sovereignty, dealt with the local Indians, established the post at Fort York, and abandoned Fort Toulouse, and the occupation of Fort Chartres was proceeding for the moment. All military matters were properly in hand, and as he reported the accomplishments of the last six months to the secretary at war in London, Farmar thought it appropriate to suggest that his nearly twenty-four years in the army might deserve recognition in the form of some further appointment in the civil government of this far-flung territory; the royal governorship was no doubt in his mind.[20] Unbeknownst to Major Farmar, George III had already acted with regard to the boundaries, political structure, and governing personnel of his new colony.

While the 34th Regiment was making its way from Havana to Mobile, the Board of Trade, the Privy Council, and the king (with the earl of Bute's advice) were determining the future of French Louisiana and Spanish Florida. After several months of consultation and consideration, a proclamation was issued, October 7, 1763, establishing the new colonies of East and West Florida. East Florida included the peninsula and was bounded on the west by the Apalachicola River. West Florida extended from the Apalachicola to the Mississippi, its southern boundary the Gulf of Mexico and the line through the lakes and rivers established by the Treaty of Paris. Its northern boundary was set at the thirty-first parallel but subsequently moved farther north to a line drawn due east from the juncture of the Mississippi and Yazoo rivers. The administration of West Florida was vested in a governor appointed by the Crown and advised by a council. Provision was made for an elected representative assembly, to be summoned by the governor, its acts subject to review and approval by the Privy Council. Customary English legal and administrative systems were to be instituted; the rights and lands of the Indian tribes in the colony were carefully protected; and financial support of the government of the colony was to be provided by parliamentary grants. It was as wise and efficient a system as the eighteenth-century British empire could produce, but much would depend upon the men who worked within it.[21]

Personal and political interest determined that appointment as governor of West Florida fell to George Johnstone, a young Scottish naval captain. Johnstone's touchy, contentious disposition and fiery temper were better suited to the quarterdeck than to the council chamber, and his love of writing letters filled with classical and literary allusions surpassed his ability to deal harmoniously with his colleagues. Governor Johnstone did not reach West Florida until October 1764; until then, Major Robert Farmar governed Mobile, but subject to the orders of a new commander in chief in North America, General Thomas Gage, who supplanted Amherst in the fall of 1763. A competent and patient administrator, Gage was also the new colonel of the 22nd Regiment, which was currently somewhere on the Mississippi River. The 22nd would also receive from home a new lieutenant colonel, David Wedderburn, like Johnstone a young Scot with useful political and military connections.[22] For the present, however, Farmar's problems were sufficiently close at hand.

The French inhabitants of Mobile, some in the town, others scattered on either side of the bay and on the lower stretches of its tributary rivers, were Farmar's concern as soon as he raised the British flag over Fort Charlotte. The manifesto he had had printed at Kingston was immediately read and posted about the town to advise its people of their rights and obligations. It was hoped that assurance of toleration of their Roman Catholic faith would encourage them to remain under British rule. As Farmar's manifesto gave the French three months to take the oath of allegiance or eighteen months in which to dispose of their property and depart, there was ample time for their opinion and prospects to swing from one extreme to the other. At the outset, D'Abbadie openly encouraged the inhabitants of Mobile to return to French New Orleans, and Farmar was enraged. Few offered to take the oath, and many began selling off their livestock. By mid-December it appeared that their reason lay in the implicit obligation to support the king of England against even the king of France.[23] In January 1764 Farmar feared that of ninety-eight French families in the district, only ten would remain; he did not press for a decision, however, and they let matters slide as long as possible.[24] There was employment to be had from the British and supplies to be sold to them. Some, like the proud Chevalier Montault de Monberaut, sought special considerations for their services. Others, like Louis Favre, were invaluable as interpreters, and as the only men of the 34th Regiment who were trained as gunsmiths had died in Cuba, competent French repairmen were in great demand. On April 7 Farmar reported that only eight French inhabitants had taken the oath. He hoped, however, that news of the cession of Louisiana to Spain would persuade many to return to Mobile, and he planned to send an officer to New Orleans "to implant a favorable Idea of the English Constitution, and be a great means of fixing them under our protection." Such hopes were largely disappointed, even when news of the cession to Spain was published at New Orleans in September. In August, Farmar noted more cheerfully that "the French are daily coming in to take the Oaths of Allegiance," and ultimately 112 Mobilians took the oath within a year of British military occupation.[25]

The French inhabitants of Mobile received generous treatment at the hands of the British government. Governor D'Abbadie, at New Orleans, sought General Gage's consideration in their behalf, and their own request for further time in which to dispose of their property was given favorable attention in London. Governor Johnstone was directed to recognize their property rights on the basis of occupation and cultivation and to allow them a reasonable period in which to complete their real estate transactions if they decided to leave the province.[26] Although Major Farmar would find himself embroiled in disputes over certain French properties in Mobile, French Mobilians would give him far less trouble than the Anglo-Americans who began to flock into the town in 1764.

Unlike some of his fellow officers in West Florida—and George Johnstone—Robert Farmar was not prone to put all of his problems, in writing, before his superiors. It is evident that when he did so he had reached the end of patience. A few episodes emerge from the first year of his government of Mobile that may be taken as exemplary of the difficulties he faced and the turbulence that was characteristic of the town.

The first Anglo-Americans to reach Mobile after the British occupation were itinerant Indian traders and their somewhat more respectable employers, who secured property, built storehouses, and became the leading figures of British Mobile. They came from Georgia and the Carolinas, and whether packhorse drivers or established merchants like John McGillivray, they were rough American frontiersmen with little respect for law and order or the Indians from whom they secured their peltries. When they came to town, they celebrated with a bottle in one hand and a gun in the other. They were "Strangers to the Paths of Vertue, and sunk in Dissoluteness and Dissipation"; helpless civilians were fair game and uniformed redcoats their natural enemies.[27] The servants or, as Farmar termed them, the hirelings of John McGillivray were a particularly troublesome lot of army deserters and fugitives from justice from the older colonies. Their violence, when they brought their skins to Mobile, made the streets unsafe, and they "continued in so riotous, debauched drunken manner of life that they were a nuisance to every family . . . and a pest to society." Twenty years of army life must have hardened Major Farmar to scenes of public drunkenness, but matters reached a crisis when McGillivray's bullies insulted the daughter (or daughter-in-law) of the Mobile area's leading French resident, the Chevalier Montault de Monberaut. Lieutenant Philip Pittman brought young Mme. Montault in tears before Farmar and no doubt spoke most gallantly in her behalf, demanding justice for a fair damsel in distress. Pittman invariably moved Farmar to action, if only from anger, and the major ordered out a corporal's guard to apprehend the rascals. The gang was readily found but not so easily corralled. Shots were fired, the corporal was knocked down, and all the ruffians except a fellow named Richard Jones escaped arrest. More troops were mustered, and the remaining malefactors soon were captured and held for trial. McGillivray and his followers made an insolent show of their objections to a military court, but Farmar proceeded with the hearing. Jones, apparently the chief offender and described by Farmar as "a wretch, bred amongst Savages & a Scourge to Society," was sentenced to 250 lashes; the rest of the gang were acquitted.[28]

Military justice was harsh, but it might be tempered by social considerations. A more respectable Indian trader who was caught stealing an officer's horse was tried and sentenced to be whipped, but Farmar remitted the corporal punishment. On the other hand, Charles Conner, a liquor dealer, was arrested and had his casks smashed when Farmar learned from a French habitant that he was selling rum to the Indians—an accusation Conner naturally denied.[29]

It is not surprising that Robert Farmar was sensitive to "the demands of a french Lady of the first rank," but his concern for a poor Indian was rather more remarkable and much to his credit, even if his primary concern was with Indian policy rather than British justice. Daniel Ward, a Mobile merchant, sold a damaged and useless brass kettle to an Indian in exchange for four skins. When the Indian returned to Ward and demanded a refund, Ward refused, arguing that the Indian knew what he was buying in the first place. On January 30, 1764, the Indian complained to Farmar, and the major ordered Ward to make restitution and to post bond for his good behavior in the future. Ward was shocked and "surprized Major Farmar should encourage such damned Rascalls in that manner, . . . in other places, an Indian for behaving so, wou'd be kick'd out of doors." Three times Ward refused to comply, and the fourth time Farmar sent a file of soldiers to seize him and place him under arrest in the regimental prison, the Black Hole. Ward was transferred to the officers' guardroom within an hour, and before the day was out he agreed to exchange the damaged kettle for a new one. He persisted in refusing to give bond, however, and Farmar ordered him to leave Mobile within a month. The reaction of Ward's fellow merchants was drastic: the next day they closed their shops and refused to do business with any army officer. After two days of angry confrontation, the merchants reopened their doors, and Farmar accepted Ward's bond for two hundred pounds as a guarantee of honesty in his future dealings with the Indians.[30]

General Gage, like Amherst before him, had a low opinion of Indian traders. Sir Jeffrey had sent firm orders to Farmar to punish any traders who might breach his instructions, and when he heard of these episodes, Gage heartily approved the major's summary treatment of that "Rascally Sett" who "must be kept within Bounds."[31]

Farmar soon found that he was not to have a free hand at Mobile, however. In spite of the three months it might take to send a letter from Mobile to New York, and two more months to receive a reply from headquarters, General Thomas Gage kept a sharp eye on his frontier regiments. Having received Farmar's November 17, 1763, report (addressed to Amherst) on the occupation of Mobile, Gage replied in March 1764, approving the major's prompt action in stopping D'Abbadie's efforts to suborn the French at Mobile, but regretting that disputes had arisen and urging civility toward Farmar's neighbors at New Orleans. At the same time, Gage wrote to the Frenchman, apologizing for Farmar's "brusqueries," trusting that there would be no further problems, and hoping that the arrival of Governor Johnstone would smooth matters on the Gulf Coast.[32]

Farmar's local arrangements drew Gage's criticism, and, urged by the War Office, he ordered the staff at Mobile reduced to no more than a fort major and barracks master. With a kindly eye to family interests, Gage approved Captain John Farmar's retention of the former position—he was not unmoved, perhaps, by John's concern that, having only won his captaincy in the field at Havana in 1762, he might be reduced to a lieutenant's pay. Major Farmar's family connections would not suffer by staff reductions, in fact. His deceased eldest brother, Jasper, a successful New York merchant, had established business interests with Paul and Christopher Miller; his sister Mary had married Paul Miller, and a brother, Thomas Miller, was a merchant captain who made his way to Mobile by February 1764 and was involved in business transactions with Robert Farmar. By March the Miller family in New York had gained Gage's favor, and a Miller (either Paul or Christopher) was being considered for the position of barracks master if he would go to Mobile. By May, Miller had not only secured that appointment but also those of storekeeper and bateaukeeper for Mobile. He planned to sail from New York in about seven weeks and named his brother Thomas as his deputy until his arrival.[33]

More immediately, Farmar faced the dilapidated condition of Fort Charlotte, set as it was amidst tribes of hostile Indians and garrisoned by a few hundred enfeebled veterans of the Havana campaign. During the spring and summer of 1764, Farmar set to work shoring up bastion platforms and casements whose arches were ready to collapse. The common soldiers' barracks were so bad that two of the fourteen small rooms for officers were turned over to them, and "tho' in a ruinous condition" the commanding officer's quarters were occupied by the surgeon and his mate. One of the two bakehouses was converted into soldiers' barracks, and in order to save the "unreasonable" rent being paid to house himself, two officers, and the commissary, Farmar proposed to live in the other. As the construction of new barracks seemed inevitable, Farmar proposed they should be two-story buildings, "by which means the officers would have sufficient as well as airy rooms and not be exposed to the inconvenience daily of being plundered by the savages, who have been ever used to come in and out as they pleased."[34]

Farmar's concern for the security of Fort Charlotte was well founded. In March he reported that Indians "assemble in large Bodys under Arms, and fire at our Men in the Woods," although a month later all appeared "very peaceable." Farmar's fears lay in his expectation that, with spring, "all the chiefs, as well those who always were in our interest as those who are but lat'ly become our allies, will certainly visit us to demand their yearly presents." Unhappily, the goods received from the Indian Department were "so very trifling and insufficient" that Farmar dared not distribute them. "The giving one party and not the other wou'd occasion such heart burnings amongst them, as must in every shape be prejudicial to the national interest, as well as His Majesty's service." The Indian superintendent, John Stuart, seemed to have no idea of the number of Indians who expected gifts—Choctaws, Creeks, Mobilians, Chickasaws, Tensas—and the 350 firelocks Farmar had received simply would not go around.[35]

The effects of a summer at Mobile had yet to be experienced. Submitting his returns on August 1, Farmar noted that the regiment was short five officers who had never joined, and within the next four days he lost two more lieutenants to fever. "A great many of our Effectives are very old and Infirm, and ought to be Discharged; and others again who have Enlisted only for a term of years are not worth detaining, . . . take them altogether we have scarce a Compleat Company who can be looked upon as Soldiers fit for Duty." The sickly season, for which Mobile soon became infamous, lasted into October, when Farmar wrote, "The Raging fever both amongst Officers & Men . . . still continues, & we have no other hopes than that the approaching cold season will effectually put a stop to it." It hardly mattered that there was no Protestant clergyman at Mobile nor regimental chaplain to administer the last rites to the dying.[36]

Such routine concerns were overshadowed, however, when the disturbing news reached Mobile that the 22nd Regiment, far from being well on its way to Fort Chartres, had been turned back by belligerent Tonica Indians at the Roche d'Avion, a mere two hundred miles above New Orleans, and was returning to West Florida. It had taken Major Arthur Loftus nearly two weeks to reach New Orleans from Mobile, and another month had passed before the 22nd was ready to begin the long haul up the Mississippi. On March 20 Captain Lieutenant James Campbell, in the lead canoe, came under heavy fire from Indians hidden along the shore, and finding it impossible to land his troops or to proceed, Loftus promptly began a precipitous retreat. He was back in New Orleans by March 22 and ended his flight at Pensacola, April 7. By the first of April, Robert Farmar had received the bad tidings; the news reached Gage's headquarters in New York a month and a half later.[37]

The embarrassment of the Loftus expedition was clearly due to British failure to prepare the way with parleys and presents for the Indian tribes along the Mississippi. Farmar had urged the pacification of those Indians by means of a conference before Loftus's departure, but Lieutenant Colonel Robertson had rejected this very sensible idea as an "unnecessary expence." "It would in all probability have saved a much greater," Farmar observed. Among the British officers at Mobile there was absolute certainty that French influence had been decisive in stirring up the Indians, and they made no secret of their opinion. Loftus all but accused D'Abbadie of ordering the attack; French settlers at Pointe Coupée were said to have been "verry industrious," even "instrumental in exciting" the Indians. Farmar was now fully convinced that no course would serve but to assemble an Indian congress "and fairly buy them from the French." General Gage, who had personal memories of Braddock's fate when ambushed by the French and Indians a decade earlier, agreed that "the French will under Hand give us all the Trouble they can, and endeavour to keep us from the Illinois." But peace imposes restraints on generals, and Gage wrote soothing words to D'Abbadie and silenced Major Loftus. Farmar was ordered to send the 22nd Regiment up the river again in August and to "pave the Way with Presents." Assistance in dealing with the Indians was on its way to West Florida in the person of John Stuart, Indian superintendent for the Southern Department, and Gage trusted that he would lend support to the second British effort.[38]

Robert Farmar had already heard from Stuart and had forwarded the superintendent's friendly messages to the Chickasaw and Choctaw chieftains to the west, but so few Indian presents had arrived—and so few did Farmar expect to receive—that he dared not assemble the tribes again for fear of offending their expectations. All that Farmar could do that summer was to effect Gage's orders to bring the 22nd back to Mobile (where they too sickened and died), begin again the costly negotiations for boats at New Orleans, and dispatch agents to smooth British relations with both the French on the Mississippi and the Indians along its banks. His prospects were not improved by the loss of a shipload of supplies on the bar at St. Augustine, and Loftus did not think it would be possible to begin a second attempt on the river before January 1765. Mobile was, meanwhile, desperately overcrowded. "This place at present carries the appearance of a little hamlet formed of Negro Hutts," wrote Farmar, "rather than a well peopled town in Canada; besides the French are coming in daily to take the oaths of allegiance, and have scarce even such cabbins to put their heads in."[39]

Faced with planning a second thrust up the Mississippi, Farmar took every precaution. Campbell and Pittman were sent west, the first with instructions to establish himself at Manchac, to clear the Iberville River, and to win the friendship of the riverine tribes between New Orleans and Natchez; the latter to attempt to reach the Illinois. At New Orleans, Governor D'Abbadie was cooperative, and Captain Campbell contracted for sixty Negro workmen to be employed on the Iberville project. Proceeding up the Mississippi, he distributed presents to Houmas, Chittimachas, Alabamas, and Tonicas and won their assurances of peace. "Between savages and nigroes I am agreeably amused," he reported. He returned to Mobile in December, full of enthusiasm for establishing a post at Manchac. Lieutenant Pittman ran into difficulties. His arrangements to join a convoy of French bateaux headed north fell through, and D'Abbadie warned him against any further efforts in that direction. He returned to Mobile complaining bitterly, and Farmar sent Lieutenant John Ross and Hugh Crawford, an interpreter, to complete his assignment

And as if Indian opposition to the Mississippi expedition were not enough, in August Farmar heard from white traders among the Creeks that both Mobile and Pensacola might expect to be attacked by that warlike tribe in the autumn. A conciliatory message was immediately dispatched to The Mortar, Emistisiguo, and other prominent Creek chiefs, together with firm reminders that English presents and English justice went hand in hand.[40]

October 1764 marked the first anniversary of Robert Farmar's occupation of Mobile and also the arrival of two newcomers to the colony who would greatly complicate his life and work. Superintendent John Stuart landed at Pensacola on October 4, and, hoping to do something to advance the business of his department, he sailed westward on October 13, accompanied by Lord Adam Gordon, a peripatetic Scottish army colonel who was making a grand tour of the North American colonies. Landing at Mobile (where he was disappointed of finding transportation to New Orleans), Stuart got a cold reception from Farmar. The superintendent proposed to visit the Mississippi in order to pacify the Indians; Farmar advised him that he had already taken steps to accomplish that end—Stuart need not bother. Nor did the major offer Stuart much information regarding the Indians when the superintendent and Lord Adam questioned him. Finding in Farmar "a backwardness & disinclination . . . to cooperate," John Stuart departed after only three days, having contracted the fever prevalent at Mobile and little else. From Pensacola he complained bitterly to Gage of having been ignored by Farmar and of having left Mobile "as much a stranger to the state of Indian affairs there as when I went to it." He wrote to Farmar, pointing out that as superintendent, he, not Farmar, was in charge of Indian affairs in West Florida and asking that Captain Campbell's instructions should be provided to Charles Stuart, the superintendent's cousin, who was being sent as a representative of the Indian Department to negotiate with the tribes along the lower Mississippi.[41] Such a letter, studded with the names of the commander in chief, the secretary of state, even that of His Majesty, from all of whom Stuart claimed authority, did nothing to smooth relations with Robert Farmar.

John Stuart's natural resolve to exercise a proper authority was strengthened when he returned to Pensacola and found that during his absence Governor George Johnstone had landed. The newly arrived governor was delighted to cooperate, to dispatch agents in every direction, and to meet the Chickasaw and Choctaw at Mobile on December 20. Invitations were issued on November 3, in spite of the advice of John Buckle, a Mobile Indian trader whom Stuart adopted as his local adviser. Young Charles Stuart was sent to Mobile on November 9 as John's representative to the tribes on the Mississippi. He found Farmar grumbling that the superintendent "had wrote him in a very Cavalier Stile" and quite unwilling to disclose Captain Campbell's instructions to a member of the Indian Department. More significantly, Charles learned that orders for the 22nd Regiment to return to England had been received, and on August 1 Gage had ordered that the next Mississippi expedition should be carried out by the 34th Regiment under the command of Robert Farmar. Before Superintendent Stuart could intervene, Farmar had sent Buckle, along with Lieutenant Thomas Ford, to talk with the Choctaw and persuade them to meet him on the Mississippi, and (so it appeared to Charles Stuart) he had, for that purpose, laid hands on the presents the superintendent had intended to distribute at his proposed Indian congress.[42]

Farmar was hardly rid of John Stuart when he heard from Governor George Johnstone. On October 25 the governor wrote to announce his recent arrival in Pensacola and to request that Farmar would publish his royal commissions at Mobile "as soon as it is convenient" and "with all due solemnity." He invited Farmar to visit him in Pensacola at the earliest opportunity, 'because I am sure I must receive great benefit in my proceedings in settling the Government from one so judicious and well acquainted with the country and the particulars to be considered." Intending to please, Johnstone added that he would support Farmar's private "pretensions" to the ownership of Dauphin Island. There followed an exchange of correspondence marked by the greatest verbal courtesy. On November 2 Johnstone advised Farmar of the news that the 22nd Regiment would be relieved in the spring, leaving the opening of the Mississippi River to the 34th, and on hearing Lord Adam Gordon's recital of the sickliness of the Mobile garrison, the governor sent three hospital mates to care for Farmar's fever-stricken redcoats. Unfortunately, the governor also decided to send Lieutenant Alexander Maclellan to New Orleans as his personal envoy to expedite the work there.[43] Farmar now began to realize that advice was the last thing George Johnstone wanted. It was obvious that Stuart had ingratiated himself with the governor and had convinced him that Farmar was negligent in pursuing preparations for the Mississippi expedition and was incompetent to carry out Indian policy.

The major politely rejected Johnstone's suggestions. His own Indian agents were already on their way north, and this was not the time to hold a congress with the Choctaws. It was pointless to send Lieutenant Maclellan to New Orleans, for he would be outranked by Captain John Lind, whom Farmar had stationed there some time ago. And as the governor had indicated that he planned to come to Mobile in a fortnight, Major Farmar would not visit Pensacola—for fear that their paths might cross at sea.[44]

On December 1 Governor Johnstone and Superintendent Stuart, his health now recovered, embarked for Mobile. Landing the next day, they were met by Farmar on the dock, where the major pointedly snubbed Stuart by refusing to shake his hand or even speak to him. In the small society of colonial Mobile it was impossible that personal hostility could be hidden or ignored, even had the major or the superintendent been inclined to do so. Two days later, they met on the street. Words were exchanged, Farmar asking, "Pray, Mr. Stuart, what do you look upon yourself to be?" This brought on a "very warm altercation" and Farmar's frank admission that Stuart had deeply offended him by questioning the Mobile commandant in the presence of Colonel Lord Adam Gordon, thereby belittling the major's local military status. This matter, at least, was thoroughly aired, and the feud between Farmar and Stuart was patched up—although the insults would be remembered.[45]

If Major Farmar's relations with John Stuart were prickly, his first personal contact with Governor George Johnstone was explosive. Johnstone brought with him to Mobile the exalted concepts of his authority that had already produced ominous disturbances between civil and military officials at Pensacola. The governor claimed the right to give orders to army officers and demanded "supreme authority in every military department." "In his whole conduct," wrote the major, "he has . . . endeavoured to wrest that authority out of my hands . . . yet I think I could not with any propriety quietly give up all our little privileges because I am only *merely* the Major of the 34th Regiment."[46] Those few words sum up a host of black looks and calculated slights on the part of both men, and Farmar's attitude was shared by most of the army officers at Mobile, including Arthur Loftus. The two majors had not been on the best of terms after Loftus's humiliation at the Roche d'Avion, but their mutual hatred of George Johnstone instantly healed that rift. The extent of the hostility generated at Mobile in December 1764 can only be measured by the steps subsequently taken by Governor Johnstone. His malice would pursue Robert Farmar for the next five years.

Their epistolary paths had already crossed, and with the enemy in sight, Johnstone, a former navy captain, promptly gained the windward advantage by questioning Farmar's arrangements for victualing the Mississippi expedition, by extolling the virtues of Lieutenant Maclellan, whom Farmar had ordered to avoid any interference with Lind's work at New Orleans, and by supporting John Stuart's views regarding Indian affairs. Farmar answered Johnstone's ranging shots with a broadside: "Mr. Stuart has both mistaken himself and me, and forgot that he ought to pay some regard in his conduct, to the Character that is due to the Commanding Officer of His Britanick Majesty's Troops in West Florida."[47]

Johnstone answered in kind: "The particular style of your last letter gives me uneasiness, because I think it forbodes a disposition to differ without a cause, which I wou'd endeavour to avoid even where there is sufficient provocation. I am far from disputing . . . the Glory which the King will derive from any actions where you are employed, but I hope to be pardoned for enquiring the particulars as far as my duty requires to add my mite to the General Joy." Johnstone declared Stuart's conduct to be correct and found Farmar's orders to Maclellan "unjustifiable." As for the major himself he was not the commanding officer in West Florida but "merely the Major of the 34th Regiment at Mobile," and the governor found his obstructions "extremely mortifying."[48]

Johnstone soon brought about one of the many remarkable confrontations between civil and military officials for which West Florida became notorious. "Some Disputes having arrose between Gov. Johnstone and Major Farmar concerning the different powers vested in each by their several commissions, it was agreed between them to discuss those matters in the presence of two persons of credit chosen by each." So began the transcript of the formal meeting held at Johnstone's quarters on December 14. The governor's seconds were John Stuart and Lockhart Russel, Johnstone's private secretary. Farmar was accompanied by Major Loftus and Captain Lind. Typically, Johnstone had prepared an agenda and threw at Farmar twenty questions relative to the military powers a governor ought to possess. Farmar took a high position on every point. To the concluding question, "Have I any direction over the military in any manner whatever?" Farmar replied, "I believe not."[49]

For the moment it was a stalemate, and both Farmar and Johnstone had other business to occupy them. The governor made a commendable effort to ingratiate himself with the French inhabitants of Mobile and was much taken with the Chevalier Montault de Monberaut. Major Farmar had once more to report to headquarters the decayed state of Fort Charlotte and that the cost of firewood in the garrison was so great that his officers declared themselves "at insupportable expence, even to cook our victuals; as near half the pay of a subaltern is expended in that article alone." Among his own mounting expenses, there was the cost of 5,235 gallons of brandy contracted at New Orleans for the soldiers who would soon be heading up the Mississippi—"without which they cannot possibly undergo the inconceivable fatigue of continual rowing, a quantity is also included in the above for the Indians, a commodity absolut'ly necessary, having always received it from the French." The brandy had yet to be paid for, as he could not secure cash locally in exchange for treasury bills; the whole body of merchants in Mobile, Farmar reported, was not worth five hundred pounds in specie.[50]

In his letters to Gage, Farmar initially played down his differences with Governor Johnstone. He recognized that Johnstone's "intentions are no ways favourable for me," but merely wished that "His excellency was more moderate, at least in his disposition." The major had yet to learn how immoderate the governor could be. That very day he would receive Johnstone's demands for information, in writing, regarding the state of the troops, forts, Indian presents, public records, provisions, boats, regimental staff, and a host of other matters legal and military. The governor accused Farmar of having resolved "to drill things off to the last, & to retard the government of this country taking place." The tone of Johnstone's latest epistle warranted Farmar's description: "imperious haughtiness . . . founded barely on the Ignorance of a Serjeant."[51] No army officer, neither Major Farmar nor General Gage, could be expected to bow to such intervention in service affairs.

Johnstone soon found stronger grounds for complaint. The schooner *St. John*, owned by the merchant George Bruce, was stopped from sailing by the sergeant of the guard. On being shown clearance papers issued by the proper civil officials, the sergeant declared that they "signified not a farthing, that he must see a clearance from Major Farmar or receive his order, otherwise he would sink him."[52] Bruce appealed to Johnstone, and the governor demanded an explanation from Farmar and fired off a salvo to General Gage, protesting the insulting conduct of both Farmar and Loftus: "The whole of his [Farmar's] government here, has been such a wanton abuse of power & such a proflagation of public money, attended with so many mean & imperious circumstances, that really I believe it were impossible to find a proper comparison in so small a compass of time & so small a society in the history of mankind."

In particular, Johnstone noted that Farmar had insulted John Stuart not a minute after the superintendent and the governor had landed at Mobile. Even before the soup had been removed from Farmar's table, Major Loftus had insulted Johnstone by telling him that he had no right to a state of the garrison. This little episode alone produced voluminous charges and countercharges before Loftus reluctantly admitted that he had indeed told Johnstone to hold his tongue. The affair was finally smoothed over through the good offices of Captain John Farmar and Lieutenant Colonel Wedderburn, but not before it had occupied considerable time and attention on the part of the colonel, lieutenant colonel, major, and a captain of the 22nd Regiment.[53] Further, it was eighteen hours before Farmar saw fit to post a lone sentinel at Johnstone's door, and fourteen days before the governor received any information from Farmar concerning the western part of his province. After his protest against the stopping of Bruce's ship, Farmar had ordered that no ships whatsoever should be halted by the officers of Fort Charlotte, thereby neatly emasculating the customs service.

Johnstone turned next to evidence of Farmar's abuse of power and his profligate expenditures. He had sold flour in New Orleans, employing a Jew named Palacio. He had sold the Tombecbé fort to Jeremiah Terry for two hundred dollars. He had made various private deals, at 5 to 50 percent commission, with other Mobile merchants. The noble Chevalier Monberaut had been turned out of his house, even out of a bed in his daughter-in-law's house, in favor of a sick soldier, and he now had no place to sleep but on the floor. Mme. Grondel had sold her house to the army for use as a hospital, and a forty-dollar interpreter's fee had been deducted from her payment. There was also the case of James Millony (or Maloney), who died in August 1764, leaving an estate of two thousand dollars, which Farmar had administered. When about three hundred dollars in debts had been paid off, Anne Ireland appeared on the scene, claiming that she had been Millony's partner as well as his mistress, and that the estate represented the profits of their partnership and ought to be at her disposal rather than Farmar's. Obviously, everyone in Mobile with a complaint to air had found the governor a sympathetic listener, whether his story was true or not.

More significant was the tale Johnstone reported from Lieutenant Philip Pittman. It seemed that Pittman, observing that Farmar was paying an extravagant price for lime used in the restoration of Fort Charlotte, had proposed to produce it more cheaply by employing some of the troops and allowing them a small sum for their labor. Farmar had agreed to Pittman's scheme; but finding that the lime could be produced at a cost of three bitts per barrel, he had insisted that Pittman submit a bill charging five bitts a barrel and split the profit with him. Farmar had also required Pittman to carry on his books an extra man and a Negro slave belonging to the major, each receiving three shillings a day. Pittman had accepted this arrangement but had cleared his conscience by confessing all to Governor Johnstone.

Further, the governor charged that "the King's boat was employed between this & New Orleans with an agreement with the sailors who were borne as soldiers, that half the profits which the boat should earn should be divided between them & the Major."[54] Johnstone supported his accusations with thirty-three appended documents—enough to keep General Gage occupied for some little time. Separately, the episodes ranged from comic to absurd; together they painted a picture of corruption that demanded investigation. In fact, Johnstone's subsequent formal charges against Farmar, as well as those of Lieutenant Pittman, originated in this letter. It would take years to resolve the issues they raised.

George Johnstone was not a man to hide his "sinister intentions" and "unfriendly, ungenerous representations"—as Robert Farmar described them. He notified the major of the accusations he had sent to New York, and three days later Farmar dispatched to Gage a memorial signed by all of the officers in the garrison of Mobile except Captain Lieutenant James Campbell. From major to ensign, the officers of the 22nd and 34th regiments protested that despite their efforts to honor Johnstone, he had not even allowed them the status of gentlemen. Loftus had been publicly insulted, Farmar catechized, a sick officer thrown out of his quarters, and their persons and goods had been endangered by the governor's encouragement of complaints against them from "the vilest set of mankind (Indian Traders &ca)."[55] When later he learned of the officers' memorial the governor described it as a feeble riposte by Farmar to Johnstone's own charges against the major: "He was advised, by Men more wicked than himself, that the best Method of blunting the Edge of those Representations, was to send a complaint against me." The memorial, Johnstone continued, was "hudled up in three weeks after I landed at Mobile, and signed by many (whom I never saw or conversed with) as a Duty in the Esprit de Corps."[56]

Happily, the first visit of Governor Johnstone and Superintendent Stuart to Mobile came to an end about January 7, 1765. The weather had been atrocious, causing illness, sharpening tempers, and probably delaying His Excellency's departure as it did that of Captain Campbell and Lieutenant Pittman. Johnstone had formed his opinion of Mobile—"The state of the town in filth, nastiness & brush wood running over the houses is hardly to be credited"—and he was needed at Pensacola. In his absence from the provincial capital, civil authority had virtually been suspended; justices of the peace were unable to maintain order, and army officers were threatening to flog anyone who laid hands on a soldier. James Macpherson, the poet-secretary to the council but no Ossianic hero himself, pleaded for Johnstone to return.[57]

The month of official disputation at Mobile was not without some useful results, however, for the principals occasionally recognized that they had common concerns. Farmar successfully defended his efforts to contact and pacify the Indians who might affect—either adversely or favorably—his ascent of the Mississippi. His agents had departed before Stuart arrived, and the superintendent accepted the fact that there was little he could do about them. Farmar admitted that he had cornered the available supply of Indian presents, at a cost of £3,247.5.4, but it could not be doubted that he would need such gifts as he traveled from Fort Charlotte to Fort Chartres.[58]

Captain James Campbell had returned from the Mississippi on December 8 to report most enthusiastically on the condition of the Iberville River and the desirability of establishing a post at Manchac. Farmar succeeded in winning Johnstone's good offices with the navy, and together they proposed to Captain Sir John Lindsay that he provide a sloop to convey supplies and munitions up the Mississippi to the Iberville. With such assistance they hoped to "immediately form a Post there by which means we shall continue our negotiations with the Indians without interruption, and in a great measure command the whole country." Johnstone faithfully pursued this project after he returned to Pensacola, inspired at least in part by the opportunity to name the place Fort Bute, in honor of his political sponsor.[59]

Other matters were not advancing so smoothly. Farmar had sent Captain Lind to New Orleans in October 1764 to expedite the acquisition and construction of boats for the Mississippi venture. Four boats had been left by Loftus at the Balise, the mouth of the Mississippi River, and when Governor D'Abbadie refused to allow the employment of French soldiers for their recovery, Lind negotiated with Antoine Bienvenue to bring them up to New Orleans for 800 livres. The French governor also declined to loan Lind 10,000 livres to cover various other expenses. François Lambert advanced the Englishman 6,800 livres, and M. Roulin provided a like amount, but when Lind sought 15,000 more from Gilbert Antoine de St. Maxent, the two quarreled and there were accusations of sharp dealing on both sides. Captain Lind finally concluded arrangements with the Jew Isaac Monsanto and left for Mobile on November 27—to D'Abbadie's considerable relief: "He is considered very mercenary, and his sojourn here has more than amply substantiated this rumor."[60] Farmar's initial opinion of the Frenchman was confirmed by Lind's report: D'Abbadie "is very profuse in empty promises and deceiptful assurances; when at the same time I am pretty confident, He'll do everything to retard the undertaking, where he can shew any plausible reasons for such behaviour, or by a nice chicanerie avoid any personal appearance in it."

Lind and Campbell, between them, had spent over two thousand dollars for work at New Orleans, on the Iberville, and among the Indians, yet everything was now at a standstill for want of cash. Farmar doubted that he could get the 34th Regiment farther than Natchez in the next year, and he could do nothing about Lieutenant Pittman's great expenses at New Orleans except forward his bills to the commander in chief in New York.[61]

In January 1765, after Johnstone disappeared from Mobile, Farmar could concentrate upon plans for the expedition northward. His first concern was for boats. From New Orleans he heard that those Loftus had left behind were all rotten; those that had been taken to Pensacola had been surveyed by Lord Adam Gordon, their bottoms having fallen out. Repairs were said to be progressing at New Orleans, however, and Farmar would not grieve to hear of the death of Governor D'Abbadie on February 4. Relations with the Indian Department finally began to improve. Farmar and Charles Stuart agreed to employ the Frenchman René Harpin de la Gauterais as an advance emissary to Fort Chartres.[62] Money was a problem as usual. Contracts for supplies and equipment would not be filled by New Orleans merchants unless they had cash in hand, and that commodity was so short that Captain Campbell feared he must sell his commission in order to meet his obligations. Farmar could provide little assistance when it came to raising cash.[63] Johnstone might be out of sight, but he was not far away. He protested that he had heard much ridicule of law from Farmar, and much about military honor—to which Farmar responded that civil government was not greatly abetted by studied persecution of the military.[64]

By February 1765 the smoke of battle on the Gulf Coast had been seen in New York, and General Gage was not pleased. The commander in chief took his responsibilities seriously, and it galled him when subordinates failed to keep him well advised on developments in the most distant posts. Major Robert Farmar was not his most regular correspondent, nor did mail from Mobile always reach its destination. Gage complained that he had heard nothing from Farmar, in response to repeated inquiries, until August 7, 1764, and he had already penned a blistering note regarding Farmar's silence when the next packet from Mobile reached New York on November 26.[65] The major was admittedly remiss in submitting the accounts and reports Gage desired, and he may have hoped to escape that task altogether. In December 1764 Farmar heard (erroneously, as it turned out) that the 34th Regiment's Lieutenant Colonel John Reed was about to retire on half-pay. Hoping that Reed's successor would join the regiment and assume command, Farmar asked for leave of absence.[66] His request reached New York in February 1765, along with his first accounts of expenditures on the various projects that had been initiated from Mobile and reports of his first contacts with Stuart and Johnstone. The general was delighted to hear of progress in clearing the Iberville but surprised to learn that Farmar faced financial difficulties. He blamed Farmar for not having informed him earlier, condemned his fiscal measures as improper, and required him to adhere strictly to orders henceforth. As for leave of absence, any consideration must await the actual appearance of another field-grade officer at Mobile. "I can't till then," wrote Gage, "think of it." As for Johnstone and Stuart, the general desired that Farmar would "pay that respect and deference which is due" and "shew no signs of contempt to such civil government as shall be established."[67] Unfortunately, Johnstone's lengthy tirade against Major Farmar would be the next letter from West Florida to cross Gage's desk.

The commander in chief was naturally disturbed by the charges and countercharges that began to flood his correspondence in February 1765. His professional concern for the rights of the service were balanced by his sense of propriety and desire for harmony between the civil and military branches of government. He had at once to protect his officers and mollify the governor. If he seemed to give undue credence to Johnstone's accusations, he acted properly and promptly to clear the air and defend the honor of Major Farmar. He soon recognized Johnstone's style, and his formal prose barely hid the distaste he certainly felt. In a series of letters to West Florida, Gage warned Farmar of the governor's charges and advised him that they were of so heinous a nature that he must expect them to be investigated. If Major Farmar had acted impartially and justly, he had nothing to worry about; if he had acted otherwise, he must be held accountable, but only to the king and council, not to any inferior provincial court or authority. The general privately hoped that Johnstone would desist from his trifling complaints and urged the governor to use his influence to quash any idle prosecutions of military officers. "A Regiment thrown in by chance to govern a Province must commit many illegal Acts, and any People who have suffered, justly or not, will be glad to take Revenge when Opportunity offers, tho' they might have deserved in equity what they have suffered. And it is presumed that the British inhabitants of West Florida are not People of greater consideration and character than those who have flocked to other new settlements."[68] The general's sage observations had little effect on the Gulf Coast.

From Pensacola, Governor Johnstone launched an offensive against Robert Farmar that drove the major to plead for General Gage's protection. The governor intervened in the affairs of the Mobile commandant whenever he could find an excuse, intending, Farmar concluded, to delay the Mississippi venture. Old sores were reopened. As early as January 24, Daniel Ward was persuaded to prosecute Farmar for false imprisonment; a month later an order for Farmar's arrest was issued by Attorney General Edmund Rush Wegg, and trial of the case was scheduled for the first Tuesday in March.[69]

About the first of March, Johnstone, on no better terms with the military establishment at Pensacola, returned to Mobile in order to participate in the approaching Indian congress. He received no military courtesies from the garrison, and Farmar's life became considerably more difficult. So constant were their recriminations that even the governor complained, "There is no settling the slightest matter with Major Farmar without a quire of paper."[70]

The major was doing his best to maintain the army's credit at New Orleans by transmitting whatever commodities he could lay his hands on to merchants who were procuring boats and supplies for the Mississippi expedition. He was soon involved as merchant and middleman, shipper and ship owner, for he and Miller were the owners of a formerly Spanish launch, turned over to Farmar by Captain William Bayne, which they refitted as a sloop and put to good use. The vessel was named *Little Bob* in honor of Farmar's infant son Robert Adolphus. Small consignments were entrusted to junior officers and sent to New Orleans whenever opportunity offered. Cash was so short that by early March, Farmar had drawn on General Gage's credit for £1,405.18.8 owing to the New Orleans merchant Monsanto. Work on the Iberville required another draft of £863.6.8 on the Treasury in order to save Captain Campbell from being arrested—an action the major credited to Governor Johnstone's instigation. To raise money, Farmar was forced to trade in deerskins. On one occasion Johnstone held up the shipment of a consignment, demanding the payment of £178.19.6 to the customs office, until John Stuart supported Farmar's argument that the transaction was necessary if the Mississippi effort were to proceed. At the first of the month the governor stopped the transfer of ninety-five barrels of army flour intended for the expedition and to be shipped aboard the *Little Bob,* on the ground that it was destined for the Illinois country—which lay outside the province of West Florida. Farmar protested vehemently and found it necessary to cajole Lieutenant Colonel David Wedderburn of the 22nd Regiment, arrived in West Florida on February 23, into calling a meeting of the field officers and captains of the garrison to decide whether the flour might even be drawn out of army stores. It took five days to settle that question. The governor then managed to delay the sailing of the supply ship for yet another five days by supporting Provincial Secretary James Macpherson's efforts to extract fees for passes from the army officers leaving for New Orleans. Farmar refused to pay, declaring that the secretary might "with the same propriety . . . stop an Army as well as that small Party." Of Governor Johnstone he wrote to Gage, "He trys methods daily to do us all the disservice he can."

Complications centering upon the *Little Bob* were far from over. The vessel, a twenty-ton sloop with six men under the command of Daniel Maclean, cleared out of Mobile on March 3 and returned about midnight, April 6. Master Maclean, in spite of Farmar's direct order, had loaded five hogsheads of claret at New Orleans, and during the early morning hours of April 7, he transferred them to the ship *Charlotte.* Later in the day Maclean went down the bay to help remove a cargo of flour from the brigantine *Bumper,* aground in the shallows off Mobile Point. On his return to town, Daniel Clark, deputy customs collector, seized the *Little Bob* on charges of smuggling. Farmar and Miller were immediately involved as the owners of the ship. They sought the advice of Attorney General Wegg, who was also judge of the vice-admiralty court, and their spokesman in Pensacola, James Noble, was able to convince Judge Wegg to release the ship on the ground that it had no contraband aboard when it was seized. Farmar and Miller instituted action against Customs Collector Jacob Blackwell, demanding four hundred pounds' damages, and Governor Johnstone added Wegg's name to his list of enemies.[71]

Farmar also complained that Johnstone put out stories of Indian hostility calculated to dispirit the troops destined to follow Loftus's course up the river. But what Farmar found hardest to accept was the fact that Johnstone was "countenanced or rather supported by Lieutenant Colonel Wedderburn," whose rank gave him precedence at Fort Charlotte.[72]

David Wedderburn's role was that of a well-intentioned peacemaker, and consequently he fell out with all parties. Young Wedderburn had much in common with his fellow Scot Johnstone. The governor admitted that it was commonly said that "the good correspondence between Colonel Wedderburn & me proceeded from a very narrow foundation namely that we were both born on the other side of an ideal line." He preferred to attribute their friendship to "both of us being capable of understanding common sence & plain reason."[73] Wedderburn privately thought that Johnstone overstepped his authority and that Farmar, "not knowing his own powers, gave one point up today, & took it back the next, Said, and unsaid, puzzled, and quibbled 'till every part of civil & military Government was thrown into a most terrible confusion." Less wisely, he imagined it his own lot "to draw light and precision, out of darkness and confusion, to make anarchy produce Government."[74] He cooperated with Johnstone in stopping the transfer of flour to New Orleans until, pressed by Farmar, he determined that its removal would not endanger the garrison's supply. On March 1 he stopped Ensign James Wainwright from sailing to New Orleans, but when Farmar protested that Wainright's departure was essential to the preparations for the expedition, Wedderburn gave Farmar general permission to send off small parties without formal notification. Two days later Johnstone advised him that Lieutenant Edward Sedgwick had left the colony with a legal action hanging over his head and that Sedgwick had traveled under the major's orders. As a sop to the claims of civil authority, Wedderburn revoked the permission he had given to Farmar. At the same time, however, he warned Johnstone that Farmar must command the Mississippi expedition; he could not be held in West Florida nor be tried by a provincial court. Only a general court martial could adjudicate the governor's charges against Major Farmar, and no such body could be assembled under present circumstances. He urged Johnstone to let the matter rest and to trust that General Gage would do the right thing by all parties.[75]

Later in March new quarrels arose. Johnstone refused to allow Farmar to use government shipping unless he contributed to the maintenance of the vessels he employed. The major was required to pay 90 percent of the cost of sending a seventy-five-ton ship carrying only eleven tons of stores for the army between Mobile and New Orleans—an obvious reason that Farmar had to draw another £355.6.1 on the Treasury.[76]

The news from his agents on the Mississippi was not calculated to raise Major Farmar's spirits. Lieutenant Ross reached Fort Chartres on February 18; a month later Farmar heard from him that the Indians of the Illinois country were decidedly hostile, and Pontiac was reported to be approaching with three thousand warriors intent upon closing the river to the British. Grain was so scarce at Fort Chartres that the arrival of a hundred men, let alone a regiment, would create famine. Farther south, the Iberville project was stalled, and it now appeared that little had actually been accomplished toward clearing a water route from Lake Maurepas to the Mississippi. Lieutenant Pittman, who was highly critical of Captain Campbell's work, found few Negroes at work and the Iberville impassable. Farmar could only observe that Campbell and Pittman had both made up to Governor Johnstone and were rivals for his favor. When the regiment reached Manchac, he would discover the true state of affairs and hold a court of inquiry to determine responsibility for whatever might or might not have been done.[77]

Amidst these trials, Farmar wisely did his best to avoid George Johnstone. The governor invited the major to meet with him, Stuart, and Wedderburn to review plans for the Mississippi expedition, but Farmar refused to discuss any military matters with civilians or the movements of the 34th Regiment with the lieutenant colonel of the 22nd. He would meet with Stuart to discuss Indian relations, but the superintendent wished to talk about his correspondence with General Gage—and with Wedderburn present. So no one spoke to anyone for days.[78]

By the end of the month the governor had snared Farmar in the toils of the law. On February 27 a warrant was issued for Farmar's arrest on Daniel Ward's plea of false imprisonment, and Farmar's trial was set for March 5. Farmar was also forced to make bail for five hundred pounds in the case of James Maloney and was confined to the province—although that restriction was raised to allow the major to lead his command to the Illinois. Farmar hoped to embark on his voyage soon, but he feared the delays Johnstone and Wedderburn might impose. He could get none of the eight thousand dollars held by the paymaster, Jacob Blackwell, because that gentleman, a member of Johnstone's council and collector of customs at Mobile, had ruled that the 34th Regiment were temporary sojourners in West Florida who had no claim upon his funds. Wedderburn had dismissed Farmar's nephew Christopher Miller as barrackmaster and had given that post to Johnstone's protégé Lieutenant Maclellan. Captain John Farmar also felt some pressure. Fearing that he would be ordered back to England with the 22nd Regiment, he reminded Gage, "As I am a soldier of fortune and have serv'd a long time, I wou'd prefer remaining here with an addition to my pay, to going home, tho' it is not one of the most desirable countrys to be in." Gage's commission as fort major would resolve his problem, he suggested. At least the strength of the regiment had been increased by a draft of twenty-nine men from New York and by the arrival of Captains Dundas, Forbes, and Pownall. Their presence would allow Farmar to send his friend Captain Lind to the northern colonies on recruiting duty, for he now needed subalterns more than captains.[79]

Between March 26 and April 4, 1765, Mobile was the site of a most important conference with the Chickasaw and Choctaw chieftains. Superintendent Stuart, with Governor Johnstone and Lieutenant Colonel Wedderburn, represented British authority. Stuart sought the Indians' assistance in facilitating the movement of Farmar's expedition up the Mississippi and urged them to use their influence over the lesser tribes. Although Farmar was asked to consult on plans for the congress, he seems to have taken (or been allowed) no part in its proceedings other than providing the fifes and drums of the 34th Regiment for the concluding ceremony.[80]

Throughout late March and all of April, Farmar struggled to get his regiment aboard ship and off to the Mississippi and his advance parties north to Fort Chartres. John Stuart's Indian Department agents, Pierce Sinnott and La Gauterais, were at New Orleans but were unable to proceed for want of money to hire boatmen, although Acting Governor Aubry and that useful merchant Isaac Monsanto were cooperating. They got away about March 14, accompanied by four Illinois chiefs who were troublesome but might be of help when they reached Fort Chartres. Late in April, Farmar heard again from the Illinois and triumphantly reported to Gage that Lieutenant Ross "publickly walks the streets" at Fort Chartres. In fact, Ross had already given up his efforts and turned downriver to New Orleans.[81]

Although Farmar had hoped to embark early in April, the Indian congress, financial difficulties, and bad weather kept him at Mobile week after week. By the thirteenth he was loading ships, which he had had to secure from Pensacola. On April 20 he signed contracts with Samuel Israel, Alexander Solomons, and Joseph de Palacios, prominent New Orleans merchants, for the 160-ton brig *Alexander,* and with Captain Thomas Tuder, of the brigantine *Polly* of New York, at thirteen shillings per ton for one month and the eight days they might require to return to Mobile from New Orleans. Predictably, Farmar's transports were aground in the bay at that very moment and would remain fast in the mud for the most of the next week—by which time the weather turned foul. At least this turn of events enabled Farmar to work up the financial accounts Gage demanded; they were dispatched to headquarters on April 25.[82]

In the midst of these preparations, Farmar received Gage's letter outlining Johnstone's charges and declaring the general's intention of having them investigated by a court martial. Farmar drew up a point-by-point denial of the charges, gathered supporting evidence, and, matters having gone this far, expressed the opinion that he had, in fact, given in too far to Johnstone's interference. Had Wedderburn not arrived, he would have taken a firmer line with the governor. He was willing to give proper support to civil government, of course, "but personal adoration has been expected in which I must own to your Excellency there has been some disappointment."[83] General Gage, who thought there must be "some contagion in the climate" at Mobile and feared "that cursed spirit of party has been at the bottom of this affair," had already taken steps to resolve the quarrels in West Florida. In mid-March he appointed Colonel Henry Bouquet as brigadier general in the Southern Department, but his first choice had yet to leave for the Gulf Coast, and Robert Farmar would sail for the Mississippi long before the arrival of a competent and respected officer could clear the air. Recognizing the confusion that must result from the painful slowness of communication, on May 23 Gage issued orders for Major Farmar to report to Mobile to face an inquiry into his conduct—orders that would find him at Fort Chartres.[84]

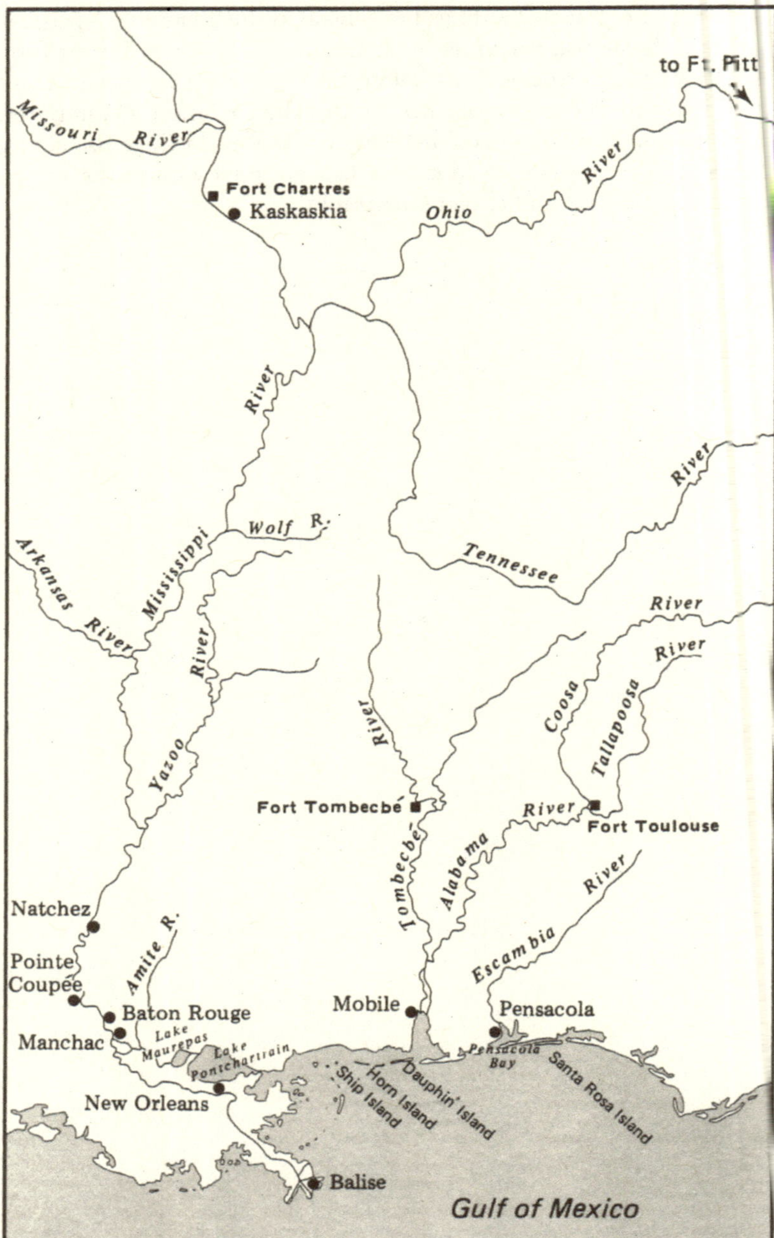

The Mississippi Valley

IV.

Up the Mississippi to the Illinois

On May 1, 1765, Major Robert Farmar joined his two hundred redcoats and their dependents aboard the transports *Alexander* and *Polly* in Mobile Bay, and on May 4 they set sail for New Orleans. Fears that the *Alexander* was too heavily laden to negotiate the shallow waters of Mobile Bay imposed this delay, requiring Farmar to hire a small schooner to take off some of the ship's cargo; he also set ashore a small contingent of men under Lieutenant Handfield that had been intended for garrison duty at Fort Bute. Once at sea, the expedition's course lay to the west, well out from the coastal islands, then south as they followed the low outline of the delta to the East Pass and the little post of the Balise, where French pilots would guide them into the calm waters of the Mississippi. During the next week or so, the transports moved cautiously through the sinuous bends of the lower river, using sails, boats, and occasionally warping, by means of lines attached to trees on the river banks, to negotiate the channel. Above English Turn, where Farmar would have noted the French defenses, batteries of ten twelve-pounders on either side of the river, signs of habitation became increasingly evident as they approached the capital of Louisiana. On May 15 *Polly*, bearing Major Farmar and a part of the regiment, reached New Orleans, but *Alexander*, having gone aground several times and having lost an anchor in the river, did not get up to the city until May 22. By that date Farmar had established a camp just upriver from the town and on the western bank, thereby creating an appropriate and necessary distance between the English and their French hosts.[1]

New Orleans and its environs, in 1765, held a population that Philip Pittman estimated rather generously at seven thousand, and it offered a welcome touch of civilization to British visitors from either Pensacola or Mobile. Behind the levee and central square, shops and markets invited prospective customers, whatever their language or desires. Major Farmar had much business to transact with his contractors, and there were formal visits to be made to Acting Governor Aubry and other French officials. The traffic across the river was at first heavy. Aubry graciously agreed to the bivouacking of a British regiment on foreign soil and proved most cordial and helpful as Farmar pursued his affairs in the city. Other Frenchmen were less inclined to cooperate. The merchants with whom he dealt demanded payment in full and on the spot in good treasury notes before anything could be done. Palacios, Monsanto, Maxent, and the rest would have their pounds before Farmar had their services; the earlier visits of the major's emissaries had merely whetted their appetites.

The presence of Lieutenant Pittman on the expedition caused some embarrassment. His last appearance in New Orleans had led to a violent scene in which he attacked an elderly Frenchman named Dupart. In order to protect him from the vengeance of Dupart's family and friends, Aubry had put him under house arrest. The governor now advised Farmar to restrict Pittman to the English camp, for he could not answer for the consequences of a meeting between the lieutenant and Dupart's supporters, including some Indians who were visiting in the town.[2]

Indian relations were on everyone's mind. From the townsfolk came tales of the dangers facing the regiment farther up the Mississippi. On May 27 a sergeant and nine men of Lieutenant Fraser's party arrived in New Orleans, and their account of affairs at Fort Chartres was so alarming that Farmar hesitated to forward it to Gage at New York for fear it should become known to his men. And reminders of Loftus's failure were close at hand as the men of the 34th encountered deserters from the 22nd Regiment in the streets of New Orleans.

Desertion had seriously weakened the Loftus expedition, and Farmar was greatly concerned to stop "so dangerous & Pernicious a practice." Once ashore in New Orleans, a soldier had only to declare himself a deserter and he came under the protection of French law, even in the presence of British officers. Singly and in pairs, Farmar's redcoats began to slip away, sometimes encouraged by the masters of merchant vessels moored at the levee, who promised the men not only escape from the army but lucrative employment. Horrified by "the public encouragement (or rather protection) given to deserters," the major appealed to Aubry for assistance. Observing that he could not hope to accomplish his mission to the Illinois unless desertions were prevented and that New Orleans was "an asylum for the deserters" who were encouraged by "ill-disposed people and masters of vessels," he urged Aubry to seize and return the regiment's runaways. The governor replied that, lacking specific instructions to do so, he could not act on Farmar's request. He did, however, arrest and return one sergeant who had boldly walked away from the British camp with three hundred *piastres gourdes* stolen from the company chest.[3]

Hoping to entice his deserters back into the ranks, Farmar announced that all who returned by June 16 would be pardoned their crime. Few responded to his appeal, and Farmar feared that they would be outnumbered by new deserters "once they begin to tug at the oar." Men recently drafted into the regiment were the most prone to desert, and Farmar lost thirty-eight men—nearly one-fifth of his force—before he got away from New Orleans. It was "most shamefull," but he assured General Gage that "all the arts of man cannot prevent it."[4]

The weeks passed slowly as Farmar and his secretary, Lieutenant Hunter Sedgwick, cursed and cajoled Frenchmen into providing supplies and completing repairs on eight of the twelve boats the regiment would use ascending the river. By June 21 Farmar's preparations were virtually concluded. Supplies were loaded and swivel guns installed, and he planned to head into the current that came down from the Illinois on Sunday, June 23. His departure was apparently delayed until the twenty-eighth or twenty-ninth of the month. In spite of wild rumors of the dangers ahead, he anticipated a quiet voyage, for Lieutenant Fraser had joined him with assurances that Pontiac was now more cordial toward the English and that the small tribes along the Mississippi would be overawed by the friendly Choctaw and Chickasaw.[5]

Whereas Major Arthur Loftus kept a daily journal of his abortive effort to ascend the Mississippi in 1764, Major Robert Farmar recounted his experiences in no more than a few laconic letters to General Gage and other British officials. Initially, like Loftus, Farmar set his men to the oars at daybreak and kept them at their task, with only a short halt at noon to feed and refresh them, until nearly dusk. Progress against the current was inevitably slow in the heavy, crowded bateaux, and there were snags and sunken logs, contrary winds, and occasional storms to be encountered.[6] The river was awesome, and Lieutenant Pittman was not the only one to observe that it was also remarkably muddy: "I have filled a half-pint tumbler with it, and have found a sediment of two inches of slime. It is, notwithstanding, extremely wholesome and well tasted, and very cool in the hottest seasons of the year; and the rowers, who are then employed, drink . . . and never receive any bad effects from it."[7]

About the second week of July, certainly by the twelfth, the 34th Regiment reached Point Iberville, thirty-two leagues above New Orleans, and there Farmar encamped his men for two weeks.

At the Iberville, Farmar found Archibald Robertson, an engineer who had been dispatched from Pensacola to direct the work on Fort Bute. Poor Robertson had gotten no assistance from Captain James Campbell, who was already on the spot but soon left to join Farmar in New Orleans, and when Farmar arrived Robertson was down to ten men, who could accomplish nothing. Farmar refused to employ the men of the 34th Regiment in Robertson's behalf or to leave any able-bodied men behind—although two sick soldiers remained at Manchac when the regiment moved north.[8]

While his men rested from their work at the oars by loading ten cannon brought up by H.M.S. *Nautilus,* which necessitated shifting the cargo of every bateau, Major Robert Farmar set out to determine the truth regarding work done toward clearing the Iberville and the prospect of ultimate success in converting it into a route bypassing New Orleans. James Campbell and Philip Pittman both claimed credit for the little that had been accomplished toward that end, and each blamed the other for the lack of greater—or even significant—results. There were also M. Dupart's charges against Pittman (and Pittman's countercharges) to be considered. On July 14 the major assembled a formal court of enquiry to determine the facts. According to Pittman, Farmar's action was a surprise, the court was held in secret, and the senior officers of the regiment did not serve on it. Captain Campbell, who was bitterly critical of Pittman, had already complained to Gage of the young man's jealousy and hatred; he declared that Pittman could not get a dog to follow him from New Orleans to work at the Iberville and that he was a conceited fool who kindled the fires of dissent wherever he went. Campbell supported Dupart's accusations, and Lieutenant Pittman was forced to admit that he had dealt with the Frenchman without knowledge of his arrangements with Campbell. Ignoring his own high-handed treatment of the old man, Pittman blamed the troubles in New Orleans on the Frenchman's determination to gain revenge by literally taking his scalp. Both Farmar and Pittman submitted reports of the court of enquiry to General Gage, the lieutenant protesting that he was being unjustly persecuted by his commanding officer. The personal animosity fired at Manchac would blaze repeatedly in the months to come.[9]

A cursory investigation of the Iberville disclosed that it was not a viable route for commerce, even though an occasional canoe might navigate its length at high water. Nonetheless, engineers would dream of transforming it into an inland waterway for years to come.

To add to Farmar's problems, Lieutenant John Henry announced that he would no longer serve as a deputy for John Stuart's Indian Department because he received only three shillings a day, and of that sum one shilling had to be paid to a sergeant who assisted him. No one else would accept the appointment, and Farmar was too busy to assume the responsibility. As he wrote the night before he left, he found the post at the Iberville in a miserable situation, and he left it in an unhappy one. One bright note was heard at the Iberville. While Farmar was entertaining the small Indian tribes of the district—Chitimachas, Houmas, and Alibamons—three Choctaw warriors recruited by Lieutenant Thomas Ford came down from Natchez to join the regiment and impress upon the local redmen the desirability of keeping the peace with the British and their Indian allies.[10]

On July 22 the boats of the 34th Regiment headed into the current of the Mississippi again. On the twenty-ninth of the month the regiment stopped at the village of the Tonica Indians, "about two miles above the last plantation of Pointe Coupée." Although reduced to some thirty warriors, the Tonica had succeeded in stopping Major Loftus and the 22nd Regiment the preceding year. They received Robert Farmar peacefully, thanks to his diplomatic preparations and the generous distribution of gifts.[11]

Beyond the Iberville, Farmar was forced to change the regiment's daily routine. "The present intollerable heat of the season obliging us to lye by in the middle of the day. I sett off betwixt two & three in the morning and row till nine, and from four to sun set in the Evening, the men being by that time sufficiently harrassed and fatigued." Such a schedule made "our progression . . . indeed tedious and slow, as we rarely attain more than three leagues in a day, and sometimes barely two."[12]

The strain of their voyage told heavily upon the men of the 34th Regiment. On the banks of the Mississippi River, August 4, Farmar held a court martial to try Angus Cameron on charges of drunkenness and insolence brought by Ensign Wood. It transpired that one night of the preceding week Cameron had caused a disturbance aboard Captain Campbell's boat. Wood ordered Sergeant Blaney to silence the man, but Cameron would not listen and, mistaking Wood for another officer, yelled that he was "a damn'd Rascal & . . . he may go to Hell." Cameron, who could only admit to the court that he was too drunk at the time to remember the incident, was found guilty and sentenced to five hundred lashes.[13]

Early departure resulted in the regiment's arrival at Natchez about six o'clock in the morning on August 11. Farmar halted on the river bank below the ruins of Fort Rosalie for four or five days in order to refresh his men, and Lieutenant Pittman seized the brief opportunity to view the site of the old French fort, which he sketched and later described in detail.

Reporting his progress to the War Office, Farmar pointed out that "the tedious delay and obstacles" encountered at New Orleans, and "the prodigious heat of the season" had so retarded his progress that he was "under some apprehensions least our provisions should fail us, tho' in that case I shall endeavour to subsist upon Buffaloe & Bear, as the French gives us plentifull accounts of that method of Supply." Uncertain what might await him farther north, Farmar wrote, "I am in hopes the Arkansas will not attack us, as I am told we are to look for an opposition only a few leagues from the Illinois from those who attacked Mr. Croghan & took him prisoner." The major's geography left something to be desired, but he assured officials at home—whose knowledge was scarcely better—"I shall endeavour to take post as near to these discontented Savages as possible, and by fair promises divest them of their prejudices."[14]

Captain James Campbell also observed that "our progress is slowe, and must be so in this excessive hott Season." "Surrounded by woods on all sides the heat of the sun is intolerable. No casualties has happened since we left Ibberville but one man fell over board and another died with excessive heat. The men in general are yet in good spirits. Every care being taken to keep them so."[15]

At Natchez, Lieutenant Ford and between seventy and eighty-four Choctaws were waiting to meet Farmar's regiment—although "to no purpose" it seemed to Captain Campbell. "The only advantage that can attend it, that the several nations on the Mississippi finding them and the Chickasaws so firm in our interest will not dare to make any attempt to disturb us, even should the French advise them, so much are they afraid of the Choctaws though a pack of begging Rascals who would Murder their fathers for a Kegg of Rum."[16] Despite Campbell's low opinion of the Choctaw, the spirits of Farmar and his redcoats were lifted by the appearance at Natchez of friendly Indians, including the son of an Arkansas chief and his attendants, and by the consequent sense of greater security as they wound their way on up the river.

The juncture of Farmar's expedition and Ford's party at Natchez represented a small triumph for British Indian policy. Ford left Mobile on May 29 with the purpose of rallying a sufficient body of Choctaw Indians in the uplands to overawe any hostile tribesmen on the Mississippi who might be tempted to attack Farmar's boats as they ascended the river. Ford reached Chickasawhays on June 5 and left three days later for the Yazoo, where he spent a fortnight. The Indians, although friendly enough, showed more interest in securing English rum than safeguarding Farmar's passage. Ford succeeded in getting eighty-four Choctaws and the chieftain Shalustamastabe to accompany him on to Natchez, arriving there on July 12. The old French Fort Rosalie was in ruins, all in weeds, no doors or shutters on the buildings, but in the officers' quarters Ford found a letter, forwarded by Farmar from New Orleans, June 13, advising that the 34th could not start north before the twentieth of that month. Lieutenant Ford could do nothing but wait, scouting the surrounding country every day and sending his Indians along the river with messages for the Tonicas and Quapas (Arkansas) in the hope of keeping them intimidated and quiet. Ford was "enamour'd with the Country" around Natchez, but concerned by his diminishing supply of ammunition and the Indians' disinclination to wait for Farmar's appearance. The Choctaw began to wander off as early as July 18 and had determined to depart as a body in mid-August, when Farmar put in a most timely appearance. Lieutenant Ford could properly believe that his efforts had guaranteed the safe passage of the regiment, and he was critical of Farmar's lack of generosity when it came to distributing presents among the deserving Choctaws.[17]

While Farmar rested his troops on the river's edge, Lieutenant Pittman made his way up the steep hill to the site of Fort Rosalie, 180 feet above the landing place. The view was worth the climb: on one side the Mississippi, 1,870 feet wide at this point, on the other, "the prospect . . . is beautifully varied by a number of little hills and fine meadows, separated by small copses, the trees of which are mostly walnut and oak."[18]

The strain of the voyage told upon the men as well as the officers of the 34th Regiment. At Natchez, Farmar held a regimental court martial on a drummer for having disobeyed the major's orders that he should not beat his wife. The trial disclosed that the woman had been frequently and blatantly intimate with the surgeon's mate, and when she was "caught in the fact," the husband had beaten his spouse on the spot. The members of the court, Lieutenants Henry, Sedgwick, and Ford and Ensign Robinson, held that the drummer was entirely within his rights. Farmar was furious at their failure to uphold his orders, declared he would flog the man anyway, and promptly classified the four officers, along with Pittman, among his personal enemies as creatures of Governor Johnstone. A second court martial was held on charges brought by Lieutenant John Ross against Sergeant Samuel Littleford. The members of the court acquitted Littleford and refused to revise their verdict when ordered to do so by Major Farmar. The frustrated commander thereupon ordered the man confined until they reached Fort Chartres and a general court martial could be assembled to try him again.[19]

On August 17 the expedition took to its boats again, and as had been true since the end of June,

> the greatest difficulty we met with was the intense heat of the Weather, the Soldiers not being accustomed to such hard labour in the most scorching Climate. I cou'd only proceed a few hours in the Morning & Evening our progress being then very slow, I was desirous to stretch a point fearing my Provisions wou'd fall short & continued rowing a little longer in the forenoon, but . . . upwards of forty men being taken ill occasioned by the heat of the Sun, many of whose lives

> we dispaired of, but were happy to find that only one died . . . was a discouraging circumstance to us all, & obliged me for some time afterwards to follow my usual notions which together with the rapidity of the current & the frequent accidents that happened to our Boats rendered our progress but small.

The expedition reached the mouth of the Arkansas River at the end of September. The French settlement would provide their last contact with civilization for many weeks, and there Farmar's best French river pilot deserted. While his bateaux remained at the little settlement on the Mississippi which served the needs of boatmen going up and down the river, Major Farmar and Lieutenant Pittman visited the French military post located nine miles up the Arkansas River. Farmar asked the French commandant for permission to hire another pilot, but he was "absolutly refused that favour." He seems nonetheless to have contracted for the services of Jean Sobym as a pilot to the Illinois and agreed to pay him five hundred livres. However, Sobym, too, deserted the expedition, and the major subsequently reported that his lack of a pilot "greatly hindered our progress afterwards, as the Islands in the great River form many different channels, we cou'd not be judges which was the most convenient for us, being unacquainted with the Navigation of ye River." At least Farmar was able, again over the French commandant's objections, to effect the release of Burton, a surgeon's mate of the 17th Regiment, who had been captured by hostile Indians while en route to Fort Chartres with Captain Thomas Morris in 1764. Farmar attached Burton to his command and took him with the 34th to the Illinois.[20]

At the Arkansas a French convoy of bateaux that had left New Orleans after Farmar's departure overtook the English boats. As the hardened voyagers would clearly reach Fort Chartres before him, Farmar commissioned one of the Frenchmen to arrange for food to be sent downriver to the regiment. His action proved fortunate. The French convoy reached Fort Chartres on October 30 and found that the place had been occupied by Captain Thomas Stirling and a hundred men of the 42nd Regiment, who had come down the Ohio from Fort Pitt, on October 9. Stirling immediately dispatched an officer and two bateaux loaded with provisions to Farmar's assistance—aid which Stirling, at least, credited with saving the expedition. The Black Watch captain also believed that if he had not been at Fort Chartres in October, the French traders would have stirred up the Indians to oppose Farmar's progress by force of arms.[21]

Wherever he encountered Indians along the river, Farmar was lavish in distributing gifts. At the Arkansas he met a party of Indians from the Illinois to whom he gave presents. "They were well pleas'd with the treatment they received," he reported, "and sent to inform their Nation of it, which contributed greatly to my not being opposed in the passage." The Arkansas Indians were also well entertained by the English visitors. Although the French commandant refused to allow Farmar to treat with them at his post, the British and the Indians got together out of sight of the fort and exchanged presents and declarations of friendship.[22]

After a few days at the Arkansas River, the 34th Regiment returned to their oars. "As we preceeded higher, the heat of the Weather abated, but as the River continued falling accidents more frequently happened, scarce a day passed (notwithstanding the pains that was taken) without some Boat running aground, or being thrown by the rapidity of the current upon logs, which often obliged us to unload them, and was sometimes the work of two days."[23]

In October, at the River Margot, known to the English as Wolf River (the site of modern Memphis, Tennessee), Farmar was met by a band of 125 Chickasaw Indians led by the trader John McIntosh. McIntosh and 14 of his followers formed a hunting party and accompanied the regiment the rest of the way to Fort Chartres. By halting frequently Farmar was able to keep his men fed, for the supplies he had shipped aboard the bateaux were now exhausted.

> Part of the Provision I received from the Agents for the Contractors at Mobile, was so bad that I was frequently obliged to serve the Troops more than their usual allowance, great part of it not being eatable, which I believe was formerly condemned, and privately conveyed into the Store; from this circumstance, had it not been for the diligence of the hunters I hired, together with the Chickasaw Indians who supplied the convoy with Buffalo &ca. for upwards of five weeks, the expedition must inevitably have fail'd.[24]

Near the mouth of the Ohio, about November 10, word reached the laboring redcoats that Stirling had arrived safely at Fort Chartres; the supply boats sent down from that post must have found the regiment at this point. Three weeks later, on December 2, Major Farmar and the 34th Regiment landed at Fort Chartres. Farmar was happy to agree that Stirling's presence "greatly contributed to my success, as I have reason to imagine that the French Inhabitants of this Country wou'd have done their utmost Efforts to have spirited up the Indians in order to oppose my passage." But it was to his men that Major Farmar gave the greatest credit, for "during all this time the Soldiers behaved with great resolution & chearfullness beyond what cou'd be expected from Troops unaccustomed to the like Service."[25] Such virtues owed much to Farmar's own iron determination and rigid discipline, qualities not universally appreciated nor even approved by some of the younger regimental officers. By the journey's end nerves were stretched to the breaking point, personalities clashed, and Farmar's authority would be challenged by his subordinates or they broken to his will.

During the next ten days Farmar familiarized himself with the fort and the surrounding country with the assistance of Captain Stirling. As senior officer and designated commandant, Farmar took it on himself to change the name of the post to Fort Cavendish, thereby honoring the colonel of the 34th Regiment of Foot, Lord Frederick Cavendish. Stirling was a bit put out by this, for he thought that as the officer who had first occupied Fort Chartres he should have had that privilege, and he advised the American commander in chief that he would have named it Fort Gage, but he acceded to Farmar's wishes in order to avoid any unpleasantness. Both officers were agreed that there was insufficient food at the fort to support both regiments through the winter and to provide Stirling with sufficient provisions to get back to Fort Pitt in the spring. Farmar therefore ordered Stirling and his men to depart by the most expeditious route—down the Mississippi to New Orleans, rather than back up the Ohio as Stirling's orders had directed. Stirling and his contingent departed before the end of the year, and Robert Farmar and his Havana veterans once more settled down in an old French fort deep in the wilderness of America.[26]

The country in which Major Robert Farmar and the river-weary veterans of the 34th Regiment found themselves in December 1765 was wonderfully different from Mobile and the Gulf Coast. A later British military visitor was moved to rapturous prose: "The natural beauty of this country exceeds the strength of imagination. It resembles most a gentleman's park in England. Clumps of trees, lawns, bubbling springs, out of the rocks and grounds, pieces of water, open woods, larger plains, in which are to be seen herds of buffalos elks, deer almost tame, pheasants, quail, duck, & all manner of game."[27] This was the Illinois country at its best, and stone-built Fort de Chartres, completed as recently as 1756, was its crown jewel and seat of government. Five French villages clustered about it. To the south, Kaskaskia, the center of the fur trade, formerly boasted a population of some six hundred white men. To the north lay the oldest French settlement in the Illinois, Cahokia, now about forty-five dwellings. St. Philippe, five miles north of the fort, was much smaller; when Philip Pittman visited there, he encountered only a militia officer with twenty slaves. Prairie du Rocher, two miles east of Fort Chartres, contained a dozen families, but Nouvelle Chartres, located on the prairie to the east of the fort, was deserted by all but three or four families—twenty-two houses stood empty. French authorities had estimated the population at fourteen hundred men, women, and children, but, anticipating British occupation, many of the French, stubbornly loyal to their king, had withdrawn to the west bank of the Mississippi. At St. Louis they created a new center from which to challenge British domination of the fur trade in the Illinois and on the Missouri.[28]

Fort Chartres—or Fort Cavendish, as Robert Farmar rechristened it—was a gem of military architecture: "one of the prettiest stone forts I ever saw," remarked an officer of the Black Watch. Captain Stirling noted the great gate, fifteen feet high; the stout bastions at each corner of the fort's irregular quadrangle were well adapted to withstand any assault by Indians; it could hold two hundred men, even four hundred in Major Farmar's view. Lieutenant Pittman noted that the stone walls of the fort, standing ten feet high, were two feet two inches thick, plastered over, "and pierced with loop-holes at regular distances, and with two port-holes for cannon in the faces, and two in the flanks of each bastion." Inside the walls were two soldiers' barracks, a storehouse and a guardhouse, the commissary's house, now turned into British officers' quarters, and the commandant's house. Major Farmar would have found his circumstances much improved over those at Mobile. Measuring ninety-six by thirty feet, his house contained kitchen, dining room, bedroom, an office, five small "closets" for servants, and a cellar. When Stirling and the 42nd Regiment arrived in October, the French commandant, St. Ange, had only one officer and twenty men on duty, and the British thought they "might be called anything else but soldiers." The flight of the French habitants had already begun; the French troops soon followed. Stirling, and then Farmar, were left to face certain grim realities: a serious food shortage, hostile Indians, and an even more hostile Mississippi River, which ate away at the bank a mere sixty to eighty paces from the fort's western wall and had advanced a half mile toward that goal in the last few years. Everyone who saw it feared that the fort would be swallowed up by the voracious current during the next spring floods.[29]

Food might be purchased from the remaining Frenchmen, and Stirling had contracted with M. LaGrange for victuals, but his prices were high, and other merchants acted as though they were doing a favor when they sold French brandy to the Highlanders at twenty shillings a gallon. As soon as he settled in, Farmar assembled the inhabitants and determined that the countryside could furnish 50,000 pounds of flour and 1,250 pounds of Indian cornmeal for his troops—221 days' rations, enough to last until July, but without any allowance for hosting visiting Indians, who expected twice a redcoat's portion. The few remaining farmers had sent away most of their cattle and were smuggling their corn across the river. Buffalo must provide most of the regiment's meat unless local supplies could be found. Captains Dundas, Forbes, and Pownall were assigned to investigate M. LaGrange's contract, and they heard his claim that he had lost money by the terms of his agreement with Stirling.

As this appeared to be the case, Farmar undertook to pay a yet higher price for fresh beef.[30]

For the moment the local Indians were overawed by the Choctaws and Chickasaws who came north with Farmar, but presents for the surrounding tribes were necessary. Stirling had found suitable gifts to be very dear; Farmar immediately purchased from French traders £546.16.6½ worth of cloth, plain and ruffled shirts, tomahawks, and gunpowder for Indian presents—and 450 gallons of brandy for his redcoats. The Kaskaskia Indians were loath to accept Farmar's gifts, however, and the Illinois Indians were averse to living peaceably with the Chickasaws. Lack of an Indian interpreter made negotiation difficult, and to Pittman it did not help that Farmar appeared "a good deal a stranger seemingly to the Laws, Customs, & Disposition of the French."[31]

To assist him in the affairs of Fort Cavendish, Farmar named as his staff Captain Edward Pownall, fort major; Captain James Campbell, barrackmaster; and Lieutenant William Baugh as his secretary. Lieutenant Pittman was dispatched to visit and report upon the outlying French posts; Ensign William Robinson was assigned command of the thirty-man garrison at Kaskaskia.

Unfortunately, the officers of the 34th Regiment were themselves far from being a happy family. Shortly after reaching Fort Cavendish, Farmar felt himself "under a necessity of ordering [a court martial] in order to support discipline in the Regiment, for such a spirit of desertion, discord and sedition broke out on the passage among some of the subaltern officers, that several men confined by me for disobedience of orders and other crimes were acquitted by regimental Court Martial ordered to try them, altho' the fact alledged against them was proved beyond a doubt."

Consequently, Sergeant Samuel Littleford was tried once again and sentenced to receive five hundred lashes. Had it been practical to delay Stirling's departure with the 42nd Regiment, Farmar would also have brought Lieutenants John Henry, Hunter Sedgwick, and Thomas Ford before a general court martial for insubordination. They had openly and in the men's hearing criticized Farmar during the ascent of the Mississippi, refused to remove their hats to the major, and thereby weakened morale and threatened regimental discipline. They had certainly failed to render court-martial verdicts to the major's satisfaction. Lieutenant Sedgwick, once a favorite with the major, was the worst offender. Farmar asked General Gage to order a court martial of these officers unless they apologized for their delinquency "publickly at the head of the Regiment." At the same time, Farmar recommended that the corporal punishment awarded against Sergeant Littleford be remitted.[32]

The young officers were quick to respond to Farmar's charges. Henry, Ford, Sedgwick, and Robinson protested to Gage that their decisions had been based upon common sense and justice. The outraged drummer who had chastised his adulterous wife could hardly be found worthy of punishment. Sergeant Littleford had been prosecuted by Lieutenant Ross as a means of discovering and silencing whoever was carrying tales to the men from the officers' mess; Ross had not wanted the man punished, and they had unanimously acquitted a "good old soldier." Further, cases of real insubordination had been forgiven by Farmar, and other officers favored by the major had been pardoned for similar words and actions. Henry, Ford, and Sedgwick suggested that Farmar's hostility apparently stemmed from the fact that Governor Johnstone had named them as witnesses against the major when they were in Mobile, and now Farmar sought to discredit them—a particularly painful situation inasmuch as they had been his staunchest supporters in West Florida.[33]

General Thomas Gage, at New York, was greatly relieved to hear in March 1766 that Farmar and the 34th Regiment had reached Fort Chartres safely (he consistently declined to accept the designation of Fort Cavendish). He approved of Farmar's handling of both Indians and Frenchmen but rejected the major's staff nominations—not even brigadiers were allowed secretaries, "and there can't be any great use for one at the Illinois." Only Barrackmaster Campbell might keep his place. The findings of the court martials were approved and Sergeant Littleford excused from suffering five hundred lashes. Gage regretted hearing of bickering among the officers, but if nothing else would serve to maintain discipline, Farmar might bring them to trial. As for the men, now enduring a hard midwestern winter, the general was sorry if they had only one blanket apiece, but that was army regulations. The men might live in abandoned French houses and plant wheat and corn in the deserted fields; they should be paid for what they produced, there being no other source of supplies. Farmar should do what was necessary for their comfort, but he should spend as little as possible in the process. He should certainly draw no more bills on the Treasury. Distrusting both the French and their Indian allies, Gage advised indulgence toward the remaining habitants, firmness toward St. Ange and the emigré Frenchmen. Illicit trade across the river might be controlled by arming a few small boats to catch smugglers.[34]

Life at Fort Cavendish during the first three months of 1766 was as hard and uncomfortable as Major Farmar had anticipated. Lack of currency strained the regiment's credit, and in February, Farmar was forced to issue personal notes in lieu of cash with which to pay officers and men. His paper was good for all purposes save the purchase of liquor by the ordinary soldiers. The scarcity of provision meant that "soldiers are frequently two or three days together without anything but bread and Indian corn as this Country cannot afford sufficient meat for the daily consumption of the Troops." In mid-March, the soldiers went without beef for six or eight days in spite of the efforts of hunting parties that constantly scoured the countryside, even taking boats up the Ohio River in search of buffalo. The plains of Illinois were sufficiently fertile to produce ample food, but the habitants "are and always have been too Insolent & Lazy to bestow any pains upon Cultivation." In order to conserve supplies, all the available flour was locked in the fort's magazine, and Farmar contracted to buy whatever the French would sell: beef at 8 sols a pound, pork at 20 sols; flour sold at $5 a hundredweight, corn at $1 a bushel; wood might be purchased at 8 livres ($1.60), candles at 30 sols a pound—all necessary purchases for officers and men alike, and, Farmar reminded Gage, for the numerous women who accompanied the regiment and must be cared for. To add to his worries, Farmar learned that the 34th's Lieutenant Colonel John Reed was coming up the Mississippi with three subalterns and forty recruits and expected to be supplied en route from Fort Cavendish.[35]

The supply situation did not improve in April. In spite of mixing flour and cornmeal for bread, reserves would be exhausted in six weeks. The men were in poor health, suffering from scurvy. "Should they be obliged to live on salt meat alone, without bread or vegetables, it will in a short time kill many of them." Farmar could not stop the smuggling of flour from the British to the French side of the Mississippi, but he enclosed three acres of ground for a regimental garden and set each company to growing its own vegetables.[36]

The French inhabitants of British Illinois were too few to give Major Farmar any difficulties, save by their preference for illegal trade with their fellows at St. Louis and Ste. Genevieve. It was perhaps helpful that Farmar enjoyed good relations with Father Sebastien Louis Meurin, the local priest who served the religious needs of the scattered villages of the Illinois country. Few of the French, however, were inclined to take the oath of allegiance to their new masters—only ninety had done so by early April, including nineteen at Kaskaskia, four at Chartres village, thirty-three at Cahokia. Farmar was more concerned by the evidence of continuing French influence with the Indians and the rumors they spread that English liquor was poisoned. Commandant St. Ange was busy among the Shawnee and cheerfully warned Farmar that the Indians on the Missouri were greatly displeased by the English presence. The French habitants did, at least, provide excuse and opportunity for some light moments. On Sunday evening, April 6, the merchant John Jennings, just arrived with a welcome cargo of supplies and trade goods from Fort Pitt, attended "a Ball, given by a Gentleman of the Army, to the French Inhabitants who made a very droll appearance, it seems this is the only day of diversion among the French."[37]

The Indians themselves were simply unpredictable. Hostilities between Kaskaskias and Fox Indians kept both French and Indian hunters close to the fort, thereby reducing the availability of fresh meat. Local Indians were also feuding with the Chickasaw, and it fell upon Farmar to patch up their differences. Wandering bands lurked about the fort demanding food, and Farmar had little to give them save liquor. He had distributed presents with a generous hand on the Mississippi, and incessant rain had damaged most of the remainder, particularly his trade blankets. Necessity forced him to purchase more from the French until supplies began to reach the Illinois from Fort Pitt. In March he entertained a band of Missouri Indians and gave them presents and a "peace belt" of wampum to show his good intentions toward tribes to the west. They left "very well pleased," and Farmar hoped that when they returned in July, English merchants would have reached Fort Cavendish, for "the Trade of the Missouri is the most advantageous of any in this extensive country." In May several tribes gathered to parley at Fort Cavendish: Chickasaw, led by "the second man of their Nation," Kaskaskia, Mitchigamis, and Illinois. They secured some liquor and got drunk, delaying any negotiations, and when Farmar refused to allow the establishment of a new Indian village north of the fort, the Illinois "went away in a huff." Finally, on May 8, Farmar secured agreement to a general peace among the Indians, one which he hoped would bind them to the English interest.[38]

The sufferings and tribulations of the late winter months did nothing to ease tensions among the British officers at Fort Cavendish. Although the four subalterns of the 34th made proper and acceptable apologies to Major Farmar in the presence of the regiment's captains, the simmering antagonism between the major and Lieutenant Philip Pittman burst into open warfare.[39]

Detached from the 15th Regiment and ordered to report directly to General Gage, young Pittman acted as if he were exempt from Farmar's authority. They had clashed at Mobile and at the Iberville, refused to speak to one another on the Mississippi, and at the Illinois, Farmar employed Captain Campbell rather than Lieutenant Pittman as his engineering officer, implying that Pittman was merely a surveyor. Pittman took his assignment from Gage most seriously and began gathering plans and maps of the area and its villages as soon as he arrived at Fort Cavendish. As early as December 13, 1765, his independent attitude drew from Farmar a warning letter. The major then refused to recognize Pittman's purchase of a house, pillaged it for planks, and used the garden for regimental purposes. Pittman was excluded from construction work in the fort, but Farmar seems to have raised no impediment to his visits to the outlying villages. On his side, Farmar believed that Pittman was discouraging local inhabitants from cooperating with him and was even seeking to discredit the bills of exchange with which Farmar had to purchase desperately needed supplies at exorbitant prices. Pittman had ample warning of his danger from his friend Lieutenant Henry, but, persuaded of his rectitude, he went his own way until March 13, 1766, when Lieutenant Ford informed him that the major had drawn up formal charges against him in anticipation of a general court martial and was placing him under arrest for "disobedience of orders, obstructing the service of the Government, and seditious behaviour." Trial would await the arrival of Lieutenant Colonel John Reed.

The 34th Regiment had seen nothing of its lieutenant colonel since landing in Cuba in 1762, but by 1765 Reed (like Wedderburn of the 22nd) felt some obligation to find his regiment. He made his way to Mobile late in the year, only to discover that he must chase them up the Mississippi. In November, Reed was at New Orleans, accompanied by three officers and forty recruits, seeking boats. Not until January 3, 1766, did he get away, and not until March did Farmar learn that he was actually coming to Fort Cavendish. Reed's voyage was as difficult and as slow as Farmar's had been; he finally reached Fort Cavendish on May 17 and assumed the command his major had held for five weary months.[40] One of his first acts was to order the hearing of Farmar's charges against Pittman.

On Saturday, May 22, Captain Alexander Dundas sat as president of a general court martial with Captains Gordon Forbes, Edward Pownall, and James Campbell; Lieutenants Baugh, Ross, Henry, Ancrum, and Ford; and Ensigns Robinson, Wainwright, Wood, and Shadwell as judges. Lieutenant Hunter Sedgwick acted as deputy judge advocate and presented charges accusing Philip Pittman of "disobedience to orders, obstructing the service of the Government, attempting to stop the public credit, disrespectful behaviour to Major Farmar and depreciating his character as Commandant." The defendant immediately protested the presence of Captain Campbell as a member of the court on the ground that Campbell might be subject to future prosecution by Pittman relative to his work on the Iberville. Pittman also pointed out that he intended to call many of the members of the court (virtually the whole officer corps at Fort Cavendish) as witnesses for his defense. The members of the court promptly—and doubtless with considerable relief—agreed with Pittman's objections. Lieutenant Colonel Reed concurred, and the court was hastily dissolved.[41]

Having neatly parried Farmar's attack, Pittman attempted a riposte. He asked Lieutenant Colonel Reed to convene a court of enquiry in order to lay his disputes with Farmar before General Gage, as Farmar had done to him at the Iberville. Unwilling to prolong the squabble, Reed refused. Pittman was determined to have revenge; he soon presented to Reed sixteen articles of accusation against Robert Farmar, and they were sent on to Gage at New York. They would resurface in Pensacola.[42]

By the time the dust from this fracas had settled, Robert Farmar had to consider other and more serious threats. He had left Mobile under the distant cloud of prosecution sought by Governor George Johnstone. While Gage bore Johnstone no love, he was a stickler for correct procedure, and he had himself found that Farmar was sometimes wanting in that department. Only a court martial could clarify the numerous, confusing charges Johnstone had made, and in February 1765 Gage determined that a general court martial should be held at Pensacola to resolve all questions. Achieving that end was not so easy. Farmar was three months distant from New York, whether in West Florida or in the Illinois country. The court martial that Gage intended to convene required the presence of a more senior officer, and no one under the rank of captain might sit in judgment upon Major Farmar. The assembling of Robert Farmar's court martial would prove to be one of the most aggravating administrative problems facing the commander in chief of the British army in North America in the decade before the American Revolution.

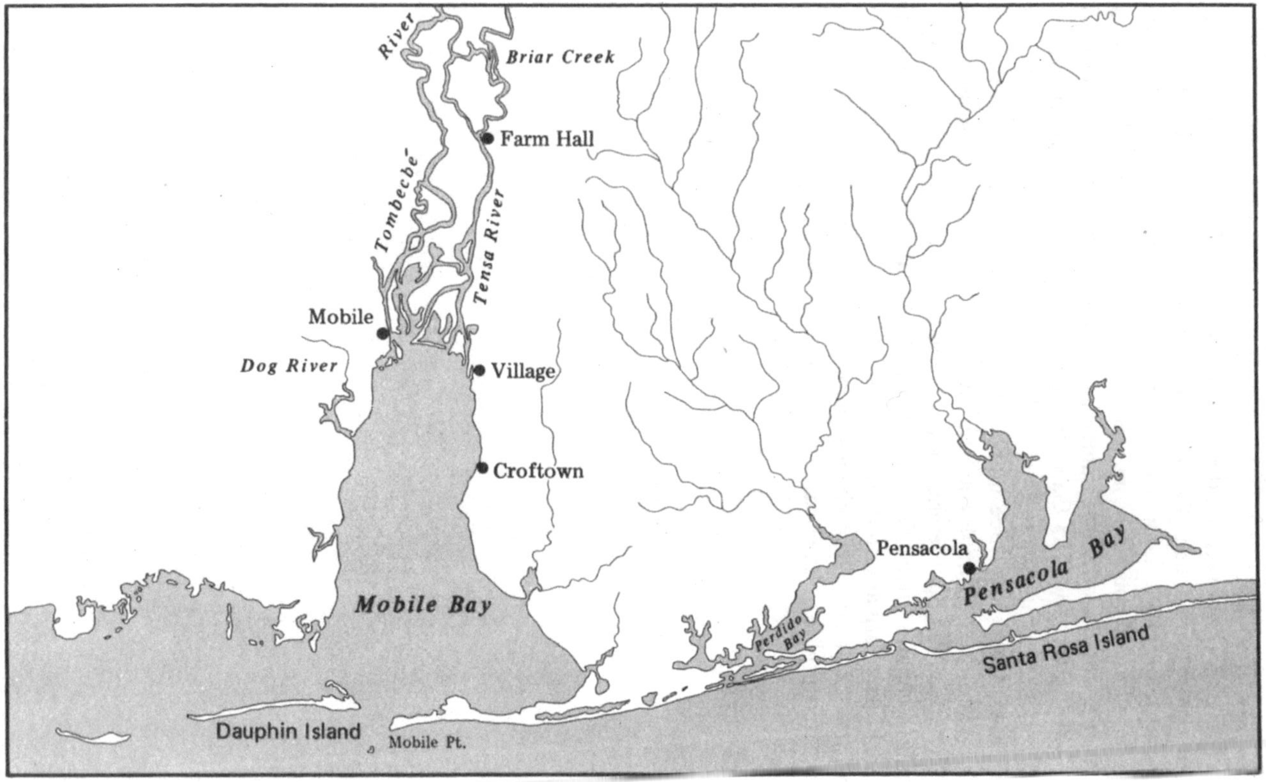

Mobile-Pensacola after Bernard Romans, 1770

V.

Court Martial at Pensacola

The formal resolution of the quarrels arising from Robert Farmar's establishment of British authority at Mobile, his successful ascent of the Mississippi, and his brief command at Fort Cavendish provides a painful demonstration of the difficulties posed by time, distance, and accidental circumstance to British military forces in North America. At New York, General Gage was half a continent distant from Major Farmar—wherever he might be. Communication with West Florida was by sea, and no matter how efficient the general and his staff might be, they were dependent upon the availability of shipping. Six weeks might pass between the drafting of orders and the sailing of a vessel from New York to Pensacola. The ensuing voyage, with inevitable delays at coastal ports along the way, might consume as much time as a crossing of the Atlantic. Men sickened and died on such voyages, and West Florida itself was "a graveyard for Britons." The Mississippi and the Ohio rivers were broad highways to the Illinois country, but even when the Indian gantlet was removed their currents were hostile, their miles seemingly endless.

Eighteenth-century British army officers were, in any case, a peculiarly independent breed; they followed their private interests with remarkable freedom, took leave with little regard for the needs of the service, and were at best few in number and widely dispersed. If their duties were light, their regiments were moved from place to place in America and rotated home to Britain with little advance notice. The circumstances in which they and their troops lived and worked were seldom conducive to satisfaction. True to English tradition, civilians had little use for them unless an enemy were close at hand, and few Americans cared to recognize or credit the economic benefits of the military presence. To envision the British army in the colonies as an armed incubus squatting over a helpless people requires a truly American imagination. The tenuous threads that held the system together were stretched to the breaking point by the simple task of bringing Major Robert Farmar to military justice.[1]

In February 1765 General Thomas Gage decided that the charges made by Governor George Johnstone against Robert Farmar must be submitted to trial by a general court martial.[2] Gage could and did discount much of Johnstone's bombast for what it was, and he firmly supported the proper independence of the military from the encroachment of civil authority. Some of Johnstone's complaints, however, raised serious questions of military propriety, and Farmar had, of necessity, run very close to the line from his first appearance at Mobile. When Philip Pittman entered the scene, the issues were clearly military in nature; charges and countercharges proliferated and required military adjudication. For that purpose as well as for the oversight of all military activity in the distant southern colonies, Gage needed a brigadier general; his first choice was the distinguished Colonel Henry Bouquet, whose success against the Indians at Bushy Run had effectively put an end to the troubles known as Pontiac's Rebellion.

Bouquet was in Philadelphia in April 1765, when he received word from headquarters that he was Gage's choice for brigadier in the Southern Department and would be stationed at Pensacola. On May 15 Gage issued orders to Bouquet to hold a court of enquiry into the charges against Major Robert Farmar and, if that investigation justified doing so, to hold a general court martial when Farmar returned from the Illinois. Gage directed that the court-martial panel must consist of officers of the rank of captain or higher, and he supplied Bouquet with materials received from Johnstone and drafts and vouchers drawn by Farmar against the general totaling £9,500 and requiring investigation.[3] On May 23 both Gage and Bouquet drew up orders for Robert Farmar, wherever he might be, to report to Mobile immediately. The general was aware that Farmar was likely to have left West Florida for the Illinois country before these orders reached him, but he could hardly have anticipated that Farmar would not receive them until May 17, 1766—a full year later.[4] As Bouquet began to review the material sent from New York, his pleasure at being appointed brigadier faded. "The distracted state of that Department, and the violent animosities of parties, opens a most disagreeable prospect for me," he first confided to Gage. He soon concluded that "the prosecutions against Major Farmar appear rather dictated by Resentment than Justice." He proposed to seek "a general reconciliation"; if that failed, "Major Farmar's Trial will unravell the Causes of all these Disputes and appreciate the Real Character of the persons concern'd."[5]

Bouquet expected to leave Philadelphia on June 20—shipping was hard to find and less than satisfactory. His ship reached Pensacola Bay on August 24, and word was sent ashore that the brigadier was seriously ill. As the town was devastated by fevers at that moment, there was little point in removing the sick man to the fort, and Henry Bouquet died, without taking up his command, on September 3, 1765.[6]

By the twenty-third of October, Thomas Gage had word of Bouquet's death, and hearing that Lieutenant Colonel John Reed of the 34th Regiment had gone to West Florida, the general hastily appointed Reed to act as brigadier. No sooner had Reed's orders been drafted than advice reached New York that Reed had wandered off in pursuit of his regiment, now in the Illinois country. In his place Gage turned to Colonel William Tayler, 9th Regiment, at St. Augustine. A series of letters was dispatched to East Florida to hasten Tayler on his way, and the accomplishment of Major Farmar's court martial was firmly emphasized in them.[7]

The silence imposed by time and distance now fell over the scene. Colonel Reed, unaware that he was supposed to be in West Florida, arrived at Fort Cavendish on May 17, 1766, and Robert Farmar received from him Gage's orders of May 1765. The change of command and Farmar's futile attempt to bring Lieutenant Pittman to justice occupied some days. Farmar had then to secure a boat in which to descend the Mississippi—no small problem on short notice and without any assistance from Reed. On June 18 he nosed out into the current that had eaten to within fifty paces of Forth Cavendish (henceforth to revert to its earlier name of Fort Chartres) accompanied only by his personal servant and one soldier on furlough. Advising Gage of the major's departure, John Reed further obscured the situation by writing that Farmar was headed for New York by way of the Ohio River and Fort Pitt. By mid-September, when Gage received Reed's missive, he had better information that Farmar was returning to West Florida. Hoping to check the unpredictable movement of his principals, Gage ordered Brigadier Tayler to place Farmar under arrest when he reached West Florida, and he provided Tayler with specific charges on which he was to be tried. To Reed and Pittman, who was now demanding that his own charges against Farmar be heard, Gage ironically expressed his surprise that all the "gentlemen" at Fort Chartres had not gone to Pensacola for Farmar's trial "if you could prove anything."[8]

Several thousand miles away, an overdue decision was being reached that would please everyone concerned in the affairs of West Florida. On September 22, the earl of Shelburne decided to remove George Johnstone from his governorship and gave him permission to return to England. Johnstone was quite ready to leave Pensacola, but not without a few last-minute efforts to entrap Robert Farmar. Upon learning of Farmar's impending return to West Florida, the governor inquired of Brigadier Tayler if he should now draw up detailed accusations against the major or if Farmar would be tried on the particular articles submitted by General Gage. Tayler advised Johnstone that Gage's articles would form the basis of investigation, and the governor complained bitterly that they did not contain half the charges he had already made. He protested against any "mutilation or suppression of particular parts," offered to provide a full and proper list of grievances, and announced that he considered the general's instructions highly partial toward Farmar.[9] Johnstone was not likely to get any satisfaction from Gage, for their recent correspondence had persuaded the general never to write to Johnstone again "on any Matter wherein I have the Misfortune to differ from him in Opinion."[10] On January 13, 1767, George Johnstone departed from West Florida—though the title of governor would remain with him throughout his turbulent life.[11]

For Robert Farmar the disappearance of Governor Johnstone smoothed the way back to West Florida. Leaving the Illinois country in mid-June 1766, Farmar came down to New Orleans and remained there for several months. He later explained that he delayed returning to Mobile in order to settle the accounts of the 34th Regiment with sundry New Orleans businessmen, but he probably also wished to avoid legal entanglements and actual prosecution and imprisonment threatened by Johnstone and others in the British colony. He could communicate with family and friends easily enough, and he would have heard at once of Johnstone's recall. In late September 1766 Brigadier Tayler knew that Farmar "is, or has been, at New Orleans, but I have not heard from him, it is said he does not come this way." Farmar returned to West Florida on December 11, 1766.[12]

On home ground again, Farmar launched an attack against one of his old enemies, Lieutenant Alexander Maclellan. At Pensacola he submitted to Tayler a set of nine general and specific accusations that Maclellan had obstructed and delayed the expedition up the Mississippi by decrying the major's credit, meddling in the preparation of boats at New Orleans, refusing bedding to the 34th Regiment and persuading Lieutenant Colonel Wedderburn to recall bedding already issued to the regiment, and by such actions having put the government to great additional expense. Maclellan had also acted as Governor Johnstone's agent and taken his orders, asserting that the civil governor "was invested with the command of the Military." The two of them had even smuggled wine from New Orleans in their own behalf—a "mean dirty transaction."[13]

Brigadier Tayler delivered Farmar's charges to Maclellan on February 21, 1767, and the lieutenant immediately demanded an explanation. The brigadier found himself acting as courier between the two officers. Farmar would offer no further explanations, and Maclellan declared himself innocent and indifferent to Farmar's charges.[14] To add to Tayler's concerns, Lieutenant Philip Pittman returned from the Illinois country in March, eager to confront his persecutor, Major Farmar.[15] Tayler could do no more than breathe a great sigh of relief when he was replaced in West Florida by a more permanent brigadier, Frederick Haldimand.

Upon learning of Bouquet's death late in 1765, Gage had determined to name in his place the distinguished Swiss mercenary of the 60th Regiment Royal Americans, Colonel Frederick Haldimand. The appointment was quickly approved in London, but nearly a year passed before Haldimand sailed from New York, arriving in Pensacola on March 24, 1767. Haldimand found Pensacola and the West Florida military establishment in a state of misery and decay. Lieutenant Governor Montfort Browne had succeeded Johnstone at the head of civil affairs, but "the spirit of party" hung heavy in the air. Fortunately, Frederick Haldimand was both a man of action and a competent administrator; he set to work to improve the living conditions of his command and to resolve the quarrels that had long plagued civil and military relations. He would find the former easier than the latter.[16]

The issue of Major Farmar's charges against Lieutenant Maclellan was dealt with quickly. On March 27, with Tayler at his side, Haldimand conferred with Farmar regarding his accusations, and the next day the major called upon Haldimand to press for action. The brigadier, who felt that the two officers might have settled their differences privately and that Farmar had been suspiciously deliberate in demanding formal trial of the charges, was unmoved. He declared that nothing could be done until Farmar himself had been tried, and he rejected Farmar's plea that it would never be possible to assemble a general court martial in Pensacola. Haldimand then packed up the documentation and dispatched it to New York—along with Alexander Maclellan, whom he sent away "for the tranquillity of the province."[17] Haldimand appreciated the utility of distancing adversaries. At the same time he allowed Robert Farmar to return to Mobile and his family, he ordered Pittman off on a surveying expedition to isolated Fort San Marcos at Apalache.[18] Farmar accepted the inevitable and agreed that he would not pursue his case against Maclellan until his own trial had been held. At the same time he pointed out that delay on that score could not be blamed on him, as he had asked for witnesses as early as April 1765 and had never received any cooperation from either General Gage or Lieutenant Colonel Reed.[19]

Nothing could be done with regard to Farmar's trial, however, until the requisite number of captains reached Pensacola. Tayler had been baffled by that problem, and Gage had thought he might send Farmar to New York for trial. As that had not been done and Farmar had apparently settled down at Mobile, the general proposed to detach five captains from various posts to the

Gulf Coast so that the court might be convened. At the same time he sent to Haldimand the complaints of Lieutenant Philip Pittman in order that they too might be acted upon.[20]

By June, Haldimand found himself thoroughly embroiled in the business. Trials would require witnesses, and while Johnstone had left charges behind, he had left no list of witnesses to support them. Pittman had provided a list of twenty-one witnesses against Farmar, but to little avail. Some were in England or Ireland, some in the Illinois country, others in New York or Carolina, and many were French merchants in New Orleans or French officers who would not come to British West Florida without compensation or direct orders to do so from their sovereign. Farmar had been asked on June 1[illegible] to submit the names of his witnesses and had protested that delays were not his fault; he had given Gage the names as early as April 1765 and might have brought sergeants and privates of the 34th Regiment with him from the Illinois had permission been granted. Haldimand observed that all of these troubles stemmed from the same source: "If Mr. Johnstone had been less violent, this affair would have been terminated long ago."[21]

Farmar came to Pensacola on June 16 to meet his wife, and on June 25 he discussed his situation with Haldimand, who sought to persuade him to reduce the number of his witnesses for practical and financial reasons. Their conversation was completely unsatisfactory. Farmar expressed great surprise that there should be any question of the government paying the expenses of all the witnesses necessary to defend an accused officer, particularly when he was accused by the government, and he cited previous court martial cases in support of his argument. "With respect to myself," he urged,

> it would be a much more humane Act to hang me up on the first tree without any form of trial than to oblige me to pay the expence of the passage of the different Officers from Europe hither . . . out of my private fortune which is by no means sufficient to answer that purpose having with the prize money that fell to my share at the reduction of the Havana purchased some Cattle & Negroes with several tracts of Land near Mobile and several on the Island of Dauphin from the French inhabitants.

The cattle, he added, had already been wrested from him by the arbitrary proceedings of Governor Johnstone and by Lieutenant Governor Browne, who had seized nearly a hundred head of cattle and their calves on Dauphin Island and who presently secured his loot by a corporal's guard from the 21st Regiment.[22]

Haldimand believed that Farmar was following the advice of legal acquaintances rather than acting on principle. It did not speak well for Farmar that he had delayed his return to West Florida; had he really feared imprisonment by Johnstone, he would not have come at all but would have gone directly to New York or on to England. Farmar was now living comfortably on his farm at Mobile, aware that it would be impossible to hold a trial in the near future and unconcerned by the embarrassment to the service and the hazards to the health of members of the court who had to live in Pensacola. Haldimand suggested that Gage suspend the charges against Farmar and that he be judged solely on negligence to the service and disobedience of orders—the only issues on which he had any cause for fear—recognizing that he could not be condemned on the other articles of accusation. On those issues he could as well be tried in New York or London, whereas the intemperate climate of West Florida and the expense of proceedings there would drag out matters endlessly.[23]

Farmar, who was much involved in preparing for his court martial and was complaining of having been insulted by Pittman, added to Haldimand's problems by demanding military quarters in the garrison at Pensacola, inasmuch as he was there in a military capacity. As there was no room in the fort for a senior officer, Haldimand was forced to ask Lieutenant Governor Montfort Browne to find a place for Farmar. On the advice of the provincial council, Browne agreed to provide a suitable billet for the major in one of Pensacola's two public houses.[24]

General Gage could see no easy solution to all these problems and advised the secretary at war that he had some time ago ordered three captains from South Carolina and East Florida to report to Pensacola. There was, however, no possibility of gathering witnesses who were scattered all over the world. "It has been a very long and perplexed Affair, with which I may hereafter be obliged to trouble Your Lordship further about." Farmar's conduct, he told Haldimand, "astonishes me to the last degree." The major had previously mentioned but never before demanded witnesses; surely he could prove his innocence without transatlantic evidence and the presence of the whole 34th Regiment. "After all the trouble this affair has given . . .. I shall push this Business as far as it is in my power."[25]

Haldimand did what he could. In August he sent Captain James Marsh and Philip Pittman to New Orleans to see if they could cajole witnesses to come to Pensacola. They had no success with individuals and, not surprisingly, found the local authorities, Spanish Governor Ulloa and M. Aubry, of no assistance in their behalf. Pittman did not return to Pensacola until November, and he was soon dispatched to Fort York on the Tombecbé River and was absent until January 1768.[26]

To Haldimand, the difficulties of assembling a proper court martial justified proceeding by less formal court of enquiry, but as others differed in opinion, he agreed to convene a general court martial at the earliest opportunity. He hoped, before the end of the year, to see the arrival of a major and a captain of the 31st Regiment, and a captain of the 21st, but he would still lack supernumeraries for them. He observed that the captains waiting at Pensacola were receiving only lieutenants' pay and would be financially ruined by delays; the army too would suffer because their posts were left in the hands of subalterns without experience. If Farmar must be tried, he would also have his revenge in the prosecution of Pittman and Maclellan. It was all most discouraging, "but until we have satisfied the law, we must submit to all inconveniences."[27]

For the officers ordered to Pensacola for the court martial, the assignment was a nightmare. Captain David Hope was so elderly and ill that Haldimand anticipated that he would die before the court convened. Both he and Captain Francis Vignolles wished to retire from their regiments. Captain Edward Crofton had suffered several attacks of fever, and Haldimand feared for his life. Captain Nicholas Sutherland, who spent thirty-two days traveling from St. Augustine to Pensacola and missed his leave home because of the trial was one of the early arrivals. He found Brigadier Haldimand uncertain whether he would hold a court or not and waiting for further orders from New York. "Is it not very extraordinary," wrote Sutherland, "that a court martial should be ordered and the evidences on both sides have been allowed to go to England. This is our method of transacting business in West Florida, but as I have no right to find fault, I shall therefore only think."[28] Pensacola was certainly not a healthy place to wait. Between 1765 and 1767, the 31st Regiment garrisoned in the fort lost 6 officers and 190 men, 20 women, and 44 children, mostly to the fevers of the place.[29]

Robert Farmar doubtless derived some small satisfaction from Haldimand's difficulties and from letters the major received from the Illinois, where he was remembered most cordially. One French habitant wrote complaining of Lieutenant Colonel Reed's "tyranny" and seeking Farmar's good offices with General Gage. There were also fears of Spanish activity on the part of the French settlers. Farmar could piously express his concern for the interests of government and the distress of the people; Gage could only acknowledge the communication—he knew all too well that Farmar's successor at Fort Chartres had proven totally incompetent in his command.[30] The commander in chief was nearly persuaded to follow Haldimand's advice regarding Robert Farmar. Although six captains had been ordered to Pensacola to form a court, death and leave had made it impossible to proceed. Perhaps a court of enquiry would be necessary, for lack of evidence would apparently make it impossible for a general court martial at Pensacola to reach any conclusion.[31]

Haldimand's patience and Gage's efforts were, however, about to be rewarded. In March 1768 the brigadier had his captains in place and his principals in hand—or nearly so. Captain David Hope of the 21st Regiment was garrisoned at Mobile, and though old and in precarious health, he could not escape this duty. Following Gage's order of May 1767, Captains Will Jenkins and Nicholas Sutherland, of the 9th and 21st regiments respectively, had left St. Augustine for Pensacola about August 7, 1767. With them went Governor James Grant's fervent hope that "those Gentlemen to the Westward will in future contrive to agree together, and allow our East Floridian Officers to live in peace and quiet at Home." Accompanying Jenkins and Sutherland was Captain Ralph Phillips of the 60th Regiment. Recently assigned to duty at Fort Augusta in Georgia, Phillips's baggage had not caught up with him when he received orders for Pensacola in mid-June. He eventually went downriver to Savannah but there he encountered difficulty finding transportation to St. Augustine. The captain of the first available ship demanded an extra thirty-five pounds at the last moment before sailing, and Phillips refused to pay it. After some little time he found William Culmer, master of the sloop *Sally*, who agreed to carry him to St. Augustine for twenty pounds but required that he also pay the ship's port fees, another twenty pounds. Passage from East Florida to West Florida would add fifty-seven pounds ten shillings to the bill, and Phillips would be responsible for demurrage of thirty shillings a day at St. Augustine. By this means Captain Phillips reached the capital of East Florida late in July, and there Brigadier Tayler canceled his arrangement with Culmer because it did not provide for a return trip. Tayler secured passage to Pensacola for all three army officers aboard Robert Harris's ship for a bargain thirty pounds, cash in advance, and they reached Pensacola on September 15. There they found lodgings that Haldimand admitted were bad. Phillips asked for relief from a duty that was both tedious and expensive; Sutherland was surely bitter at losing his leave. Perhaps the only captain in Pensacola who was happy to be there was Thomas Hodgson of the 31st Regiment. Sailing with a detachment of recruits for the decimated regiment, Hodgson had been shipwrecked on Grand Cayman Island. His party escaped with little loss of life, but almost all their baggage was destroyed. They were rescued and taken first to Jamaica and thence to New York, and only succeeded in reaching Pensacola in late February 1768. Hodgson's wanderings were, at least, successfully concluded. Captain Daniel Rea, who had been ordered down from Natchez, succumbed to the recurrent fevers of the Gulf Coast some months before the trial began.[32]

The court was finally ordered to convene on March 16. At the moment of assembling, an irate Lieutenant Pittman came before Haldimand and expressed surprise that Farmar was to be tried on the seven specific charges Gage had prepared rather than on his own more numerous accusations. He even claimed to have proof of a false contract in hand. Haldimand "tried uselessly" to explain that such evidence would not suffice, but Pittman had consulted Francis Hutcheson, the designated deputy judge advocate, and had been assured that it was valid. Haldimand was at last persuaded to consent to the presentation of all of Pittman's charges as well as those emanating from headquarters.[33]

The long-awaited general court martial of Major Robert Farmar was convened in the fort at Pensacola on the morning of March 16, 1768.[34] Major James Chisholm of the 21st Regiment presided over a panel of twelve officers: nine captains and three captain lieutenants. From the 21st Regiment came Captains C. A. Steward, Frederick Disney, Nicholas Sutherland, and David Hope and Captain Lieutenant Patrick Innes. The 31st Regiment provided Captains A. Hamilton, Francis Vignolles, Thomas Varlo, Thomas Hodgson, and Captain Lieutenant Edward Crofton. Several of these men had been stationed in West Florida with their regiments since 1765. Captain Will Jenkins, 9th Regiment, and Captain Ralph Phillips, 60th regiment completed the roster. Lieutenant Francis Hutcheson, 60th Regiment, Haldimand's brigade major, directed the prosecution as deputy judge advocate, assisted in procedural matters upon occasion by the more experienced Captain Vignolles.

The members of the court were exemplary in attendance to their duty: every man was present throughout the thirty-six days of the trial and the nineteen days of actual sitting. The court did not convene on the five Sundays between March 16 and April 20, but there were three Saturday sessions. Twelve days of adjournment were granted in order that the defendant might prepare his case and the deputy judge advocate transcribe the voluminous record of the trial. The court convened at either nine or ten o'clock and usually sat until two or three o'clock, most often a six-hour day, although there were four occasions when the court rose shortly after being called to order. In addition to the leading figures, Robert Farmar and Phillip Pittman, eighteen witnesses appeared before the court, some of them repeatedly. They included two officers, three soldiers of the 34th regiment, seven British merchants and craftsmen from Mobile, three "Jew Merchants" (a customary distinction and one requiring the attention of the court, as they took their oaths on the Old Testament alone), one Frenchman, the skipper of a merchant vessel, and the deputy Indian superintendent. To their testimony was added a vast quantity of documentation—letters, contracts, vouchers—provided by General Gage and the witnesses and principals. Two full days were spent by the court in examining these accounts. The court was certainly diligent in its efforts; there were no unwarranted delays; and as they considered thirty-one articles of accusation in four sets of charges, they deserved the praise they received from Haldimand for concluding their work in as short a time as possible.

On Wednesday, March 16, the court being sworn and Robert Farmar appearing as prisoner before the court, the charges approved by General Gage were read. Eight articles originated with George Johnstone, late Governor of West Florida, and accused Major Farmar of:

1. Sending the king's flour to New Orleans and selling it through the agency of the Jew Joseph de Palacios.
2. Selling Fort York on the Tombecbé River to the merchant Jeremiah Terry.
3. Misapplying ten thousand pounds said to be expended on Indian presents and the fortifications at Mobile.
4. "Making a job of the Publick Service" in (that is, profiting from) the operations at the Iberville River.
5. "Turning into a different channel" money that should have been spent on barracks, so that officers and soldiers at Mobile had to live in miserable conditions.
6. Insisting upon charging five bitts a barrel for lime, when it could be made for three bitts, and dividing the profits with the engineer.
7. Desiring the engineer to carry an extra (fictitious) man on his account books at three shillings a day and to employ a laboring Negro who belonged to the major at another three shillings.
8. Employing the king's boats for his own emolument and dividing the profits of their work with the sailors.

From Philip Pittman came a set of five articles which were to be considered "as far as they tend to corroborate the Charge made by Governor Johnstone." These claimed that Farmar had:

1. Shared with the sailors and soldiers on a king's boat let out to certain Mobile merchants for a voyage to New Orleans.
2. Agreed to contracts for boats made by Captain John Lind at New Orleans which provided for the payment of three thousand dollars more than the actual cost.
3. Promised to lend flour to Governor D'Abbadie, but then charged him for it and sold it at an exorbitant price through the Jew merchant Isaac Solomons,
4. and did so at a time when the garrison at Mobile was near being in great want of flour.
5. Formed a fraudulent contract with unqualified parties, to the prejudice of government.

The deputy judge advocate presented Gage's charge that Farmar had disobeyed the commander in chief's orders, an accusation that was subsequently enlarged to two articles, the latter charging that Farmar was responsible for delaying the departure of the 34th Regiment on its expedition up the Mississippi River.

As they were informed that the chief witness to Johnstone's second article, Jeremiah Terry, planned for reasons of health to leave Pensacola the next day, the court agreed to hear him at once. When summoned, Terry advised that he was greatly indisposed, and the court adjourned its session to his house in order to take his evidence. Major Farmar quickly elicited the information that when the fort on the Tombecbé was occupied in 1763, Terry had given necessary financial assistance to Lieutenant Thomas Ford for the purchase of private property belonging to the departing French commandant and vitally important to the new occupants. On October 1, 1764, as British forces were withdrawn from Fort York, Farmar and Terry had signed an agreement allowing the merchant to take possession of the fort and to store in it supplies destined for the Indian trade; in return, Terry was obligated to maintain the place at no cost to government and to evacuate immediately if the army should decide to re-establish a garrison there.[35] Terry declared under oath that he did not pay Farmar anything for the privilege he received. The court then returned to the fort and adjourned for the day.

At nine o'clock, Thursday, March 17, the court took up the first of Governor Johnstone's accusations, that regarding the provision of flour to the French at New Orleans. Philip Pittman appeared as a prosecution witness and immediately demonstrated the nature and weakness of the whole case against Major Farmar. Pittman was, by his own admission, no more than a casual and inaccurate observer of this matter. He had been present, in May 1764, when Governor D'Abbadie's letter requesting the loan of flour had been delivered to Farmar, and he had translated it for the major, but he was now unsure of the letter's contents and had then misunderstood Farmar's verbal reply to D'Abbadie's messenger. His suspicions had been aroused, however, by observing Farmar's "frequent and private conferences" with Joseph de Palacios, and he had heard Commissary Dougal Campbell and Quartermaster Lieutenant Henry speak of a scarcity of flour in Mobile. The merchants Joseph de Palacios and Samuel Israel were then heard by the court and proved quite unhelpful save as they clarified the rather casual manner in which supplies moved in and out of the military storehouse at Mobile—to the mutual advantage of both private merchants and the army. The court adjourned at one o'clock in expectation of the arrival in Pensacola of other witnesses on Friday. As they did not appear, the court spent March 18 and 19 examining accounts and vouchers received from General Gage and organizing them for future reference.

On Monday, March 21, at nine o'clock, Dougal Campbell, formerly commissary at Mobile, took the stand. He declared that, on Farmar's order of May 3, 1764, he had delivered three hundred barrels of flour requested by D'Abbadie to the firm of Israel, Solomons, & De Palacios, the merchants having engaged to replace it from the first shipment of flour arriving in Mobile. They had done so, and the garrison had never been in want of flour. When forced to it by the court, Campbell suggested that the garrison might, as a result of this arrangement, have been momentarily reduced to a week's or a month's supply of flour, but those who had been most vocally alarmed (and he named Captain Ogle of the 34th Regiment) were the least knowledgeable. He was certain that Farmar had received no gratuity for his part in the arrangement.

Alexander Solomons shed more light on the transaction. He had conveyed to Farmar D'Abbadie's anxiety over the very real shortage at New Orleans and had been told by the major of his concern for D'Abbadie's reliability and for problems that might arise at New Orleans from the transfer of sovereignty from France to Spain. Farmar was sympathetic with the Frenchman's problems, but he wanted the security of dealing with a British subject and had thought of using the Jewish merchants who moved freely between the two colonies. Solomons saw a good business opportunity and, with Joseph de Palacios, signed an agreement with Farmar on May 4, 1764, to receive three hundred barrels of flour from the army stores and to replace them from a shipment from New York that was expected to arrive at any moment, or to replace the flour from the firm's first purchase of flour from any other source. Farmar's desire to be a good neighbor and, at the same time, to guard his own resources was amply demonstrated. As for any personal interest in the deal, Solomons admitted that he had given the Major "2 or 3 Dishes of Greens out of my Garden, which were intended as a Compliment to Mrs. Farmar" and that he did as much for "most of my Neighbors, having a very good Garden."

The evidence on the first article being concluded, that on the second already heard, the court moved on rapidly. No evidence was presented on Johnstone's third and fifth accusations, and as for the fourth, Lieutenant Pittman could only say that even he knew nothing of Farmar "making a Jobb of the Operations of the Iberville."

On the sixth article, Pittman spoke like a defense witness. He explained that when he came to Mobile in April 1764, lime was being provided for building purposes by Mr. Boniel, who charged six bitts a barrel and wanted to raise his price. Pittman told Farmar that he could do it for five bitts and make a profit—though little, as it turned out. Farmar had no part in the work, and it passed on to Engineer Archibald Robertson when Pittman left Mobile. As far as the witness knew, there was no truth in Johnstone's allegation that lime was made at three bits a barrel, and it was now selling at six to eight bitts, even though labor was cheaper than it had been in 1764.

As far as laborers were concerned (Article 7), Pittman agreed that Farmar had not insisted upon carrying an extra man on the rolls, though he himself had asked and received the major's permission to put his own servant on the rolls at three shillings a day—the customary perquisite of an engineering officer. Farmar's Negro slave, a skilled bricklayer, had been employed at five shillings a day, and that was cheap when common black labor drew two shillings fourpence and rations as well.

On the last of Governor Johnstone's charges, that relating to the use of the sloop *James*, Henry Latto master, witnesses were heard Monday afternoon and Tuesday morning, March 22. As Farmar's later evidence would disclose, the *James* had been purchased and named by Lieutenant Colonel James Robertson for the use of the garrison at Mobile. Farmer had contracted with Latto (a mariner who found himself on the beach when the ship he had brought to Pensacola was sold) to operate her for the general benefit of the army. She was used to off-load ships that could not dock at Mobile because of shallow water. When not thus employed, she was sent fishing and oystering, and upon occasion she made trips to New Orleans on government business. Her crew were paid only sixpence a day, so it was agreed that when engaged in fishing they might keep half their catch, the other half being sent to the officers' mess—an arrangement supervised by Fort Major Captain John Farmar and a sergeant major of the 34th Regiment. Major Farmar had purchased a small boat and some nets to facilitate the fishing. When sailing to and from New Orleans *James* carried goods for local merchants who paid freight charges, half of which went to the sailors, half for the upkeep of the ship. There were no funds for the maintenance of the vessel, so *James* had necessarily to be self-sufficient. Inasmuch as he determined its employment, the sloop was commonly referred to as "Major Farmar's ship" and the maintenance fund as "Major Farmar's share," although he derived nothing from operations that were advantageous to all parties concerned—that is, until Lieutenant Philip Pittman came on board.

In June 1764 Pittman sailed in *James* to New Orleans, the ship then carrying ten casks of beef belonging to Francis Pousset, a prominent Mobilian, with Pittman's approbation. When Henry Latto returned to Mobile and demanded ten-dollar freight charges, Pousset objected, thinking he had enjoyed the ship's service as a favor from the engineer. Latto insisted and gave Pousset the impression that he did so on Farmar's orders—a fact that Latto vehemently denied at the trial. Returning to New Orleans in July, Latto loaded timber for a merchant named Stewart. He was under Farmar's orders to remain only two days. At that point Lieutenant Pittman took command. He asked Latto to wait until he was ready to sail for Mobile, persuaded Governor D'Abbadie to withhold the ship's clearance papers, and when Latto protested that Pittman should be responsible for feeding him and his crew for the ten days they were delayed, the lieutenant refused and threatened to flog him. Pittman also insisted that *James*'s cargo be unloaded in order to accommodate three other passengers and their baggage, cases, six or eight casks of wine—and sixty sheep. Two of the new passengers and some of this cargo were destined for H.M.S. *Alarm*, anchored off Ship Island, where Pittman required Latto to stop and wait while passengers and cargo were transferred and Lieutenant Pittman entertained Captain Rowland Cotton. At least *Alarm*'s people had paid for the service they received.

When *James* docked at Mobile, the sailors complained to Robert Farmar that Pittman had detained the sloop for his own purposes and had paid nothing for his passage. The major thereupon reprimanded Pittman, telling him that he had "acted unlike an Officer." He also explained the distribution of the freight charges and that his portion was spent on the upkeep of the ship. When questioned by the court on March 22, Pittman admitted his knowledge of the arrangement but sought to exculpate himself by arguing that it led to rumors that were to Farmar's dishonor, and the major took too little notice of it. Young Pittman was most tender where honor was concerned.

With Johnstone's charges out of the way, the court turned to Lieutenant Pittman's list of accusations. On the first, Pittman had no more to add to what had just been said on Johnstone's identical last charge. The second item, that concerning Captain Lind's contracts at New Orleans, forced Pittman to face a major procedural problem: as only *viva voce* evidence could be presented and Lind was in Great Britain, D'Abbadie dead, and merchants at New Orleans would not come to Pensacola for the trial, he could only speak for himself—which he did in a most abrasive manner, drawing from the court the observation that it had in no way obstructed his efforts. But when Pittman then attempted to introduce a letter from a New Orleans businessman, Maxent, the court stopped him in his tracks. The room was cleared, and after brief consultation the court reaffirmed its position that letters from absent persons might not be introduced. With that, Pittman declined to prosecute this article further. A witness was summoned by the court, however, and Deputy Superintendent for Indian Affairs Charles Stuart denied any knowledge of Lind's business, save as it had been mentioned by Pittman and Lieutenant Alexander Maclellan.

Pittman now insisted that as the court had called in a hearsay witness, he wished to have Francis Pousset and Harpin de la Gauterais admitted on the same basis. Pousset readily admitted that he had only heard unflattering rumors regarding Lind's activities and a payoff. When he had confronted Lind with these stories, the captain had shrugged his shoulders and declared that "he had not gone off on a fool's errand, but had sufficient authority for what he did." La Gauterais's evidence, translated for the court by Charles Stuart, was more interesting. One day while walking on the levee at New Orleans, La Gauterais had chanced to overhear Maxent saying that he and Lind had fallen out over three thousand dollars that Lind proposed to add to the contract they were negotiating. Such a charge was said to be customary for officers when unpaid for their services, and Lind was said to be authorized to demand it and to divide the sum—presumably with Maxent or (even worse) with Major Farmar.

Having made his point on this score, Pittman had nothing to say regarding his own third and fourth articles, the subject being the same as Governor Johnstone's first article and already well covered. At Article 5 the president announced adjournment, it being three o'clock.

The next morning, Wednesday, March 23, the court received a letter from Brigadier Haldimand with directions to comply with Major Farmar's request of that same day: that as Lieutenant Pittman's final complaint was not exhibited in support of Johnstone's accusations but introduced a new subject, the court would hear all of the accusations Pittman had sent to General Gage in 1766, thereby giving Farmar the opportunity to clear his name completely. There can be little doubt that the major knew the contents of the Pandora's box he was opening, and doing so took a certain courage as well as a strong sense of injured innocence. It would also extend the trial by many weary days.

At the court's direction, Pittman produced sixteen articles he had drawn up two years earlier, accusing Robert Farmar of "being wanting to the Interest of his King & Country, & behaving in a manner unbecoming the Character of an Officer & a Gentleman." They more than adequately illumined the personal animosity between Farmar and Pittman. More significantly they shed much light upon conditions and circumstances as the 34th Regiment made its painful way up the Mississippi and endured its first hard winter at Fort Cavendish. If, in the final judgment, they all went up in smoke, they were born in the heat of passion, indignation, and injured honor—and broke against the iron determination, authority, and practicality that characterized Major Robert Farmar and every successful commander on the wilderness frontier.

Having received Haldimand's direction and agreed to hear all of Pittman's complaints, the court resumed its interrupted hearing on his original fifth article. But now Pittman protested. Inasmuch as General Gage had evidently decided against trying Major Farmar on all the crimes he had committed in West Florida and at the Illinois, and as the general knew quite well that witnesses against Farmar could not be produced in Pensacola, and as only direct personal evidence might be presented in court, Lieutenant Pittman objected to the court's hearing his charges until witnesses could be brought forward. Again the court was cleared while the judges consulted. When they resumed, they announced their opinion that Pittman's protest reflected upon their authority and integrity. What obstacle had they put in the way of his prosecution? When Pittman had tried to introduce Stewart's affidavit, the court had reminded him that Stewart was not present to confirm his written statement. The rules of evidence had not been violated; no witness had been refused a hearing. Clearly the proceedings stood at a critical juncture. Farmar had boldly seized the initiative; Pittman, thrown on the defensive, had brashly and gratuitously insulted the members of the court and, by implication, the commander in chief whose authority they represented. Tempers flared on both sides. The two o'clock adjournment of this day reflected more than the heat of the afternoon.

The court met in closed session the next morning, March 24, and determined upon an equitable course for the future: it would suspend the expression of any opinion whatsoever on articles of accusation whereon either Pittman or Farmar could produce no witnesses. With the principals returned to their places, Deputy Judge Advocate Hutcheson solemnly advised Lieutenant Pittman that his protest had been overruled; the trial would proceed forthwith. Pressing his advantage, Major Farmar demanded to know why Pittman had submitted the ninth article of his new charges (which was the same as his original Article 5, which was now before the court) when he was only a witness to circumstances distant in time and place. The flustered young lieutenant won no friends on the military bench when he replied that he had consulted a lawyer and had been advised that written testimony was valid. Finding that it was not, he chose to withdraw the charge. Pittman had begun a humiliating retreat, but he had not stopped fighting.

The next charge, the new fifth article, accused Farmar of setting Pittman at odds with the officers of the 34th Regiment, of blaming him for retarding the mission to the Illinois, and of holding a regimental court martial on a soldier when Pittman had demanded a general court martial. These were hardly more than demonstrations of that pique of which Pittman acused Farmar, but they had festered in Philip Pittman's mind for three years, and now he unburdened himself.

According to Pittman, when the regiment was at New Orleans, Farmar had told other officers that the lieutenant from the 15th Regiment had put down the 34th by taking statements from soldiers at the Iberville that derogated the work of a fellow officer, James Campbell, and that Pittman meant "to hurt" Farmar himself. Hearing of this, Pittman confronted Farmar and declared that he would justify himself to General Gage. Farmar responded by threatening to arrest Pittman if he spoke and acted like that again.

When the expedition left New Orleans, Pittman was given command of boat number 11, with orders to keep station in the little flotilla as it moved upstream. Those orders, said Pittman, would make it impossible for him to chart the course of the river as he had been ordered to do by Gage, and in any case, boat number 11 was manned by the refuse of the regiment and could not keep up with the rest. As a result, on June 29 Farmar moved Pittman into Ensign William Robertson's boat and put Sergeant Francis Swindal in charge of number 11. A violent public quarrel ensued. Farmar denounced Pittman for incompetence, wandering all over the river in his boat and thereby delaying the expedition. Within hours Pittman had penned a formal demand for a court of enquiry to clarify Farmar's charges and passed it on to the major's boat. When they stopped at eight o'clock that evening at the German Settlements, Farmar had cooled off; he admitted to Pittman that he had lost his temper and that boat number 11 was indeed deficient in manpower. But at the Iberville on July 9, Farmar issued orders for a court of enquiry to be held the next morning at eight o'clock. The court was to review Pittman's report on the work accomplished at the site and his ensuing quarrel with M. Dupart. The lieutenant immediately demanded the more formal proceeding of a court martial, for he was certain that Farmar "meant to demean me in the eyes of the Officers, and even the Soldiers present." The enquiry proved most unsatisfactory to Pittman, for Dupart, who was working at the Iberville at this time, was given a chance to testify as to their quarrel and the beating and kicking Pittman had administered to the old man.

Pittman next probed the affair of Surgeon's Mate Miller, which occurred at Natchez, where the expedition rested for several days. At ten o'clock on the night of August 16, when Pittman was preparing to retire in his marquee tent, he discovered that his Negro servant had neglected to leave him a light. Pittman searched for and found the black man asleep and proceeded to kick and shake him awake, yelling at him to be more attentive as he did so. The disturbance aroused soldiers sleeping nearby; someone swore and asked if he was to be cheated of his sleep by Pittman "& my Man Friday." Pittman's warning response, "Don't be impertinent," was answered by a chorus of oaths, among which the lieutenant recognized the voice of Surgeon's Mate Miller. Pittman promptly called for the sergeant of the guard; Miller was arrested to the sound of more abusive language. The next morning Pittman offered to release Miller, but the mate swore he would have revenge, so Pittman reported him to Major Farmar (who was lying ill at the time), expecting that the major would merely admonish Miller to act like a gentleman. To Pittman's surprise, Farmar ordered a court martial, which delivered the uncomfortable verdict on August 19, that both Pittman and Miller had used improper expressions—though Miller was the aggressor and deserved censure. Pittman was quick to note that two members of the court were Miller's mess-mates. A day or two later, Miller accosted Pittman, presented a pair of pistols, and demanded satisfaction. Instead, Pittman ordered him in arrest again. On the twenty-fourth Farmar ordered a regimental court martial—only to have Pittman demand a general court martial. The court could not sit in any case, because all the captains reported sick, and Farmar refused to grant Pittman the trial he desired. Finally, on August 26, the regimental court martial was held and found that there was insufficient evidence of Miller's having challenged Pittman to a duel. To stir the engineer's ire further, Farmar issued orders that no officer should henceforth put any of the regimental staff in arrest without the prior approval of the commanding officer.

This long tirade may have amused the court, but it limited its inquiry to the performance of boat number 11. A subdued Lieutenant Pittman admitted he had not kept station as ordered—and then more happily recalled that that had not, after all, interfered with his making a draft of the river.

The next three articles, numbers 6, 7, 8, were passed over quickly, as Pittman had no personal knowledge to support rumors he had picked up from various parties at Fort Cavendish. There were, however, witnesses to be called on Article 9 (the fifth of Pittman's original charges). The accusation rested on Major Farmar's having drawn a contract with certain Frenchmen for work actually performed by soldiers. Pittman was incomprehensibly vague about the contract, but his witnesses, William Bellem and William Paxton, soldiers of the 34th Regiment, were quite clear on their satisfaction with having been employed by Captain Campbell, Farmar's choice as engineer, in demolishing abandoned houses about to fall into the Mississippi, burning charcoal, and working on the smithy for fifteen to eighteen pence a day, particularly as they were paid in rum.

Article 10 died for lack of evidence, but Pittman was his own witness for the eleventh charge. He had proposed to sell his slave to M. Carpentiere for four hundred dollars in Treasury bills. When the Frenchman offered bills drawn on Samuel Farmar, merchant of New York, the engineer refused to accept them. Carpentiere, having received his money for goods sold to Major Farmar, tried to get the New York notes changed for Treasury bills, but Farmar refused—and Pittman persisted in his demand, so the sale fell through. The major, who had little or no cash and very firm instructions from Gage against drawing on the Treasury indiscriminately, complained to Lieutenant Henry (who was apparently the regimental gossip) that Pittman had hurt his credit.

Pittman's twelfth charge attacked Major Farmar for "uttering a falsehood relative to the public service"—in reality, changing his mind without telling Lieutenant Pittman. As a member of the court testily remarked, intentions may change daily, but that does not constitute falsehood. The next two articles (13 and 14) could not be supported by witnesses, but Pittman was his own witness (and could introduce his correspondence with General Gage) to his penultimate grievance that Farmar did not allow him to act as engineer at Fort Cavendish but employed Captain Campbell instead. The final, sixteenth, charge accused Farmar of forcibly removing lumber from a house that Pittman had purchased and burning it to make charcoal. The fact seemed clear enough, but the court inquired why Pittman had no other witnesses. They were told that Colonel Reed would not allow a soldier named Jones to come downriver with Pittman—nor did Jones want any part of a court martial.

Having exhausted the list of Pittman's complaints, the court now heard the deputy judge advocate present the most serious charge brought against Robert Farmar, that by failing for two years to notify General Gage of witnesses he would require for the court martial, and by delaying his return to West Florida, he had disobeyed the general's orders. But it had been a long day; after six hours of Philip Pittman the court was in no mood to continue the session further. They adjourned until Monday, March 28.

The third week of the trial opened with a reading of the proceedings thus far. Robert Farmar was "put upon his Defence" and asked what the court readily granted, five days to prepare his answers. On Wednesday, March 30, however, the court met briefly, at Farmar's request, to hear the evidence of Dougal Campbell, who was about to leave Pensacola. Campbell testified that the major's expenditures on Indian presents at Mobile were properly covered by vouchers and that he knew of no improper use of those goods.

The presentation of Major Farmar's defense against Governor Johnstone's accusations occupied eleven hours of the April 4 and 5 sessions. From the outset Farmar distinguished himself by his modest demeanor and restraint—in marked contrast to Pittman's performance. Where his accusers were vague, Farmar was precise; extensive documentation (acceptable to the court because it was his own) supported his declarations of fact, not rumor, and his correspondence bore the dates of receipt, meticulously recorded by an experienced and responsible commanding officer. Although the court spoke only through its verdict at the end of the trial, its members were clearly won to Farmar's side at an early stage of his defense.

Observing that he had been brought before this court because of Governor Johnstone's desire to reduce all things—particularly the military establishment—to his authority, and by the personal vendetta of Philip Pittman, Farmar assured the court that he was "perfectly Satisfied with the Candour and Uprightness of you, Gentlemen, my Judges." Johnstone had sought to bring him to trial in Pensacola so that he would be subjected to the harassment of civil litigation; happily, the governor's departure had allowed prospective prosecutors to reconsider their intentions and a more honest and impartial attorney general to quash the proceedings. Pittman, whose malice was restrained by no oath when he compiled his accusations, could not even control his passion in the presence of the court. Robert Farmar would bring cool reason and proper order to the fore.

With regard to shipping flour to Governor D'Abbadie (Article 1), Farmar noted that his first concern had been the protection of the supply at Mobile. Solomons had been able to assure him on that score, and in fact a second British merchant had also offered to do so. His hesitancy in dealing with the French governor was based upon the prospective establishment of Spanish authority at New Orleans that would not be bound by D'Abbadie's personal agreements. Furthermore, the Frenchman was prone to cancel his debts to the English by raising claims against them for properties that had changed hands at the time of the occupation of Mobile. D'Abbadie was not a good risk, whereas merchants at Mobile were anxious to be of service. Even Philip Pittman had solicited the major to put the transaction in his hands, for he would make a profit on it—which made the lieutenant's subsequent accusations look most suspect.

The arrangement made with Jeremiah Terry at Fort York (Article 2) was supported by documentation and had clearly been advantageous to government; the fort had been preserved, in fact reoccupied. As for misuse of funds in repairing Fort Charlotte, Mobile (Article 3), it was painfully evident that every penny was needed, and more, if its fabric were to be maintained and British troops accommodated. The distribution of Indian presents was no less necessary.

To prove that public money had been properly spent on public works (Article 4) both at Mobile and at the Iberville, Farmar produced half a dozen witnesses to what had been accomplished. Lieutenant John Thomas of the Royal Artillery, Lieutenant Alexander Fraser, and William Marshall had seen the efforts to clear the Iberville, modest though their success had been. A master mason named John Vollums testified to work at Mobile and remarked that Farmar's slave, Tom, was "the chief Support of the Work" on Fort Charlotte. He also recalled that Philip Pittman never visited the works, unless in the cool of the evening, and tried to persuade Vollums to come to him rather than to Farmar for orders. Attorney James Ross pointed out that Governor Johnstone had sought still more money than had been allowed to Farmar; yet it was obvious, Farmar observed in dealing with Article 5, that nothing had been done save what he had done, and that as cheaply as possible (Article 6). As for padding expenses with extra men, Captain Lind's public accounts would prove that untrue—though Pittman had charged three nonexistent workmen to his account and claimed it as an engineer's perks. The slave

Tom, who worked for a dollar a day, was less expensive than any other skilled labor available, and at that time there were only two men in the regiment who were capable of laying brick. Tom's value was proven when Superintendent John Stuart bought him from Farmar for the handsome price of five hundred dollars.

The activities of the sloop *James* (Article 8) had been highly beneficial to the service. Government had saved perhaps twenty to thirty dollars in boat hire when it was used to off-load provision ships down the bay, and the supply of fresh seafood had certainly been welcomed by the garrison; rather than profiting, Farmar was out of pocket for the small boat and seine. Farmar claimed that the instance cited by Pittman was the only occasion on which the *James* sailed with private freight. The results had obviously not been happy, and it was quite probable that he had told Pittman that he had not acted as an officer should—he had not. But then, "Lieut. Pittman has in my humble opinion, introduced an entire new system of Military Discipline" regarding superior officers.

With that parting shot Monday's session ended and the court adjourned until Friday to allow Major Farmar time to prepare his answers to Philip Pittman's two sets of charges. Farmar's defense opened on April 8 with a renewed attack on Pittman's "restless and arrogant disposition." Farmar noted that he "had overlooked many Acts of disobedience and disrespect," but when the lieutenant's actions threatened regimental discipline he had ordered him in arrest. Only then had Pittman framed his sixteen "scurrilous articles," although his disaffection went back to his arrival in West Florida in the spring of 1764. It was Pittman who ought to be on trial now, but with George Johnstone's assistance he had inveigled General Gage into adding his to the governor's charges.

Inasmuch as lengthy statements had been made on many of the repetitive charges, Farmar concentrated upon those matters that were in need of clarification. With regard to Captain Lind's activities at New Orleans (Article 2), Farmar noted that Lind was the senior captain present with the regiment and spoke fluent French; he was therefore frequently employed in business at New Orleans, and it was hardly a crime that young Pittman was not consulted in such matters. Maxent had failed to receive the contract for providing boats because he wanted to be paid in full at once and in cash and insisted upon raising his price if required to accept Treasury notes. Lind had therefore contracted with Isaac Monsanto for eight bateaux of twenty or twenty-two oars and suitable equipment for 5,137 livres each, and for the repair of five boats left by Major Loftus at the Balise at 2,400 livres each, a total of 53,096 livres to be paid, part in cash, part in bills, over an extended period. Maxent was angered at losing the contract; he verbally attacked Lind when they met on the levee at New Orleans, and the captain had raised his cane and threatened to "break his bones." When Farmar and the regiment reached New Orleans in 1765, Maxent had spread awkward stories of money owed to him by the major and other officers until Farmar faced him down and secured a recantation of his falsehoods.

Having brought Lieutenant Alexander Fraser before the court as a witness to this story, Farmar then drew from him an interesting observation that all was not well among the officers of the 34th Regiment. Fraser admitted that he had refused to sit at mess with Captain Dundas, and there had been talk at New Orleans of forming "national messes," one for the English and one for the Scottish officers. So far abroad had the national antipathies of London politics spread as a result of fires lit by the Scottish earl of Bute's elevation in government and fanned by that most patriotic Englishman John Wilkes. Farmar subsequently expressed to the court his disapproval of this xenophobic flare-up.

On Article 4, regarding the sufficiency of the supply of flour at Mobile, Farmar merely referred to Dougal Campbell's earlier evidence and noted the vagueness of such phrases in the accusation as "nearly in great want." He also pointed out that Captain William Ogle, an officer whom Farmar disliked, had cause to spread rumors embarrassing to the major: one night when drunk, Ogle had quarreled with Farmar and had been forced to write a most humble apology for his behavior. (Happily, Ogle remained but a short time in Mobile; less happily, he retained his place in the 34th Regiment and would succeed to its majority).

At this point in the day's proceedings the court received a communication from Haldimand, together with a letter from Farmar to the brigadier. Haldimand noted that the charge of delaying the expedition was not among those submitted by General Gage and that Farmar did not appear to be guilty of it. The major had, none the less, requested that the issue be aired while he had witnesses present, and the court was directed to do so. In this manner the deputy judge advocate's articles of accusation were increased to two.

Pittman's Article 6 referred to insinuations made by Surgeon William Annesley at Fort Cavendish that Farmar owed him two hundred dollars. Pittman had admitted that he knew nothing more than rumor about the affair; Farmer explained to the court that when he had brought Annesley before Colonel Reed, the surgeon had confessed that there was no debt. and Farmar produced Annesley's abject written apology to the regiment for his "imprudence and folly."

Article 7, accusing Farmar of defrauding Captain James Campbell, was dismissed when Alexander Solomons vouched for the payment of the engineer's bills. Article 8 brought forward two soldiers of the 34th Regiment,

William Bellem and William Mallet, who testified that the meat shortage at Fort Cavendish had been so severe that they went without beef for fifteen days, but as a result of Major Farmar's efforts they had been able to secure game, ducks, and geese in its place. Articles 9 through 12 dealt with the management of necessary work at Fort Cavendish, where firewood and furniture were greatly needed and a smithy and forge were required for the repair of both soldiers' and Indians' guns. Farmar had tried to employ two reduced French officers who wished to remain at Chartres village, but Pittman had frightened them off, so the major had had to bring in a Frenchman from Kaskaskia. The major's use of bills drawn upon his brother, Samuel Farmar of New York, was a matter of convenience, for the cost of much of the work being done was too inconsiderable to warrant the use of Treasury bills. The French had been encouraged to demand government paper by Lieutenant Pittman, who told them they would get a 15 percent premium on Treasury notes at New Orleans. The succeeding articles were passed over quickly with Farmar's trenchant observation that Pittman's tenderness toward reputations was not his alone; Captain Campbell had every right to defend himself against Pittman's criticism of his work; similarly, Major Farmar, as commanding officer at Fort Cavendish, was within his rights to name as overseer of the works anyone he chose. As for M. Carpentiere's abandoned house, turning it into charcoal was the best possible use that could have been made of it.

Farmar next took up the charge of having broken Gage's orders by delaying his return to Pensacola. It was, said the major, the first time in twenty-eight years that he had been accused of disobedience to orders. The letters themselves bore the most exculpatory evidence: issued in New York between May 15 and June 15, 1765, they had gone to Pensacola, where Colonel Reed had opened them and read them in order to satisfy his and Governor Johnstone's curiosity, and they had only been delivered to Farmar at Fort Cavendish by Reed on May 17, 1766. Not until June 11 would Reed assume responsibility for the Illinois post, nor would he then facilitate Farmar's journey by allowing him to take any soldiers as boatmen. To make matters worse, the first boat Farmar secured was stolen by a couple of deserters, and he could not get another boat until June 19. He then left Fort Cavendish with only his servant and one discharged soldier and floated down to Ste. Genevieve, where he was able to hire some Frenchmen to row him on downriver. Although he avoided telling the court just when he arrived at New Orleans, there was no question that he had had to settle business matters there relative to the regiment's boats and financial obligations. Accounts signed by Monsanto proved he was so engaged on November 19, 1766. He had previously advised Brigadier Tayler of his situation, and when his business was concluded, he had taken the first available ship to Pensacola. He was innocent of the charge or any intention of delaying the proceedings against him.

The next morning, April 9, the court met for less than an hour, for Farmar begged for a postponement because those who were transcribing records for him were engaged in their own private business. The court agreed to hear his defense on the charge of "delaying the expedition" on Monday. So on April 11 Robert Farmar set forth those circumstances that had frustrated Gage's hopes for a speedy occupation of Fort Chartres and had almost frustrated those of the 34th Regiment. In brief, Farmar had expected that a second attempt on the river would be made after Loftus's failure, and Captain Campbell had been sent to the Mississippi in June 1764 to try to pacify the Indians on the river. Gage had ordered the 22nd Regiment to renew its efforts on May 22; those orders were received on August 16, at which time Loftus's men were at Pensacola and the condition of the boats necessary for the river trip was unknown. Gage had, in fact, already issued new orders, on August 1, assigning the expedition to the 34th Regiment, orders that only reached Mobile on September 30. Captain John Lind was immediately dispatched to New Orleans to make arrangements for boats and supplies, but at the same time Governor Johnstone began those objections, interruptions, and lawsuits that plagued Major Farmar for more than six months and placed him in bail for five hundred pounds in one case that was still pending. Further, Johnstone's emissaries spread the word that Farmar's credit was questionable, that even his Treasury bills would not be honored. Lieutenant Colonel James Robertson had had cash with which to speed the 22nd Regiment on its way; Major Farmar had none. As a result, when Farmar reached New Orleans, he found that all work on his boats had been stopped by Monsanto, and that accounted for his remaining there from May 15 to June 27.

Alexander Solomons now appeared as witness to Farmar's "indifferent credit" with the merchants of New Orleans. He also asserted that French businessmen were told by Johnstone's associates that Farmar's bills would not be paid unless the governor endorsed them. William Marshall echoed Solomons's evidence and insisted that Farmar and his officers had been most diligent in getting the expedition under way. He particularly praised the efforts of Ensign Wainwright, whom Farmar described as "bred to the Sea" and especially competent where boats were concerned. Lieutenant Alexander Fraser, who had been to Forth Chartres and left in a hurry, noted that when La Gauterais came down to New Orleans, he told the major that he "might as well think of flying to Heaven as going to Ilonois." Fraser had been prepared to speak optimistically of their chances, but the major had advised him to spare the argument, because he was determined to persevere. On that note, and with fulsome compliments to the court, Robert Farmar concluded his defense.

Philip Pittman, on the other hand, was not one to let matters rest. He submitted to the court a letter and a paper replying to various parts of Farmar's testimony and declaring that Farmar had reflected upon his character. He also presented a list of questions he wished to put to witnesses whom he proposed to call. The court was cleared, considered Pittman's material, then called him in, and the deputy judge advocate advised him that the subjects he had raised were "foreign to the Trial"; they tended only to justify himself, and he was not on trial but merely present as a witness.

On Tuesday morning, April 12, the charges and the defense being closed, Francis Hutcheson requested time to transcribe the proceedings, and the court adjourned until Saturday, April 16, when the record was read in open court—a task that consumed five hours. On Monday, April 18, the court met to give their formal opinions. They acquitted Robert Farmar on twenty-five of the thirty-one indictments: all of Governor Johnstone's and the deputy judge advocate's charges. On twenty of these counts they were unanimous. On six of Philip Pittman's articles they suspended judgment, as had been agreed on March 24. As they went through the long list, item by item, their views became clear. Farmar had acted humanely, prudently, and properly. Of Johnstone's charges they declared, "The Language is indecent and Scurrilous," the obvious intention of them "as malicious as the Substance of them is Groundless." Turning to Pittman's twenty-one accusations, the court observed that in one case "Major Farmar's name is not mentioned in the whole of the Evidence"—"there was no such Transaction." Of another they said, "The Charge is absurd." They found that Major Farmar had found fault with Lieutenant Pittman "for very sufficient reasons." Many of Pittman's complaints were "vague," "undeterminate in nature, founded on hearsay, and inserted to blacken Major Farmar's Character," "childish," "false, scandalous, & malicious." Of one they proclaimed, "This article being of so uncommon a nature, and conceived in Terms so scurrilous & improper, a doubt arose concerning the nature of the Lye." And they were appalled by "the indecency" of Pittman's preamble to the list of sixteen articles; Robert Farmar had, in their opinion, acted as an officer and a gentleman and had paid the strictest attention to the interests of his king and country. With regard to the charges of disobedience of orders and delaying the expedition, the most important as they derived from General Gage himself, the court declared that Farmar had come down to New Orleans with "all the expedition in his power," and rather than delaying the ascent of the Mississippi, he had used every means to forward it and had acted with the greatest perseverance.

The verdict was in, but the case was not yet closed. On Wednesday, April 20, the court met once more to approve some last-minute corrections made by Francis Hutcheson, then the massive document was signed by James Chisholm, president, and the deputy judge advocate.

As the members of the court rose, their duty fulfilled, Haldimand triumphantly advised Gage of their accomplishment, assuring the general that the court had taken great care in its task and had reviewed all the documents. Hutcheson, as deputy judge advocate, had managed the prosecution to the best of his ability, but not being fully cognizant of all procedural matters, he had turned to old Captain Vignolles, who was of great assistance when he was not drunk. In fact, said Haldimand, it was to Vignolles that most of the credit for conducting the trial was due. The court's report filled 170 pages of large paper. The brigadier would now return various members of the court to their proper posts and send Robert Farmar and Philip Pittman to New York, as the 34th Regiment was en route to Ireland. On the twenty-ninth of April, Haldimand entrusted the finished copy of the proceedings to Captain Hamilton and sent him off to New York with four months' leave. Captain Sutherland now got his leave to return to England; Captains Jenkins and Phillips were sent back to St. Augustine; and Captain Vignolles would soon be allowed to retire, broken in spirit and overwhelmed by debt.

The general satisfaction of the military community in West Florida with the conclusion and outcome of Robert Farmar's trial was reflected by Lieutant George Phynn, who remarked, "I heard the whole prosecution . . . and there was not one evidence said a thing in support of any of the many and heavy charges exhibited against him. . . . I think Major Farmar has been greatly injured by the mear surmise and chimera of one man's brain."[36]

There remained the settlement of expenses for the trial. Major Chisholm and eight captains had been housed in Pensacola at government expense. Rentals ranging from $40 to $80 were owing to the accommodating Messrs. Gordon, Hodge, Moore, Watson, Luche, and Burton—a total of $361. In addition, Dougal Campbell and Alexander Solomons had come from Mobile as witnesses and were due $39.3 and $73.7 respectively. Three captains had also been transported to and from Mobile, another $26; other witnesses traveling from New Orleans increased the bill by $120. Haldimand also included the expenses of Captain Daniel Rea, $28 from New Orleans to Pensacola, although Rea escaped serving on the court by dying. Captain Ralph Phillips submitted his own account to Gage. The cost of his trip from Fort Augusta amounted to £178.8.8, of which £21.8.1 was private expenditure not chargeable to the army, but he hoped to be recompensed a total of £157.0.7.[37]

Robert Farmar did not accompany the record of his trial to New York. He pleaded very important private business in West Florida, and Haldimand allowed him to remain on the Gulf Coast until further orders from General Gage were received.[38]

The brigadier's decision was made in response to Farmar's plea that the troubles brought on by Governor Johnstone's hostility would require eight or nine months to be resolved. Early in 1765 the acting attorney general,

Arthur Gordon, and the provincial secretary, James Macpherson, had at Johnstone's insistence preferred a bill in Chancery against Farmar. As the major was about to leave for the Illinois, he had been put on £500 bail against his reappearance. When Lieutenant Governor Montfort Browne succeeded Johnstone in 1767, Farmar had petitioned him as chancellor for dismissal of the charges, "but from excessive ignorance and want of equity he made himself a party in the cause" and ruled against Farmar. When the major then protested that Browne could not act as judge in his own case, Browne reversed himself but left the issue undecided. Farmar was truly caught in the toils of the law until a new governor should arrive. There were also two common-law actions, in one of which Farmar had been awarded £350, but a motion against the judgment had been accepted and action delayed during the court martial, because Farmar's enemies hoped that he would leave the colony after the court martial and a more favorable settlement might be secured from his attorney. Major Farmar admitted that he had once wished to go to New York, but having no business there and much in Pensacola and Mobile, he asked Gage to allow him to stay in West Florida, "where I have finally determined to fix my abode," until His Majesty's pleasure with regard to the court martial had been signified.[39] Farmar still had some thought of bringing Pittman to trial, but he got no encouragement from Haldimand, who suggested that he could best do so in New York. The brigadier had had his fill of courts martial. In any case, Farmar felt that he could not leave West Florida until the official approval and publication of the court's and the king's decision in his case, and he would forego a trip to New York for the dubious pleasure of prosecuting Lieutenant Pittman.[40]

From New York the great bundle of court martial proceedings went to London on June 19, and on August 10, 1768, the judge advocate's office advised General Gage that they had been placed before George III, and His Majesty had confirmed the honorable acquittal of Major Farmar on all of the original charges. The judge advocate observed, however, that the court had been "irregular" in taking cognizance of Pittman's second list of sixteen charges, inasmuch as Pittman had declared himself unprepared to prosecute them. The crown would neither ratify nor approve the court's action on these articles, but it would not take any further action with regard to them. Major Robert Farmar was restored to duty.[41]

By the end of October, Gage had received word of the final decision, and in due course he expressed his great pleasure at the happy conclusion of the business. The substance of the sentence was included in general orders issued to all regiments under Gage's command in North America. Gage also advised Farmar that, as the 34th Regiment was without a field officer, the major would do well to join his regiment as soon as he could conveniently settle his private affairs.[42] Good news travels slowly, however. No vessel sailed from New York for West Florida until late January 1769. By that time, Farmar's request to be allowed to remain in West Florida had been forwarded to Gage, sent on to London, and approved by the secretary at war on November 1, 1768.[43] Farmar did not receive the news at Mobile until April 1, 1769. Thanking Gage for his consideration, Farmar indicated that he hoped to leave for England some time late in May, but he intended to absent himself from Mobile only a short time, for the "depredations that have been committed on my property in consequence of that mass of calumny that was so maliciously and invidiously exhibited" against him required his personal attention.[44] He was also now deeply involved in provincial politics. When he boarded the brig *Africa,* in company with Elias Durnford, he was the official bearer of a set of strong remonstrances from the inhabitants of both Mobile and Pensacola against Lieutenant Governor Montfort Browne.[45] Quite different fates awaited the two West Floridians in London. Elias Durnford would return as the new lieutenant governor of the colony—and for the moment, acting governor. Robert Farmar would encounter bitter surprise and disappointment.

Major Farmar reached London in July 1769 and apparently remained in England until June 1770, in spite of his anticipation of a quick return.[46] The business that engaged him centered first upon the conclusion of his military career. Although the particulars do not appear, the major's tribulations and the complications leading up to the court martial led some to believe that he wished to leave the army. By May 12, 1769, General Gage understood that Farmar intended to sell his commission and retire, and when Farmar reached London, he discovered that, in fact, his commission as major of the 34th Regiment had been disposed of without his knowledge on November 22, 1768. The purchaser was Captain William Ogle, no favorite of Robert Farmar, but the senior captain in the regiment currently stationed in Ireland.[47] Given the latitude allowed to senior officers in the British army—and Farmar was the thirty-seventh major in seniority in the whole army, fourteenth among majors actually serving in November 1768—in all likelihood he intended to retain his commission for an indefinite period and to sell out at the most opportune moment. A majority was now officially valued at six hundred pounds, but a shrewd negotiator could probably do better than that, even though George III disapproved of the haggling that customarily accompanied such transactions. There were doubtless many visits to the Horse Guards and much recrimination before Farmar accepted the inevitable.

From the army he turned to the Colonial Office for assistance, and to the secretary, Lord Hillsborough, he submitted a memorial setting forth his case. After twenty-nine years in the army, with service at Havana and on the Gulf Coast, he had been "most unjustly accused of many crimes" by Governor

George Johnstone "on the bare insinuation" of Philip Pittman. He had been under arrest for two years and three months before his acquittal in 1768. Soon after receiving leave in April 1769, he had embarked for London, "and on his arrival here found to his Great Astonishment that his Commission was disposed of on the 22nd of November last without his Consent or knowledge or the least foundation whatsoever more than that in the year 1765 or 1766 he in a letter to Lord Frederick Cavendish [Colonel of the 34th Regiment] Intimated a desire of disposing of his Commission as soon as he was acquitted of the Charges laid to him." Asserting that the sentence of the court martial had not yet been made public, Farmar declared that being deprived of his commission was deprecatory to his character and "a great Injury." In view of the vacancy resulting from the death of Governor John Eliot, Farmar asked for the governorship of West Florida "as a mark of royal favour for his long & faithful services," a demonstration of satisfaction with his innocence, and compensation for "the trouble & Expence he unjustly sustained by those unmerited accusations."[48] If he had any real hopes of such an appointment, they were in vain. By the first of March 1770, the governorship of West Florida had been given to Peter Chester.

Robert Farmar's next order of business in London concerned the properties he had acquired or at least claimed in various parts of West Florida. He was all too well aware of the ease with which political pressure and legal prosecution could affect the tenure of land in the colony, and if he was destined to spend his life there, he wanted security. On Monday, May 21, 1770, the Lords Commissioners for Trade and Plantations, better known as the Board of Trade, heard the petition of former Major Robert Farmar for confirmation of his lands in West Florida, part of them held by purchase from French habitants and part by virtue of grants from Indians. The board agreed to consider Farmar's petition on Thursday and gave him notice to attend. He was present on May 24, but to no avail. Their lordships declared that they could not comply with his request "as there was not precedent of any confirmation of titles and lands in America claimed under the circumstances stated in said petition."[49]

Farmar doubtless visited the Treasury offices while in London, endeavoring to achieve a settlement of his complex military accounts.[50] General Gage had forwarded his own accounts with Farmar to London in May 1769. He had little expectation of coming to terms with Farmar from New York, and he hoped that when the major settled with the Treasury, allowances might be made for sums he had advanced to Farmar. Farmar, too, memorialized the Treasury on the subject of his expenditures. He asked for 5 percent on the money he had drawn on the Treasury and for an "extra expenses" account, among other matters. Gage approved the 5 percent supplement because

Farmar obviously could not meet all of his obligations on a major's salary; charges for transportation and sixty pounds' house rent for two years, along with expenses incurred by the court martial, were also acceptable, for Gage agreed that after all was said and done, former Major Farmar was "entitled to the Consideration of Government."[51]

There was little else that Farmar could do, though perhaps he took the opportunity to visit old military friends, perhaps even his distant relatives the Fermors and his wife's family. He could, at least, broadcast his injured innocence to the public, and steps to that end must have been taken before he returned to West Florida. It would have cost him something to get the long record of his trial copied, and probably something more to persuade the publisher, Johnston, to print it up, but by January 1771 London booksellers were offering to sell for three shillings and sixpence a pamphlet entitled *Proceedings of a General Court-Martial Held at Pensacola, in West Florida, on Wednesday, March 16, 1768, and Continued till Wednesday, April 20, 1768.* Considering the subject, the pamphlet got good reviews and reasonably wide notice. The *London Magazine* observed that "these proceedings contain the trial of Major Farmar, who was accused of very heinous offences, and very unjustly we may conclude, as the accusers produce no evidence whatever of his delinquency. The Major was acquitted by the Court Martial, and the sentence of that court was confirmed by his majesty, notwithstanding which he is [wounded] as an officer, and destroyed in his military reputation."[52] The *Monthly Review* expressed sympathy for an officer who was deprived of his rank; the *Gentleman's Magazine* and the *Critical Review* noted the publication without comment.[53] Although Robert Farmar had the best of it at his court martial, Philip Pittman triumphed on the literary scene. In November 1770 his *Present State of the European Settlements on the Missisippi* was published. It was destined to become the classic description of the scenes in which he and Robert Farmar had clashed.[54]

With his military career at an end, Robert Farmar returned to Mobile and to his family; in West Florida he would always be known as Major Farmar. By the beginning of 1771, he was well engaged in his new career as a planter and politician.[55]

VI.

Planter and Politician

The last years of Robert Farmar's life centered upon the acquisition and development of his properties in West Florida, some in the western parts of the province, others in and near Mobile. His holdings, whether acquired for speculative purposes or occupied and farmed, were sufficient to make him a leading planter in the colony. Possessing early and lasting connections with traders and shippers into Mobile, he was a figure of importance to the economic life of the town and surrounding Charlotte County. As Mobile's first British "governor," for so many viewed him, and as its pre-eminent military figure even in retirement, he was inevitably drawn into colonial politics. Indeed, property and politics were intimately connected in West Florida, as in every part of colonial America. Politics provided a key to the acquisition of property, whether by royal mandamus or gubernatorial grant, and property was the basis of political influence, whether in eighteenth-century England or America. As their properties had elevated the Farmars to prominence in the affairs of Pennsylvania and New Jersey, so his interests in the land of a new colony propelled Robert Farmar into the politics of West Florida.

Major Farmar's interest in Mobile real estate was forced upon him by the circumstances of the British occupation of the town in 1763. His obligations to his troops required him to look beyond Fort Charlotte for their care and housing, nor could his own needs be met by the claustrophobic accommodations within its walls. The exchange of private property that accompanied the transfer of imperial title at Mobile offered an opportunity for departing Frenchmen to turn a cash profit and for Anglo-American speculators to lay hands upon properties that might prove highly valuable in the near future.[1] As the commanding officer at Mobile, Farmar was initially satisfied to make use of government property, transforming one of the fort's bakehouses into his personal quarters. It was necessary, however, to secure private properties for many government purposes and difficult to determine the legal rights of French proprietors who claimed that everything outside the fort was privately owned. In January 1764 Farmar negotiated the purchase of Jean Baptiste Rousseré's house for $400 (£93.6.8) for the use of the Indian interpreter. Another house was purchased from Mme. Grondel in September for use as a hospital. For this Farmar paid £186.13.4, although he understood that it had been built by the French government and the Grondels simply pretended that it had been given to them. But as Farmar remarked, "It would appear rather an act of oppression in me to seize on those Houses" without knowing the truth. In January 1765, anticipating the arrival of workmen from New York, the major spent £200 New York (£116.13.4) for a house and lot owned by Hugh Kennedy Hoy.[2] These were all government purchases, but both Farmar's superiors and those who sold him the properties held him accountable for the financial transactions.

When Major Farmar landed in Mobile in 1763, he observed that the French storekeeper's house contained goods that Governor D'Abbadie distributed to visiting Indians. As properties belonging to the king of France were subject to direct transfer to the king of England, Farmar charged D'Abbadie that the house and contents should be put into his hands. The Frenchman advised the major that the house belonged to Mme. Socie and was private property. Farmar's suspicions of the French had already been raised; after having been told by Commandant DeVelle that there were no such records in Mobile, he had caught the French notary trying to remove the town archives to New Orleans. He proceeded to occupy the Socie house and told D'Abbadie that he would keep it until Mme. Socie showed proof of title—which she never did. In January 1769 the house was claimed by the woman's son, acting as attorney for his mother, who by then was married to a reformed French officer and living in the Illinois country. Young Socie proffered evidence of ownership to Lieutenant Governor Durnford, and Brigadier General Haldimand inquired of Farmar how the house had passed into British hands. Farmar's explanation left the question of legal ownership unresolved, and Attorney General Wegg concluded that the house was indeed private property. Haldimand promptly ordered the place restored to the possession of the Socies.[3]

Mme. Grondel's house was also the source of numerous complications. Marie Louise Dutisné, the wife of French Captain J. P. Grondel, seems to have left her house in Mobile in the hands of Joseph Badon. Papers for transfer of ownership were drawn up by Mr. Hendrie so as to vest possession in Farmar rather than in His Britannic Majesty, for whose service the purchase was made. Farmar caught the mistake and had it corrected, but apparently a copy of the first draft had been sent to Mme. Grondel. When it surfaced, the major had further explaining to do.[4]

Major Farmar's position as commandant at Mobile involved him in a variety of property transactions wherein it was sometimes difficult to distinguish the army officer from the private gentleman, and as in the case of the supposed sale of Fort York to Jeremiah Terry, Farmar's enemies were quick to accuse him of malpractice. The casual nature of many French property claims encouraged French inhabitants to deal with the senior officer present and Farmar's relations, the New York merchant family of Miller, were doubtless aware of the opportunities the situation offered. By April 1766 Governor Johnstone, no friendly observer, referred to "Messrs. Miller, in Company with Major Farmar," as "the brokers for French Purchases."[5]

In addition to town property, Farmar extended his acquisitions to the north of Mobile on June 11, 1764, when he purchased 542 acres from François Daran—a property on the Tensa River that had been held by Mme. Populous, widow of the French officer Boissy.[6] But not all of Farmar's real estate ventures were successful. Early in January 1765 Farmar petitioned the governor and council for a parcel of Mobile property which he had already fenced at his own expense. His request was denied on the grounds that the lot had been granted to a committee of citizens for the establishment of a church.[7]

The most notorious—and least successful—of Farmar's French purchases was that of Dauphin Island. The strategic significance of the island lying off the entrance to Mobile Bay had long been apparent to the French, but by 1763 it was, like other offshore islands along the coast, little more than a sea-girt cattle pen. A sergeant's guard and a harbor pilot, the only representatives of French officialdom, had been withdrawn when the English occupied Mobile, and most of the island remained in the hands of private Frenchmen who grazed their cattle in relative security from marauding Indians. Soon after his arrival in Mobile, Major Farmar sought to establish a legal interest in Dauphin Island by purchasing the claims of Messrs. Dedres, Doran, and Bruce, from whom he secured bills of sale. The livestock on the island—seventy-six cattle and three pigs—Farmar bought from John Orona and Mary Dubo for four hundred dollars. These were sold in February 1764 by Henry Fairchild for Farmar and Thomas Miller in exchange for two male slaves named Peter and Prince.[8]

Unfortunately, at about the same time, the newly appointed lieutenant governor of West Florida, Montfort Browne, then engaged in recruiting emigrants in England and Ireland, received a royal mandamus for an unspecified 20,000 acres of land in the new colony for himself and his brothers. Montfort sent the papers to his brother William, then in North America, and William selected Dauphin Island as a desirable location, assuming it to comprise the assigned acreage. When surveyed, the island proved to contain only 2,600 acres, but Governor Johnstone insisted that if the Brownes wanted Dauphin Island they must surrender their claim to the remaining 17,400 acres of the original grant.[9]

Upon arriving in West Florida, Browne found that his claim had been challenged by Farmar and the issue brought before the governor's council by the rival parties. On February 5, 1765, the council considered Farmar's claim to the purchase of the rights and stock of the French inhabitants and his petition for a formal grant of the island. Governor Johnstone simultaneously laid before the council the royal order granting 20,000 acres to Edmund, Thomas, William, and Montfort Browne, along with William's letter of October 21, 1764, asking that those acres be located on Dauphin Island. Noting that Farmar's supporting documentation neither mentioned him nor showed any right in him, the council rejected Farmar's claim and offered the island, then estimated to comprise 7,000 acres, to William Browne in satisfaction of the full grant. William declined to accept this proposal, ostensibly because his brother Montfort was expected to arrive shortly (and no doubt because his presence would improve the Brownes' prospects). Unable to resolve the dispute at once, the council agreed to give Robert Farmar the opportunity of presenting further proof of purchase by March 1, 1765; otherwise it would consider the land to belong to the Crown and to be free for granting to other parties.[10]

William Browne quickly reconsidered his position and wrote to the council on February 6, 1765, accepting Dauphin Island in fulfillment of the Brownes' 20,000-acre grant. On April 2, 1765, the council received Farmar's papers: a new petition, bills of sale to Farmar from the Frenchmen Dedres and Doran, and from the English merchant Bruce. Without indicating their reasoning, the council rejected this evidence and ordered that the Browne petition be accepted.[11]

As Major Robert Farmar was then deeply engrossed in final preparations for moving the 34th Regiment to New Orleans and up the Mississippi (he boarded ship May 1), he appears to have taken no action before leaving Mobile. He returned at the end of the year 1766 under the cloud of impending court martial and found that Lieutenant Governor Browne had occupied Dauphin Island, seizing nearly a hundred head of cattle and calves, and had ensured his possession of the island with a corporal's guard of the 21st Regiment.[12]

George Johnstone's departure from West Florida in January 1767 removed one of Robert Farmar's enemies but elevated Montfort Browne to the executive position in the colony. Farmar was not anxious to confront the lieutenant governor while in the midst of his military problems, so nothing was done with regard to Dauphin Island for some time. Browne enjoyed possession, and Farmar sweated out the court martial, which was not concluded until April 20, 1768. Freed of that incubus, Farmar turned his attention to Dauphin Island.

Perhaps painful experience with Johnstone persuaded Farmar to move more carefully against Lieutenant Governor Browne. He prepared his attack by laying the political groundwork, sought to take advantage of his opponent's weakness, then struck with apparently overwhelming force. It was good military strategy, but Major Farmar proved unequal to the West Florida lawyers.

Among his more noteworthy actions, Governor George Johnstone, in accordance with the king's instructions, had brought together the first West Florida Assembly in November 1766. There were many local matters to be pursued by an active legislature, and the assembly proved both useful and popular. It also began to show that character of independence noted in every American colonial assembly. Johnstone escaped with his reputation intact; he had at least brought the assembly into being. His successors would not be so fortunate.[13]

Montfort Browne wisely kept his distance from Governor Johnstone while they were both in the colony. In 1766 Browne had dared to summon a meeting of the council while the governor was away from Pensacola; in the opinions of Johnstone and the members of his council, Browne had attempted to usurp the governor's prerogatives. Johnstone made it clear that he felt "grossly and violently insulted."[14] Perhaps Browne, formerly an army officer also thought it politic to separate himself from the governor's unpopularity and tribulations with the military establishment in West Florida. If he thought to gain favor by such a course, he was wrong. When he assumed the role of acting governor upon receipt of the news of Johnstone's dismissal in 1767, he rapidly established his place as one of West Florida's most unpopular characters. Upon meeting the general assembly in May 1767, Browne found himself opposed by a formed opposition which he described as "a set of giddy unthinking young men . . . who called themselves the supporters of the late Governor."[15] Browne dismissed the assembly in June.

When necessity forced the lieutenant governor to convene a new assembly in December 1767, he found his enemies well entrenched; among them were Dougal Campbell and James Ross, both representing Mobile. A brief winter session passed without major incident, but during the long summer recess Browne began to lash out at his foes, and Daniel Clark was removed from his place on the governor's council, having been found to be "at the head of a Scotch Party."[16] The threatened removal of troops from the colony brought the assembly together again in August, but the terms of its election writs forced a dissolution in October 1768. Legislative and financial necessity persuaded Browne to order new elections in January 1769, and among the representatives from Mobile were Major Robert Farmar, his friend Dougal Campbell, and his lawyer, James Ross.

Major Farmar took his place in the commons house on Wednesday, January 25, 1769; he was one of eleven assemblymen present. As James Ross had been elected from Pensacola as well as Mobile, he resigned the latter seat, leaving Farmar the sole member present from Mobile. The major was promptly named to the Committee of Privileges and Elections and to the Grand Committee for Grievances, which was authorized to correspond with the colonial agent in England. Farmar was a constant attendant to his duties. As a member of the privileges and elections committee he reported to the house their decision in the disputed Campbell Town election, and he undoubtedly supported the committee's opinion that the Speaker of the commons house had the right, denied by Lieutenant Governor Browne, to issue a warrant for filling the vacant seat for Mobile.

On the last day of this short session, February 2, the commons in committee of the whole took up "the present state of the Province," and Farmar reported their conclusion to the house—sure sign that he had taken an active part in their deliberations and supported their findings. Among other matters, the house called for an investigation of the public accounts, the collection and application of public money, and an inquiry into the securities given by the holders of public office—all highly sensitive issues touching the prerogatives of the governor.

At that point the commons received Browne's message announcing their adjournment until March 10. The house reacted brusquely. They resolved that Browne had obstructed and frustrated their plans "for the *welfare of this Colony,*" that those persons who had advised adjournment were "enemies to His Majesty . . . and to the settlement and welfare of this Province" and had destroyed all harmony "between the branches of the Legislature." To demonstrate their independence, the commons then voted to adjourn themselves until March 10.[17]

Much was hoped from the new governor, John Eliot, who arrived at the beginning of April. The old assembly was dissolved and new elections were ordered. Lieutenant Governor Browne's administration came under investigation by Governor Eliot, and Robert Farmar was elected to the new general assembly. Unhappily, on May 2 Governor Eliot committed suicide, and Browne was restored to the head of government.[18] By that date Robert Farmar, triumphantly acquitted by court martial, was engaged in violent confrontation with Montfort Browne.

On Monday, May 1, 1769, having returned to Mobile from Pensacola,

Farmar gathered several determined friends aboard two boats and sailed down to Dauphin Island. His own party consisted of Dougal Campbell, now a Mobile merchant but formerly commissary at Mobile and one of Farmar's witnesses in the late court martial; Henry Litto or Latto, formerly skipper of the sloop *James* and much indebted to Farmar for employment; William Harris; and a Negro servant. On Dauphin Island were Richard Hartley, Browne's resident manager; William Kimbe, a laborer; Hartley's servant Robert Love; and a female housekeeper. At about two o'clock these men were seated at dinner in Hartley's house when they heard distant musket fire. Hartley dispatched Love to see if the shots might indicate the presence of a band of Indians, but the servant returned to report the approach of a boat. Hartley and Kimbe went down to the shore to meet their visitors and invited them to the house. Campbell told Hartley that they had come for oysters, and both parties began to walk up the beach to Hartley's house, formerly the residence of the harbor pilot. Shortly after leaving the beach, Hartley and Kimbe saw a second party of armed men who had apparently landed elsewhere. These were James Waugh, George Martin, and Thomas Gronow, good Mobilians who were no friends of Lieutenant Governor Montfort Browne. Martin and Gronow reached the house ahead of the others, forcibly ejected Deborah Coughlin, the housekeeper, from the house and began to throw furniture out the door. Litto and Harris rushed to join their confederates and slammed the door against the confused pair of Browne's men.

Turning to Farmar, Hartley asked if they had come to rob him, to which the major replied that the island was his. Together they entered the house, Hartley protesting and Farmar proclaiming his right to everything in sight. As kitchen furniture and utensils were rapidly disappearing out the window, Hartley ordered Kimbe to recover them, but Farmar and his friends seized Kimbe, and the major forcefully applied the end of his stout stick to the small of Kimbe's back (causing considerable pain, according to Kimbe's later account). Hartley grabbed at Farmar, but the others roughly seized him, tearing his jacket and cutting his cheek. Both of Browne's men were thrown bodily out of the house. George Martin then kept them at bay with his leveled musket. Hartley demanded to see Farmar's authority for such highhanded action, but the major refused him any satisfaction and threatened to lay Hartley by the heels and send him to jail. Nor would Farmar even allow Hartley to leave his bed and chest in the house, safe from rain, though the poor fellow was permitted to deposit them in an open shed. Hartley and Kimbe soon withdrew from the scene, though they did not leave the island until Sunday, May 28. Some of Farmar's party remained at the overseer's house throughout the month.[19]

News of the Dauphin Island affair soon reached Montfort Browne. His friend Lionel B. Westropp, acting Indian agent at Mobile, advised the lieutenant governor on May 12 that not only had Farmar seized Dauphin Island, he had, "at the head of a Scotch party, who it is well known have been your Enveterate Enemies, . . . waited on all the french Inhabitants here, with a paper which severely reflects on your Honors conduct." When questioned by Westropp, the Frenchmen said they had heard that Browne was appointed governor at Natchez or in the Illinois country; Farmar had solicited their support and signatures in behalf of his own appointment as governor of West Florida. Farmar had told them that he was going to England to seek that place, and he had made many promises to them, should he succeed.[20]

Browne shortly brought the matter to the attention of Attorney General Edmund Rush Wegg and complained to the American secretary, Lord Hillsborough, in London, of his grievances. Of Farmar he wrote: "This Gentleman is endowed with all the Violence & Subtilty of His American Brethren from being both Civil & Military Governor of this province at one time; he has long since become an Assembly man and leagued with the more despicable of the People, merely to form a party among them, to serve him in a Variety of law suits in which he is ever embroil'd."[21]

The law moved with surprising speed when activated by the lieutenant governor. Depositions having been taken from Farmar's accomplices on June 12, the next day Attorney General Wegg, Provost Marshal Alexander Moore, and James Allen Martin, as justices of the peace, were ordered to impanel a grand jury at Pensacola on Friday, June 30, to inquire into the Dauphin Island affair. There being an insufficient number of jurors on hand on the thirtieth, the case was held over to 9 A.M. Saturday, July 1, when the jury assembled to hear the witnesses Hartley, Kimbe, Love, and Elenora Walker. The defendants were represented by their attorney, James Ross, and witnesses Dougal Campbell and James (John?) Waugh. The jury sat until midnight, then adjourned to Monday, July 3, when it inevitably found "the Entry and Detainer to be forcible." On Wednesday, Chief Justice William Clifton reported the jury's findings and ordered the restoration of Browne's property, the formal order to be issued July 12.[22]

Lieutenant Governor Browne forwarded copies of the proceedings to London and observed to Lord Hillsborough that he expected Farmar to do him "all the Ill Offices in his power."[23] He would not be disappointed in that, for Farmar was certainly active in mustering opinion in the colony against the unpopular lieutenant governor. Both Farmar and Dougal Campbell were justices of the peace for Charlotte County and could organize opposition to Browne at Mobile. In fact, the jury that condemned Farmar's forceful action on Dauphin Island probably regretted acting in support of the lieutenant governor. Although William Godley, foreman of the jury, was a member of

Browne's council, he had been appointed by Governor Eliot; five of the twelve jurors (Walter Hood, James Aird, James Amos, Patrick Morgan and William Southall) had already signed a petition asking for Browne's recall.[24]

During much of the time Farmar's seizure of Dauphin Island was in litigation, the general assembly was in session. Perhaps court duties and obligations explain the absence of both Attorney General Wegg and Major Farmar from the meetings of the assembly. Farmar certainly had friends enough in both houses to carry on his feud with Browne. His attorney, James Ross, was a leading member of the "Scotch party"; his friend James Waugh was the brother of the Pensacola assemblyman David Waugh; the presence of the army captains Patrick Innis and Edward Crofton (the latter prominent in the affairs of Mobile) in the council may also have strengthened the opposition of Farmar's friends.[25] In any case, by the end of the session in June, Lieutenant Governor Browne's career in West Florida lay in ruins. He would soon be recalled to London to explain himself, and Robert Farmar would set the same course in hope of recovering something of his dreams of military, political, and propertied advancement.

If Dauphin Island was not to be had, Robert Farmar cast his eye on other offshore islands. The major's brother, Captain John Farmar of the 22nd Regiment, had also been involved in land deals while in the colony and had secured a claim to one-tenth of Horn Island before he and his regiment returned to England. Captain Farmar died there on July 24, 1766, leaving his property in the hands of another relative, Thomas Miller, mariner, of New York and West Florida. Before he left for England, Robert Farmar arranged to secure John's interest from Miller, the indenture requiring the payment of thirty-six pounds. Miller himself claimed another tenth of the island, and that was transferred to the major on October 6, 1769, for five shillings and rent of one peppercorn per year. The negotiation was concluded November 28, 1769, on the payment to Miller of ninety-eight pounds ten shillings for the cattle on the island.[26]

Farmar, while in London, took his case regarding West Florida property to the Board of Trade. On May 9, 1770, Farmar petitioned the Board of Trade and Plantations for confirmation of unspecified tracts of land, including houses and 140 head of cattle, which he had purchased from Frenchmen shortly after arriving in Mobile. He declared that at that time he had no intention of settling in West Florida; he had entered into these transactions because there were no other English purchasers at Mobile at the moment and the French were anxious to sell their property and leave the colony. The latter part of this statement, at least, was accurate. Farmar also told their lordships that after the Creek Indian conference certain chieftains had compelled him to accept a tract of land on the east side of Mobile Bay called

Apalache Old Town, a property which extended as far east as the Perdido River.[27] On May 21, 1770, the board heard the major's petition and ordered it to be taken into consideration on May 24. Farmar was ordered to attend at that time. On the designated Thursday, Farmar appeared, only to be advised that the board could not comply with his request "as there was no precedent of any confirmation of titles to lands in America claimed under the circumstances stated in said petition."[28]

More promising were the two tracts granted to Farmar by Governor Eliot upon his petition of April 24, 1769, and confirmed by letters patent, January 6, 1770. One was a thousand acres located thirty miles above Mobile, and six miles north of the Tensa settlement, on Briar Creek. The other grant, on Shavebaugh's Creek, lay within the boundary of land belonging to the Indians. As settlement of such land was forbidden, Farmar proposed in 1776 to exchange it for a more useful grant.[29]

After his return to West Florida, Major Farmar pursued land claims in the western reaches of the colony, as did many others. On September 22, 1775, he secured two grants totaling five thousand acres, about twelve miles southeast of Natchez, on Sandy Creek, one abutting on the land of Captain Amos Ogden, the other near Manchac.[30] On April 5, 1777, he secured a grant of six hundred acres near Thompson's Creek, and that same year he asked for two five-hundred-acre plots on Briar Creek and Pine Island in place of his previous grant in Indian territory.[31] By January 2, 1778, Farmar claimed some forty-three hundred acres held by family right, but only eighteen hundred acres had actually been surveyed.[32] It would appear, however, that by 1778 the major had secured over ten thousand acres in various parts of the colony.[33]

With properties in Mobile and on both the Tombecbé and Tensa rivers, Farmar was as eager as any provincial to see peace among the Indians and security at home. As Lieutenant Governor Durnford described it, these rivers, the Alabama river system, formed "the Western Barrier of America,"[34] but when General Haldimand returned to West Florida from St. Augustine in May 1770 and toured Mobile, he found the place practically deserted. The fort was falling apart from lack of maintenance, and Haldimand suggested that three of the bastions be demolished and the material used for strengthening the one remaining. Although Fort Charlotte escaped that fate, the American secretary did in fact grant to Peter Chester, the new governor, permission to dismantle the disintegrating architectural pride of the Gulf Coast.[35]

The restoration of a military presence at Mobile and the restoration of Fort Charlotte owed much to Indian troubles, a war between the Choctaw and Chickasaw. Prowling natives found cattle less risky prizes than scalps, and

Farmar spoke for many Mobilians when he demanded protection. "Mr. Farmar frequently addresses himself to the Governor in Council," wrote Haldimand, "from whom he demands that I send an officer with a detachment to the River Mobile in order to protect the inhabitants and protect a new plantation which he has established there & which the Indians have threatened to destroy because it is outside the limits like several others."[36] With an aversion to risking the health of his men at Mobile and little more than a token force at his disposal, General Haldimand was led to observe, "If every person like Mr. Farmar is to have demands of troops comply'd with, to protect and guard his plantations, I suppose you will have occasion for three or four more regiments" in West Florida.[37] The presence of the outworn and understrength 16th Regiment at Mobile may have increased the settlers' sense of security, but peace came only as a result of Indian exhaustion and Governor Chester's diplomacy. Farmar's interest in that successful effort was evidenced by his presence at the Indian congress held at Mobile by Superintendent John Stuart, December 31, 1771, along with Chickasaw and Choctaw chieftains and the "Principle Inhabitants of Mobile."[38]

Major Farmar's prominence was also demonstrated by his return to the general assembly as a member of the commons for Mobile in 1771. The new governor, Peter Chester, ordered the election of the assembly in April, and elections were held about mid-May. As Campbell Town had been abandoned, the house was composed of eight members from Pensacola and a like number from Mobile. Indentures were signed between the freeholder electors and the provost marshal limiting members' terms to one year. Although originally directed to convene on June 6, only six members were present on that date; as several of the Mobilians were expected to arrive in the next week, Chester prorogued the session to June 13 and then again to June 24. On that morning Edmund Rush Wegg informed the governor that there were still only six members in town and until several members from Mobile, now expected to arrive hourly, appeared, no quorum could be secured. The first pair of dilatory Mobilians turned up in the afternoon, and Governor Chester decided to open the session on June 25. Only nine men were then in attendance, the maximum number present throughout the session. Mobile was represented by Speaker Wegg, Robert Farmar, and Alexander McIntosh, old hands in the assembly, and by John Miller, a new member from a West Florida family closely related to Farmar. Either Farmar or Miller or both would serve as members of all the commons' standing committees.[39]

As chairman of the committee to prepare an humble address of thanks to the governor for his opening speech, Major Farmar was immediately involved in setting the tone of the session, including notice that the commons intended "to prevent any loss which might arise to the Members who reside in distant parts by a too long vacation from their private affairs at this busy season." Both Miller and Farmar were deeply involved with the drafting of necessary tax measures; they showed no inclination to increase existing taxes, even for so worthy a cause as meeting the expenses of the criminal court. Farmar's attendance in the house when business was being transacted and on the many days when the house adjourned for lack of a quorum was unflawed until July 18, when he dropped from the scene. Miller, who had missed but one day, continued faithfully in attendance until the prorogation on July 30.[40]

In January 1772 Governor Chester decided to dissolve the assembly because members had been elected for limited terms—a practice he held to be improper. Writs for an election were issued, returnable on March 9, but the polling at Mobile took an unexpected turn. The freeholders approved the names of eight "principal inhabitants," including Robert Farmar, but insisted upon restricting their tenure to one year. The provost marshal so reported to the governor and council on March 9, and although the Pensacola delegation was itself large enough (if all were present) to form a quorum, the council was advised that only two would attend the commons if the Mobilians were not seated. Efforts were made to persuade the recalcitrant electors of Mobile to conform to the governor's wishes, but they persistently refused. On April 23, Governor Chester abandoned the attempt to bring an assembly into being and declared it dissolved. As the elected members for Mobile were all experienced assemblymen, it may be assumed that they approved—if indeed they had not inspired—the stand taken by Mobile on the issue of limited terms. Farmar had been involved in proceedings relating to the governor's tampering with representation in the last assembly, and Miller (although not returned in 1772—perhaps he was out of the colony) would be a leading foe of gubernatorial authority in the next assembly. Governor Chester was quite prepared to forego the meeting of an assembly in the immediate future, and with the approval of the new colonial secretary, Lord Dartmouth, he declared, "Should the District of Mobile still persist in their claim, I shall forbear to send them any writ."[41]

During the next half-dozen years, Robert Farmar's career centered upon the development of his property holdings. His last acquisitions consisted of two tracts of land far up the Tombecbé River, one described as a high bluff on the river known as Architicpy, including eight hundred acres, the other a thousand acres some 130 miles north of Mobile. Both grants were signed on August 6, 1778.[42] His ambitions for more and better land, particularly along the Mississippi, were pursued by the best means available—and under Governor Peter Chester that meant in collaboration with the governor's ubiquitous secretary, Philip Livingston. On April 8, 1777, Farmar sold Livingston six hundred acres back of Thompson's Creek, valued at £280.[43] Late in December

1777, Farmar was in correspondence with the secretary, "entreating the favour you would procure me two warrants for five hundred acres each to be laid out on Piney Island, Brier Creek," as a prior location had proved too small to accommodate his needs. It is evident from this letter that Farmar was dabbling in real estate in conjunction with Livingston, each being in a position to do the other a favor. An accompanying plat shows Farmar's three thousand acres, bordered on the south by land belonging to Amos Ogden, as good soil for hemp, flax, and indigo.[44]

In the final inventory of his estate, Major Farmar's properties were listed and evaluated as follows: (1) a house and lot in Mobile, $2,000; (2) an island sometimes referred to as Farmar's Island, on the Mobile river, one mile north of the town of Mobile, $125; (3) 3,000 acres on the Mississippi River, about twelve miles southeast of Natchez, $3,000; (4) 2,000 acres located about four miles from the river and three miles from Baton Rouge, $2,000; (5) the home plantation of Farm Hall on the Tensa river, $2,500; (6) another plantation, $185; (7) a tract of 1,800 acres located on a creek, $1,200; (8) two tracts on the Tombecbé River, $1,000; and (9) three-eighths right to Horn Island and its cattle, not appraised.[45]

In 1836 the heirs Louis de Vaubercey and Curtis Lewis advertised the Farmar lands as 3,000 acres on Sandy Creek below Natchez, 1,000 acres near Baton Rouge, 1,000 acres on the Tombecbé River four miles north of St. Stephens, 800 acres twelve miles above St. Stephens, 1,280 acres on the Tensa River and Briar Creek, 640 acres near that same location, 300 acres on an island above Mobile, 57,000 acres on the east side of Mobile Bay, a tract on Dauphin Island, a large lot at Government and Emanuel streets and another lot on Conti Street, Mobile.[46]

Robert Farmar's standing in his community was reflected by his reappointment as justice of the peace for Mobile in 1774 and again in 1777.[47] He took his civic duties seriously. In a postscript to his letter to Livingston, Farmar noted, "I did propose attending the ensuing Court [at Pensacola], but my Health will not admit of it." The years of soldiering on battle fields and river bottoms were beginning to take their toll, but there were still battles to be waged.

The American Revolution came to West Florida only gradually. As opposition to British government built up in the northern and Atlantic coastal colonies between 1773 and 1776, West Florida remained calm. Backwoods "Virginians," as they were known, began to come down the rivers to settle on the Mississippi in increasing numbers, and among them were many rough and lawless men; but to the coastal towns came also more cultivated folk, sometimes wealthy and sometimes poor unfortunates who fled from their boisterous neighbors, seeking a haven of peace and loyalism in West Florida.

Neither group attracted much attention among settled West Florida planters like Robert Farmar. The major and his kind might watch distant developments with some concern for the British American empire which they had helped to create, but Mobile and Pensacola were far from Boston and New York.

Merchant shippers to and from the Gulf Coast were the first to feel the fires of war when they encountered Yankee privateers. Other merchants noticed the cordiality between the young Spanish governor at New Orleans, Bernardo de Gálvez, and rebel merchants such as Oliver Pollock, who arranged the purchase of military supplies for the Americans and their shipment to the north. The Spaniard's seizure of British colonial ships and contraband cargoes in 1777 forecast his attitude in 1778 when James Willing and his band of piratical Americans raided the British settlements on the Mississippi River and created panic as far east as Mobile.[48] Robert Farmar was one of sixteen "principal inhabitants" of Mobile who then signed a petition seeking reinforcements for Fort Charlotte.[49]

The Willing Raid forced Governor Peter Chester to act upon earlier orders from the American secretary to summon an assembly in order to provide a militia for the security of West Florida. Chester had no love for assemblies, nor for Mobile. He reduced the town's representation to half that of Pensacola and gave equal representation to both Manchac and Natchez on the Mississippi, clearly intending to swamp the opposition at Mobile. Elections were held at Mobile in May 1778, the return ordered for June 6. The voters of Mobile gave their voices to Robert Farmar and three others, but because of delays in hearing from the western districts, Chester put off the assembly until October 1. By that date Major Robert Farmar's seat was vacant.[50]

In the absence of other information, it must be assumed that in spite of complaints earlier in the year, Farmar was in sufficient health to offer himself to the Mobile electors when they polled in May and to anticipate serving in the assembly. But the major was sixty-one years old, and he admitted to the ailments of advancing years. He had survived the rigors of Cartagena and Havana, the blood-letting of Fontenoy, Laffeldt, and Rocoux, and the no less deadly fevers of Mobile for many years. With the American Revolution, Robert Farmar's world was coming to an end. Whether he bowed before the ravages of the years or to flux or fever, his life ended sometime after August 1, 1778, when his last will was drawn up at Mobile.[51] Farmar was not present when the assembly convened on October 1, and his death was acknowledged by John Miller (sitting for Pensacola on this occasion) in the commons' session of October 8.[52] On November 25, well after the assembly had been adjourned (it would not, in fact, meet again) Peter Swanson, a merchant of Mobile and partner of John Miller, signed a "Memorial of the Speaker and other Members" in the capacity of "Member elected for the district of Mobile In the Room of Robert Farmar deceas'd." As Swanson was never seated in the assembly and, on November 17, had signed a "Letter of Thanks from the Principal Inhabitants of the Town of Mobile" to the members of the Commons House who had opposed Governor Chester, his claim to membership must have derived from a by-election held between November 17 and November 25 in the expectation that the assembly would meet again.[53] Swanson was an active spokesman of Mobile's displeasure with Peter Chester—a role that Robert Farmar might well have filled had he met his last muster.

VII.

Old Soldier at Home

The professional soldier who commanded at Fort Charlotte and was thought of as the military governor of Mobile, the investor in western lands, and the member of the West Florida General Assembly may be described with some assurance. His was a public career. The private man, his loves and losses, is less easily discovered. Little evidence remains with which to delineate the man whose military portrait most certainly discloses the face he intended to present to the world. Yet something may be said of this younger son of American colonial gentry, a family man in his own right, at the end a Mobilian of unique distinction.

His character may first be drawn from his works. In his youth he enjoyed the advantages of a prosperous and distinguished lineage: a good education, political connections, and military opportunity. As a young man he displayed to Governor Lewis Morris the self-assurance that was the natural attribute of his class and which, to a critical observer, might be termed the brash pride of youth. Years of hard service in the 19th Regiment hardened and honed the professional soldier to the burdens of duty, obligation, and responsibility. Wealth, wit, and connection could speed promotion in the eighteenth-century British army, but Captain Robert Farmar does not appear to have enjoyed those advantages. His virtues were of the mundane sort—diligence, application, eventually seniority. As a junior officer commanding men under fire, he performed efficiently, bravely, and successfully. Ligonier praised the 19th Foot for their steady performance at Rocoux, but it was a stricken field. It mattered little to the army whether Captain Farmar was among the eight regimental officers wounded. At Havana, Colonel Guy Carleton responded gallantly to the Spaniards' surprise assault, but it was Major Farmar whose men chased the attackers into the sea. Farmar's subsequent assignment to direct the occupation of Mobile reflected no more than the absence of the lieutenant colonel from the 34th Regiment—nor was it an attractive military plum, quite the contrary.

In Mobile between 1763 and 1765, Major Farmar displayed proper concern for His Majesty's rights against the petty trickery of disgruntled French officers and enforced treaty terms upon the whole population. His was the sole responsibility for maintaining law and order among Indians and Indian traders—not the easiest of "subjects." The firmness with which he did his duty won him few friends. James Adair, no unbiased observer, declared that Farmar acted "to gratify his pride, and aggrandize his power"—"the merchants and other gentlemen at Mobile, of generous principles, despised it." "Except for a couple of officers of the commander's own principles, all the rest blamed if not despised him for his haughtiness and ungenerous principles."[1] Farmar's difficulties with Governor Johnstone show him to have been overburdened, touchy, sometimes irascible when confronted by an overweening, insensitive young Scottish naval officer who sought to exercise an authority that no self-respecting army officer could easily accept.[2] Perhaps it is most ironic that Farmar should be confused in the minds of twentieth-century historians with his arch-enemy, George Johnstone.[3]

The arduous voyage up the Mississippi and the months of isolation at Fort Cavendish brought out sharp differences between the major and some of his young subordinates. Responsibility weighed heavily upon his shoulders, not theirs, and among them were recent arrivals to North America who had little or no experience of campaigning in the wilderness. Nor had they the task of provisioning and financing an expedition under the watchful eye of General Thomas Gage and the British Treasury. The abrupt temper and rigid discipline of the commanding officer grated upon their tender sensibilities.[4] Suffice it that Major Farmar succeeded in his task; under Lieutenant Colonel John Reed, the regiment soon fell apart and returned home no more than a skeleton of the force Farmar had led from Havana to the Illinois.

The most obvious flaw in Robert Farmar's military performance was that of administrator of funds grudgingly and belatedly provided by a peacetime government intent upon saving British taxpayers' money. In that arena Farmar faced in Gage a stern, meticulous, demanding superior. If the major's problems may be cited in defense of his somewhat casual bookkeeping, credit must also be given to Gage's patience, for the general was no less rigorous when dealing with other officers on the fringes of British North America. He found not a few to be more culpable than Robert Farmar, and he ultimately concluded that Farmar's circumstances warranted the Treasury's kind consideration.

The greatest and least of the charges against Major Farmar were brought to the fore during the court martial at Pensacola. There Farmar defended and explained himself with most becoming dignity, and while the prejudiced accusations of Philip Pittman, an insubordinate junior, and George Johnstone, an interfering civilian, were not apt to be supported by the long-suffering officers of the court, those gentlemen attended most carefully to General Gage's charges. Their honorable acquittal of the major on all counts was the final verdict of the army to which Farmar devoted most and the best years of his life. It must be the verdict of history as well.

Behind the martial sash and silver gorget was another Robert Farmar, a member of a far-flung clan and head of his own familial establishment.

The accidents of empire brought Robert, John, and Jasper Farmar together in Mobile as the 34th, 22nd, and 21st Foot took up their regimental assignments in West Florida. The two brothers had no doubt maintained professional contacts long before 1763. John had been at Havana with the 22nd Regiment, and Robert employed him as his personal emissary when they reached Mobile. The major must have rejoiced at his younger brother's fortune in being able to return to England and grieved at news of his death. In 1763 Robert sought from Thomas Miller "a special authority to act for him as Executor" of John's estate and eventually became possessed of a part of it.[5] The major was in the Illinois country when his nephew Lieutenant Jasper Farmar of the 21st Regiment was stationed at Mobile, but family connections would have been maintained, and Jasper remained in the colony until 1769, when he departed for St. Augustine.[6]

Robert Farmar's relations with his nephews, the Miller family, were intimate throughout his residence in West Florida. The New York merchants early sought a place in the commerce of the new colony, and the major found them extremely useful—nepotism was the norm in all aspects of eighteenth-century business. Thomas Miller settled in West Florida in the summer of 1765 because of financial necessity. When he renewed correspondence with John Ellis, the king's agent for West Florida, he explained that the "misfortunes in my affairs in New York has at length thrown me into his Majesty's Province of West Florida." At that moment Thomas Miller judged that the colony would be "useful to the Mother-Country, when Prudence, that amiable Exile, is admitted into it; but till that happy Event, its Prospects are dreary."[7] Thomas Miller did indeed prosper in West Florida, and became one of the colony's foremost merchants.[8] John Miller, probably Thomas's son, was himself a merchant of note in West Florida and continued his career on the Gulf Coast and the Mississippi long after British dominion ended.[9] His connection with Robert Farmar in the assembly and with William Swanson in both politics and commerce illustrates the ties that bound West Florida together.

Christopher Miller resided in New York and served as agent for his relatives in West Florida. A surviving letter addressed by Farmar to "Dear Kitt" discloses that Robert and Christopher shared business interests, particularly regarding Horn Island. A minor official having failed to act promptly on a matter of importance to Miller, Farmar promised to "convince him that I hold his impertinence in its just esteem and shall never more treat with him personally." At the same time, the major, displeased with the evidence given by Israel Solomon at his court martial and suspecting that Solomon's "venality was satisfied for the evidence he gave," urged Kit to "expose him to all your Hebrew acquaintance, tho' poor Devil everything has turned out contrary to his expectations." Farmar also asked Miller, as well as his own brother, Samuel, to keep him informed of the progress of the court martial proceedings through New York and on to London. There was some thought that Christopher might move to West Florida; he already held some town lots in Mobile. With the right capital investment, urged Robert, "I could procure you Twenty Prime Negroes so that the rest of the money you would have to live on for two years or Build if you choose it, as you would even the first two years be almost able to maintain yourself; be assured it is no chimerical scheme."[10] It does not appear that Miller pursued his uncle's suggestion.

For himself, Robert Farmar held property on the northeast corner of what became Government and St. Emanuel streets in the town of Mobile. Major Farmar's family probably lived in this residence during their early years in West Florida. Farmar's house was located near to and facing Fort Charlotte, and because of its proximity it was demolished by Lieutenant Governor Durnford in 1780, in order to clear a field of fire from the fort when Spanish attack was imminent. When Major Farmar's holdings were appraised in 1780, the town property was valued at two thousand dollars. A few years later, Mrs Mary Farmar, hoping for compensation from the British government, placed its worth at six hundred pounds.[11] After Farmar moved to his plantation on the Tensa River, he probably maintained the house for occasions when he had reason to visit Mobile.

It was quite appropriate for a young and junior army officer to cling to bachelorhood for many years. Military responsibilities did not preclude engagements of the heart, but a captain dependent upon his pay was not in a good position to marry and assume family obligations in the eighteenth century. Well-dowered brides were widely sought but seldom caught. It is uncertain when Robert Farmar married, but it seems likely that he took a wife only after he secured his majority. She was Mary Anderson, a Yorkshire woman, obviously a good bit younger than her husband. Perhaps she accompanied the major, as officers' wives sometimes did, on the Havana expedition and on to Mobile. She was most probably there when their second child was born, a son christened Robert Adolphus Farmar. The event would have been cheerfully anticipated by the officer corps at Mobile, and from deep in Indian country

Lieutenant Thomas Ford hastened to send his compliments when he heard the happy news in 1764.[12] Major Farmar seems to have celebrated the birth of a male heir by christening his sloop *Little Bob.*

The family came to include five children: the oldest, a daughter named Anne Billopp, then Robert Adolphus, next Elizabeth Mary and Catherine Louisa, followed by Thomas John Theodore.[13] If this chronology is correct, the entry in the Reverend Nathaniel Cotton's register of births and christenings requires explanation, for it lists Ann Billop Farmar under the date March 28, 1769.[14] It seems most likely that Anne then received a belated christening or perhaps confirmation because of the lack of a proper Anglican cleric in the colony before Cotton's arrival and the inconvenience of meeting with him at Pensacola. As late as April 1769, Farmar described his family as consisting of wife and two children. In 1776 the major declared that between January 1770 and October 6, 1773, his family had increased by one, presumably Elizabeth.[15] As Farmar was petitioning for land granted by family right and would have benefited by mentioning all of his children, it may be assumed that the two youngest children were born during the last few years of his life, 1773–78. Although subject to question, this chronology is not contradicted by available evidence, nor is it exceptional for the eighteenth century.

It was not in the town of Mobile, however, that the Farmar family put down roots. Apparently shortly after the satisfactory conclusion of his court martial, Robert decided to settle permanently in West Florida. He cast his eye upon the rich alluvial lands of the Tensa River, which flows lazily into the northeastern corner of Mobile Bay. A short distance up that dark river, Farmar found suitable land on both sides of the stream, that on the eastern side distinguished by a high bank secure from flooding which is still known as Farmar's Bluff.[16] Farmar secured this property by purchase from John Dedres and Francis Duran. There the major built the home he called Farm Hall, and there he lived from 1771 until his death in 1778.[17] The house sat on the east side of the river, and on the west side lay his corn fields. The home farm had sixty-two toises frontage (roughly four hundred feet) and was at least forty arpents (roughly thirty-four acres) deep; it lay between the plantations of S. Michel and M. Popolous. The property west of the river contained seventy arpents (roughly sixty acres) of river frontage and was bounded on the north by a bayou. The land was valued at twenty-five hundred dollars when appraised in 1780. There was no settlement to the north or east of Farm Hall, though toward Mobile the land had been claimed and occupied. Farmar built upon the edge of that land designated for British settlement; the Tensa property he secured in 1770, a few miles farther north, lay within the Indian boundary line. Farmar established himself on the frontier of civilization in

West Florida; hence his repeated demands for protection from marauding Indians.[18]

There is no description of Farmar's house, but it was clearly a sizeable dwelling, designed to accommodate the family and its guests. A kitchen stood apart from the house, and at least one other building was described as "large." There were pens, stables, slave quarters, all the appurtenances of a working plantation. As befitted his rank and station, Farmar lived in considerable style and comfort, yet only two rooms possessed fireplaces, and cold February weather discouraged spending any time in an unheated part of the house.[19]

The master's bedroom contained a large mahogany bedstead with feather bed and bolster. Rose-colored blankets and blue and white cotton curtains set off the room. A mosquito curtain could be hung when required. In other bedrooms were to be found a large black walnut bedstead and two beechwood tent beds, one with chequered curtains, the other with curtains of printed cotton. Ample supplies of blankets, sheets, and bed linens were kept at hand.

The house contained six tables, including the large oval mahogany dining table. There were five mahogany Windsor chairs and nineteen others, including the major's leather-covered easy chair with upholstery secured by brass tacks. Three mirrors, two described as large, decorated the rooms and a mahogany bureau with drawers provided readily available storage space, though much must have been kept in four trunks. In addition to candles, Farm Hall was lit by two glass oil lamps with glass shades.

When the major wished to dine in style, his table might be set with a variety of twenty-eight china dishes or the fifty-two-piece set of blue and white tea-table china. There were miscellaneous plates and dishes for ordinary use. A dozen and a half wine glasses were available to set off the silver: seventeen silver tablespoons, nineteen teaspoons, four silver serving spoons, three silver serving dishes, silver salt and pepper and various other pieces valued at over two hundred dollars. The two and a half dozen knives and forks, like the carving set, boasted ivory handles.

The major's military mementoes were prominently displayed: a gold medal his silver gorget, and a silver snuff box. On the wall would be hung his silver-hilted dress sword and a more utilitarian small sword with steel hilt, also a fusee; his pair of silver-mounted pistols probably remained boxed. On a mantel stood a gold "horizontal watch" with a gold seal (valued at one hundred dollars). For dress use Major Farmar could have donned either gold or silver buckles; his gold-headed can was undoubtedly familiar to fellow Mobilians and assemblymen. To pass the time pleasurably with a guest, the host possessed both a backgammon table and a chess table with chessmen. Mrs. Farmar probably spent many hours seated at her spinning wheel.

Kitchen and sheds contained the usual pieces, including eleven iron pots for cooking. A chest of tools was highly valued at sixty dollars, and two whipsaws and six crosscut saws at fifty dollars; and there was the necessarily large number of axes, scythes, hoes, and other farming equipment.

Robert Farmar's library occupied several shelves in the house and reflected both his and Mary's taste. A large family Bible, two prayer books, Humphrey Prideaux's *Old and New Testament Connected in the History of the Jews*, and Archbishop John Tillotson's popular *Sermons* proved their orthodoxy. Sets of Joseph Addison's *Spectator* and Richard Steele's *Tatler* and *Guardian* were at hand, as were Alexander Pope's *Complete Works* and an abridged *Roman History*. Beside these stood Jonas Hanway's *Travels*, Thomas Otway's *Plays*, Arthur Young's *A Six Months Tour Through the North of England*, *The Turkish Spy*, and Charles Wentworth's novels. Almost requisite in such a library were Milton's *Paradise Lost* and Samuel Butler's *Hudibras*. Two dictionaries were available, and a mariner's compass found its place beside the books.

The immediate value and agricultural potential of any plantation could be measured by the number of slaves the master owned.[20] In 1769 Farmar stated that he owned sixteen Negro slaves; by 1773 this number had been increased by forty-five.[21] In 1780 Farm Hall employed a total of fifty-five slaves: twenty-eight men, thirteen women, ten boys, and four girls. Together they were valued at $14,121. The number of his slaves made Robert Farmar one of the leading slaveholders in the colony. The value of Farmar's blacks varied from $500, that of York, a cattle hunter, to a mere $50 for unskilled men and women. The average value of a male slave was $313, but in addition to the highly prized York, Paul and Juba were assessed at $428 each, Sampson at $400, Adam and Polidore at $380. These men undoubtedly possessed special skills not only valuable to the plantation but recommending them for profitable hiring out to other employers. Among the women, eight were valued at over $300, the highest regard being given to Hester and Queen ($350 each). Negro boys were worth on the average $143.5, girls $132.5.[22]

In addition to his slaves, Major Farmar would have employed several white overseers or workmen. In 1769 he employed two such "hirelings." They do not appear in the plantation record, but the major did not attempt to raise such crops as rice and indigo without supervision.

For both work and riding the major kept thirteen horses worth more than $20 on average, and sixteen asses worth $136 in all. His cattle numbered some three hundred, valued at $10 a head. There were also a sow and five shoats, and doubtless chickens ranging freely.

Farm Hall was, by West Florida standards, a large, well-endowed plantation, and the Farmars were part of the frontier aristocracy.[23] Farmar's prosperity, like that of his fellows, depended upon finding a cash crop, and in that he, like them, fell short of much success. Part of the problem was circumstantial. When the British arrived in West Florida, the market demand was for beef. Open-range cattle raising in the marshes and piney woods of the coast was not a gentleman's work, nor were the black cattle of the region apt to be prime steers. Indians took a cavalier view of ownership, and that gave particular value to the offshore islands, West Florida's natural cattle pens. With that in mind Farmar had invested in both Dauphin and Horn Island, with small satisfaction. In 1780 those knowledgeable Mobilians William Gordon and James McGillivray refused to assign any value to the three-eighths of Horn Island that Farmar owned, observing that they did not know what cattle were there, and animals were the principal value of the property.[24]

The experience of other southern American colonies and the benign Gulf Coast climate suggested long-term options for agriculturists, and the propagandists of settlement praised the virtues of rice and indigo as cash crops. Great efforts were made by West Florida planters, but results were all too often disappointing. In 1776, Farmar expressed to an old comrade in London his appreciation of

> the condolence of real friends in any kind of adverse fortune, therefore be assured that your kind concern . . . gives a pleasing satisfaction. Was it not that the last year produced about a fourth part of what might reasonably be expected, which is near double what any of the preceeding years turned out, my patience would be entirely tired out. I've been obliged to shift the scene, after three Years tryal of Indigo, for want of a proper hand acquainted with the process of making it, and am now going on getting lumber, an article that present disputes between the present state and the Associated Colonies [that is, the United States] renders more beneficial.[25]

To a niece in London he wrote that he was

> much pleased to find the Rice came to hand in such good order. It is an Article that for these two last Years through bad management in my overseers, I have not raised sufficient for family use, indeed the Year before last not so much as a single grain.[26]

The failure of cash crops to materialize was at least balanced by the plantation's ability to produce the necessities of life from season to season. The Farmars hardly suffered, and the major hoped that speculation in land on the Mississippi might produce profits in the future. Without any doubt, he had invested all of his capital in West Florida property, cheap as it was. A major's pay could not meet the expenses that fell upon him in such a post as Mobile, and it was apt to be in arrears in any case. In the spring of 1769 the pay of the

34th Regiment was still wanting for the years 1765 to 1768, and other military perquisites depended upon the generosity of his superiors.[27] If his initial share of the Havana prize money enabled him to get a start in Florida land speculation, the whole came to him only gradually; the final distribution of prize money was not made until October 1771.[28] Perhaps Farmar succeeded in getting an advance on that payment while he was in London; he surely was able to collect the price of his commission, which had been sold in 1768—though the sum of six hundred pounds, the official price at that date, may not have represented a very significant profit.[29] According to Mary Farmar, "He sold his Commission . . . & laid out all the money & more in the Purchase of Lands in America. At the time of Major Farmar's Death the whole of his property was valued at more than £12,000."[30] The appraisers in 1780 set the figure at $31,541 or £7,335.

Major Farmar's plantation lay on the edge of civilization north along the Tensa, but he was by no means isolated from society. There were French families living on his land as tenants, and it was probably in their behalf that Mary Farmar stood as witness to a marriage ceremony in Mobile some weeks after the major's death.[31] Friends and relatives would have made visits extending over several days, in the eighteenth-century fashion. Apparently Farmar's place was also a rendezvous for traders and their pack-horse trains as they plodded their way between Georgia and the Gulf Coast.

Among the visitors in the summer of 1775 was that indefatigable naturalist William Bartram. The itinerant botanist made his way through the woods from the Chattahoochee to the Tensa late in July and found himself at the home of "that worthy gentleman" Major Farmar. He quite accurately described the site of Farm Hall: "It is a most delightful situation, commanding a spacious prospect up and down the river, and the low lands of his extensive plantations on the opposite shore." Bartram spent some time with the Farmars in August "in consequence of an invitation . . . to spend some days with his family: here I obtained the use of a light canoe to continue my voyage up the river." Bartram later used the Farmar plantation as a base for more careful examination of the surrounding area. When he came down with fever, he enjoyed their "care and good attendance." After a few days Bartram was sufficiently recovered to roam the woods again, "the Major being so polite and obliging as to furnish me with horses to ride, and a Negro to pilot and take care of me." The naturalist's attention was caught by the plenitude of wax myrtle in the area, a shrub which was highly esteemed for producing candle wax that was harder and therefore longer-burning than beeswax. At Farm Hall, Bartram encountered Dr. William Grant, like Farmar a former military person, and the two men made their way by canoe down the Tensa and across the head of the bay to Mobile. After some less than happy adventures westward, Bartram returned to Farmar's place by boat, a days paddle from Mobile, on November 27, 1775. He was then traveling in company with an Indian trader, and they joined the pack-horse men at Farm Hall. "I took my last leave of Major Farmar," wrote Bartram, "and left Taensa" the next day.[32]

The major undoubtedly enjoyed the visits of friends and travelers; he certainly kept in touch with his old companions of the West Florida regiments after they returned to England. John Lind, who succeeded to the majority of the 34th Regiment in 1771, appears to have remained a particular favorite. In a long letter to Lind in 1776, Farmar noted:

> Your kind favour of the 7th February '75 did not reach me until the 7th of August. I have delaid acknowledging the receipt thereof till this opportunity by the Annual Ship that comes to McGillivray's House, as it is so very expensive by the Packets. . . .
>
> Be pleased to return my Compliments accompani'd with best wishes to Captn. Forbes and his Family. Mrs. Forbes has honoured him with the laudable Rank of a Citizen of Rome with which I heartily congratulate him, altho: I could wish he was better enabled to provide for so large a family, it being just equal to mine, the burden whereof I sensibly feel.

Farmar recalled Dundas as "the man of pleasure and gayety, his presence with the Regiment will be seldom, however pray remember me to him. Ross & Wood [and] Townsend is too much in the great World to consider such a Retired thing as I'm." Of other old comrades Farmar remarked, "Wilkie's windfall . . . gave me great pleasure; he now wants only another good Wife to make life pass agreeable in the decline." Some were less cordially remembered: "The association of Bromhead, Sedgwick, and Pownal must doubtless be a very regular, sober society." Of himself Farmar wrote, "Altho:, as the blackguards term it, I am poverty struck, I enjoy some domestick felicity amongst my little Girls."[33]

All in the Farmar family was not, however, as the major wished. Little Bob reached sufficient years to be sent to England for schooling, and that gave his father deep and painful concern. To John Lind he remarked, "Bob is still in England, but he makes very little progress in his studies. His Cousin writes he promises to be tall and has a manly appearance."[34] The cousin was Mrs. Davis, No. 9 Great Tower Hill, London, who kept Major Farmar apprised of his son's progress—or lack of it—as did Captain Campbell. To her Robert admitted his disappointment in the boy's casual approach to education and his failure to correspond with his distant parents:

Notwithstanding I am so angry with him for not writing, that was it not the weather is too cold to set in a Room without a fire, especially as I have a sore leg, and my little Girls have so many referances for me to decide when in either of the rooms with a fire place that it is impossible to do anything else, I would recommence a correspondency with him. . . .

You will see by mine to Mr. Davis that my expectations are frustrated in a double sense; first, and the least, is the disappointment in my Crop, the other is what relates to my sons Education, and gives me inexpressable uneasyness. Therefore [I] must entreat you will be so good as to second my solicitations that Mr. Davis will direct his re-assuming the study of Latin, and encourage the boy in his close application therein . . . ; after what he had acquired in Latin while with Mr. Bindfield, it would not have taken him much time, if applied to with assiduity to have made himself an entire Master of that language, without which, in public Assemblies and business, a man makes but a trifling figure. If he has not a Capacity of attaining it, I much doubt of his ever making a proficiency in any branch of learning, for it is the ground work and foundation of every science.[35]

Major Farmar's disappointment in the boy, who was perhaps no more than twelve or thirteen years old at the time, is understandable. The burden of supporting the lad required financial sacrifice on the part of the father. Whether Bob corrected his ways or not is uncertain. That he retained a sense of family, attachment to West Florida, and took some pride in his father's career seems clear, but Major Farmar did not live to see it.

VIII.

Farewell to British West Florida

When Major Robert Farmar died, in the autumn of 1778, the future of British West Florida was far from certain. To the north, Americans had declared their independence of George III, but they had yet to win it. Few West Floridians expected that they would do so, and the province had become a haven for loyalist refugees from the rebel colonies. Mobile and Pensacola seemed secure behind the bulwarks of the Royal Navy and the bayonets of the British army.

The explosion of American insurgency between 1773 and 1776 did not pass unnoticed, for there were strong ties between the Gulf Coast and Atlantic commercial centers. Farmar and the Millers had close business and family ties in Pennsylvania, New Jersey, and New York, and they were not unique. For a time, the former West Floridian Brigadier Frederick Haldimand acted in Gage's place as British commander in chief in North America, and he remained at the general's side when Gage returned to face unruly Bostonians. Among Haldimand's regular correspondents was Thomas Willing of the eminent Philadelphia firm of Willing and Morris, and both had taken an interest in the attempt of James Willing to establish himself as a planter on the Mississippi.[1] Ominously for the future, James Willing also formed connections with Oliver Pollock at New Orleans that were stronger than those with Haldimand at Pensacola or with his neighbors on the British side of the Mississippi.

West Floridians followed the course of events in Boston and Philadelphia with very mixed feelings. They were aware of the "Americanization" of their own provincial population as hundreds of new settlers came into the lower Mississippi valley from the hinterlands of the old colonies, and it made them nervous regarding the future. They were not concerned by the possibility of Spanish aggression from New Orleans, for since the Falkland Islands crisis at the beginning of the 1770s, they had rather anticipated that New Orleans would fall to Britain in the event of an Anglo-Spanish war. At the same time they were sufficiently aware of American grievances and British policies to take a jaundiced view of the state of imperial relations.

Major Robert Farmar, an American-born retired British army officer, found himself caught in the center of the maelstrom of loyalties. In February 1776 he observed to John Lind:

> The situation of affairs in the northern & Eastern parts of British America are really deplorable, and let what will be the consequence of the present Struggle, Great Britain as well as America will rue that ever their politics took such a fatal turn. It on your side of the Atlantic Ocean may be thought an easy matter to reduce the Americans to a state of *Slavery* (for the present proceeding of administration will admit of no favourable appelation) without considering they are descendants from those who in England made so glorious a stand for liberty, the most laudable cause a man can be engaged in. The Americans only desire to participate with the Britains in the privileges and liberties of their happy constitution, which by nature and consanguinity they have a right to expect not withstanding the unnatural pretensions the Majority of the present British Parliament Assume.[2]

Again, to his niece, Farmar wrote:

> The Eastern and Northern Provinces of British America are in a melancholy situation. The Harsh and coercive measures the British ministry and Parliament have thought proper to adopt, it is to be feared, will bring on a Civil war, which gives me great concern for our friends and near relations, for should Affairs be brought to this deplorable pass, none will be suffered to remain Neuter and Idle Spectators, but all will be compelled to declare for either one or the other part. For it is not to be doubted that since Government has used such Compulsory measures, the Americans will carry it to the utmost extremity. In this colony we have nothing to apprehend but what may proceed from the inhuman steps endeavours are using, and for which there is preparations making publickly, to effect in Congresses to be held with the Creek, Chicasaws and Chacktaw Indians, of setting these Savages upon the inhabitants of Georgia & South Carolina. This will render both Lifes and Property of the Settlers in this Colony very precarious indeed, and the disinterested are too feeble to prevent what will bring so much Grist to the Mills of a few in Power. When Britain (if she is able) has effected this mighty Work of exterpating her American Subjects, how replete will she be in Glory and an inexhaustible Treasury. This is an event that both Spain & France look for with some impatience, and to forward what tends

> so much to promote what they will at a seasonable time shew the world what is transacting for their particular interest. They make promises without intending to observe them.[3]

Major Farmar's tragically accurate analysis of the situation has hardly been improved upon in the intervening two hundred years, whether by patriot rhetoricians or historical philosophers.

The first alarm bells sounded in West Florida in the spring of 1778 in response to James Willing's raid. It was evident that the colony had desperate need of a militia and had the men and means to create one; that was the basic concern of the general assembly to which Major Robert Farmar was elected, but governor and assemblymen stood upon opposing constitutional principles, and nothing was accomplished. West Florida remained dependent upon the 16th and 60th regiments, the Waldeckers and loyalist forces sent to the Gulf Coast in 1778 and commanded by General John Campbell. They were scattered from Pensacola to Manchac on the Mississippi, where Lieutenant Colonel Dickson's force fell easy prey to Louisiana Governor Bernardo de Gálvez's Spanish troops in 1779. Mobile was obviously the next target, but the defenses of Fort Charlotte were little short of ruinous; guns and ammunition were mismatched, and Lieutenant Governor Elias Durnford, who defended the place, had only a scratch force with which to maintain himself against an army. He leveled the houses of the town that offered cover to an attacking force—including Farmar's town house—but when Gálvez prepared to open siege lines on March 10, 1780, Durnford's only hope lay in the arrival of Campbell's relief force from Pensacola, bogged down on the banks of the Tensa River near the Farmar plantation. Campbell advanced no further. Durnford capitulated on March 13, and the Spaniards raised their flag over Mobile the next day. Campbell lost no time retiring to Pensacola, leaving the British civilians at Mobile to fend for themselves.[4]

By the time Mobile came under attack, the family of the late Major Robert Farmar had been reunited at Farm Hall. Robert Adolphus returned from England and joined his widowed mother and her children. More than a dozen miles and a day's journey from Fort Charlotte, they were not involved in the action, but their prospects were grim. When Campbell left the vicinity he assigned a small force of West Florida Royal Foresters to provide some security to the settlers on the Tensa and to sweep the country of cattle for the garrison at Pensacola. Gálvez was no less anxious to secure supplies and to bind the conquered British civilians to their new masters.

Robert Adolphus Farmar found himself between two fires. He had joined Captain Patrick Strachan's company of light dragoons of the West Florida Royal Foresters.[5] Composed of the more active and daring of the local population, the little band of thirty-six men hardly deserved any more formal military description than that of irregulars. When Mobile came under attack, young Farmar was listed, March 8, 1780, as lieutenant and Strachan's second in command. Strachan's men waited at the Tensa for General Campbell's arrival, safe if inactive, but most of the company were captured on the lower reaches of the river on the night of March 17, when they were surprised by a Spanish reconnaissance party. Sixteen were taken, including Strachan; the rest scattered. Young Farmar apparently got away and made for Pensacola; if captured, he was granted freedom of movement by the Spaniards, as were Strachan and other captives.[6]

Mary Farmar and her children remained for the time at Farm Hall. Gálvez and his trusted subordinate José de Ezpeleta, who was named commandant of the Mobile district, asked no better than that the English should remain peaceably in their homes. They were promised security in their persons and property, specifically if they would take an oath of allegiance to the king of Spain, and generally for as long as eight months after the capitulation of Fort Charlotte if they gave neither aid nor comfort to the British at Pensacola. As a result, peace settled quickly upon the civilian population. It was even possible for British legal proceedings to be carried out on the banks of the Tensa. On February 1, 1780, Peter Chester, as judge for the probate of wills and granting of letters of administration, had directed the Reverend William Gordon, James McGillivray, and Walter Hood, or any two of them—all Mobilians—"to inventory and appraise the goods and chattels of Robert Farmar late of Mobile, Esquire, deceased, as shall be shown to you by John Stephenson and George Troup, Esqs., executors of the last will" of Major Farmar. Accordingly, on March 19 Troup, Gordon, and McGillivray met at Farm Hall and compiled a thorough and detailed description of its contents, equipment, and Farmar's landholdings throughout the colony. They appraised the total worth of the major's possessions at $31,541.1, and their findings were filed in Pensacola on May 29, 1780. Thanks to their efforts, a remarkable picture of a British West Florida plantation was preserved.[7]

Mary Farmar continued in residence, delicately balanced between hostile forces in Mobile and Pensacola. Early in June, Ezpeleta levied a contribution of some forty head of cattle from her, combining the satisfaction of his needs at Fort Charlotte with clear public warning to other Englishmen that illegal sales to their countrymen at Pensacola would not be tolerated. The pain of the blow was softened, however, on June 10, when the Spanish governor paid 599 pesos to Mrs. Farmar for her animals—not a bad price, but far less than they would have brought in the market at Pensacola.[8]

The Tensa plantations occupied a sort of no-man's land between the British and Spanish forces; both combatants claimed authority over them, but neither could protect them from marauding Indians, and the planters' repeated attempts to do business as usual were firmly rejected by Ezpeleta.[9]

The complications of the situation came home to the Farmar household in the person of Lieutenant John Louis Barde of the 60th Regiment. Taken prisoner by the Spaniards when Fort Charlotte surrendered, Barde succeeded in avoiding transportation to New Orleans with the other two captured officers of his regiment. At the end of May, Ezpeleta prepared to send the prisoners remaining at Mobile, including Barde, to New Orleans. He noted in Barde "an extraordinary fanaticism for his Nation" and thought his presence in the area "highly prejudicial" to Spanish interests.

Mary Farmar had other ideas. According to family tradition, young Barde had been quartered in the Farmar house (probably in Mobile, more certainly at Farm Hall after the fall of Fort Charlotte) and there met Anne, the oldest daughter. Their love blossomed and, in spite of Mrs. Farmar's coolness, came to fruition in marriage on April 6, 1780. On June 9, Mrs. Farmar called upon Ezpeleta in order to intercede for her son-in-law. She argued that Barde had surrendered his commission and was consequently in the bad graces of General Campbell at Pensacola, who would not accept the young man's resignation. Fervently she pleaded against Barde's removal to New Orleans. Whether she also mentioned her extensive herds of cattle and the need for men to guard the plantation against raiding Indians may be pondered. Ezpeleta acquiesced in her request, and the newlyweds remained at Farm Hall.[10]

British subjects could not, however, linger in the Mobile district indefinitely without taking the oath of fealty required by the Spanish government. By the end of the year 1780, Mary Farmar, her family, and John Louis Barde (free on parole) made their way to Pensacola with the little they could salvage from the major's estate. Though their departure must have been tearful, they had, in fact, been singled out by Ezpeleta among those Mobilians who had, for their cooperation, enjoyed the favor of the Spanish governor.[11]

Pensacola offered little security and less comfort. The town was terribly crowded; prices were high. General Campbell refused to utilize the Indian allies who were available to him, and the British high command could send him no more reinforcements. In January 1781 a British attack was launched against the Spanish outpost known as the Village, on the eastern shore of Mobile Bay, in which Lieutenant Farmar may have been involved, but the effort came to nought, and the fortifications raised on Gage Hill, above Pensacola, were as yet unfinished when the Spanish fleet appeared off Santa Rosa Island in March. Once past the harbor defenses and ashore with overwhelming forces, Gálvez's advance upon the English position was inexorable. Happily, the town of Pensacola and its civilian population were spared from bombardment or attack. Lieutenant Robert Adolphus Farmar did his part in manning the British defenses; Anne Farmar's husband, Lieutenant Barde, having been released from Mobile on parole, joined other officers in the same situation who left the town and submitted themselves to Gálvez.[12] From mid-April until May 8, the Spanish lines closed upon the British fortifications on Gage Hill. On the latter date a powder explosion in the Queen's Redoubt demolished the center of Campbell's earthwork system, and on May 10, 1781, the Union Jack was lowered and the British capitulated.

The defeated British forces and many civilians began to leave Pensacola about the first of June aboard Spanish transports that deposited them in New York in mid-July. The Farmar family were among those departing. From New York, Mary Farmar, her daughters, and her younger son accompanied Lieutenant Barde to Charleston after he was exchanged and ordered back to duty. The first of Major Robert Farmar's grandchildren, Robert George Barde, was born there on April 1, 1782. That same day, Mrs. Farmar and her younger children took ship for England.[13]

The West Florida Royal Foresters having faded from the military scene, Robert Adolphus Farmar formally associated himself with the 3rd Battalion 60th Foot, in January 1781, while in Pensacola.[14] He was shipped to New York along with the other troops from West Florida, and in September he secured appointment as lieutenant in Captain Thomas Taylor Byrd's company, then stationed at Newtown, Long Island.[15] On December 15, 1782, he was transferred to Colonel Dalling's company under Captain N. F. Lockell and remained at Hampstead, Long Island, until July 3, 1783.[16] It is intriguing to note that during this period young Farmar, barely out of his teens, temporarily reverted to the old English spelling of the family name and signed himself Robert A. Fermor. With the reduction of forces at the end of the American war, Robert Adolphus was reduced to an ensigncy in the 1st Battalion of the 60th Regiment, but in 1787 he recovered his lieutenancy in both regiment and army. He last appears in the *Army List* as a lieutenant on half-pay in the 92nd Regiment as late as 1792.[17]

John Barde left the army on half-pay at the end of the American war and remained in North America, living in Philadelphia briefly, finally settling at Birdsboro, some fifty miles up the Schuylkill River, where he was engaged in the local iron works until his death in 1799.[18] He was joined at Birdsboro by his brother-in-law, Robert Adolphus Farmar, who married in 1792 and brought up a family. Robert lived until some time after 1804, showed an interest in the family inheritance in lands ceded to Spain, but is thought to have been lost at sea while sailing to England.[19]

Of the other children of Major Robert Farmar, Catherine Louisa married and lived in New York. Thomas went to sea. He "made a couple of voyages" with Captain Matthew Forrest in the merchant ship *Mary*, belonging to the international Indian merchants of West Florida, Panton, Leslie & Co. Subsequently, he is said to have entered the Royal Navy and died at sea.[20] Elizabeth Mary, who probably remained with her mother in England until Mrs. Farmar's death, returned to America and, like her brother Robert, sought to recover something from the lands Major Farmar once held.

In 1783 Mrs. Mary Farmar, along with other exiled West Floridians, tried to secure compensation from the British government for her losses in America. She noted that "the whole of this property"—valued at twelve thousand pounds—"came after Major Farmar's Death, to the Widow & her Family." She remarked upon Durnford's destruction of the house in Mobile, certified to be worth six hundred pounds, and added that "the Indians destroyed a great deal of the Property." All having been lost, Mary Farmar declared that "she has nothing in this Country excepting the remains of £300 being money for which she sold her negroes—£150 of which is spent." The Loyalist claims commissioners accepted the facts set forth, but as her losses were suffered in formal warfare and at the hands of the Spanish enemy, they could only conclude, "It is with great Concern that we report . . . that we are not able to extend any Relief to this Lady."[21] Hers was the sad fate of most of the British Mobilians. Mrs. Farmar was granted letters of administration for the major's estate by the Prerogative Court of Canterbury, August 3, 1784, but she does not appear after that date.[22] She remained in England and died sometime before 1799.

Elizabeth Mary Farmar was a determined young woman who undertook in her own person to recover something of Major Farmar's West Florida properties after her mother's death. Through Colonel William Stiell, 60th Regiment, who had served in the colony before it fell to Spain, Elizabeth made contact with the great Anglo-Spanish Indian trader William Panton. Writing on May 31, 1800, from Perdido Cowpens, near Pensacola, Panton offered her what advice he could. "Unless you become a Spanish subject or are disposed to give your hand to some accomplished Spaniard," recovery of her inheritance would be "extremely difficult." "The Spaniards are however a generous people & the object is worth a trial." Panton volunteered the services of his partner John Forbes and urged Elizabeth to draw up a memorial stating her case. She should declare therein "that your parent took the family to England for the purpose of Education but always with a view of returning with you . . . , but that death arrested the good intentions of your Mother while you were all minors." The Farmar heirs might then appeal to the generosity of the Spanish government as "Orphants so peculiarly circumstanced." Panton thought the recovery of lands now controlled by the American government would be considerably more difficult. Although Tom Farmar, her brother, was the only member of the clan whom Panton had ever known, he urged, should she come to Pensacola as had been suggested by a mutual acquaintance, "you must accept of such accomodations as an old Batchelor is able to afford."[23]

Elizabeth and the other heirs made a futile attempt to support their claims by arranging for indirect occupancy in their behalf, and they secured the services of a New York lawyer to prepare their case for the claims commission for the Mississippi Territory in 1804. In spite of grants and deeds of purchase proving Major Farmar's rights under the British crown, the heirs' extensive claims upon property near Natchez and on the Tombecbé and Tensa rivers failed to satisfy the occupancy requirement of the United States.[24]

Elizabeth pursued her mission to the Gulf Coast. Arrived in Mobile, she married a French gentleman, Louis François LeGras de Vaubercey, and was resident in Mobile in 1813 when it became part of the United States.[25] Finally, on March 3, 1839, the United States Congress confirmed the heirs and legal representatives of Robert Farmar in title to some four hundred acres known as the Island, on the west side of the Mobile River and about a mile above the city.[26] Through Elizabeth and her descendants, the Farmars returned to Mobile.

The ghost of the old soldier should rest content. Although it is a long road from the Billopp mansion on the southern tip of Staten Island to Farmar's Bluff on the banks of the Tensa, Robert Farmar might recognize those landmarks in his life today. As an American by birth, he would surely take satisfaction in knowing that one flag flies over them both—as it did when he was major of the 34th Regiment of Foot.

Notes

In citing works in the notes, short titles have generally been used. Frequently cited manuscript collections housed in the Public Record Office, London, have been identified by the following abbreviations:

ADM Admiralty Papers
C.O. Colonial Office Papers
S.P. State Papers
W.O. War Office Papers

Introduction

1. Peter E. Russell, "Redcoats in the Wilderness: British Officers and Irregular Warfare in Europe and America, 1740 to 1760," *William and Mary Quarterly* 35 (1978): 629–52, and Daniel J. Beattie, "The Adaptation of the British Army to Wilderness Warfare, 1755–1763," in *Adapting to Conditions: War and Society in the Eighteenth Century*, ed. Maarten Ultee (Tuscaloosa, Ala., 1986), pp. 56–83, offer useful correctives to the popular view.

2. Most colonial historians have seen the army as a mere tool of imperial policy (assuming there was one). John R. Alden, *General Gage in America* (Baton Rouge, La., 1948) and *John Stuart and the Southern Colonial Frontier* (Ann Arbor, Mich., 1944) tapped the riches of the Gage Papers at the William L. Clements Library, but the military road was mapped by John Shy, whose study of the British army in America placed that body in continental context for the first time. It is illustrative of the problem that his book carries the insinuating title *Toward Lexington: The Role of the British Army in the Coming of the American Revolution* (Princeton, N.J., 1965).

As the writing of history is inevitably subject to revision, Anglophobia has recently re-emerged in the work of such authors as Stephen Saunders Webb, "Army and Em-

pire: English Garrison Government in Britain and America, 1569 to 1763," *William and Mary Quarterly* 35 (1977): 1–31, and Francis Jennings, *Empire of Fortune: Crowns, Colonies, and Tribes in the Seven Years War in America* (New York, 1988). Major Robert Farmar simply does not fit into their version of planned military dictatorship by bloody-minded praetorians.
3. A historical marker commemorating Major Robert Farmar was erected on Highway 225, in Stockton, in 1978 by the Baldwin County Historical Society.

I. The Making of an American Family and A British Army Officer

1. Charles Farmar Billopp, *A History of Thomas and Anne Billopp Farmar* (New York, 1907), pp. 7–8. *Dictionary of National Biography, s.v.* "Fermor." The spelling of the name remained Fermor in England; by the late seventeenth century the Irish branch of the family had accepted the spelling of Farmar or Farmer. As Major Robert Farmar persisted in the orthography of his name, that spelling is used here, except in quotations.
2. Billopp, *Thomas and Anne Billopp Farmar,* p. 9, suggests that Jasper Farmar was a royalist during the civil war, lost much of his property, and was poorly compensated for his loyalty after the Restoration in 1660. Richard and Mary Dunn, in William Penn, *The Papers of William Penn,* ed. Richard Dunn and Mary Dunn (Philadelphia, 1981–), 1:138, n. 164; 2:484–85, n. 11, indicate that he "had been active in the army during the commonwealth" and was "a Cromwellian soldier."
3. Penn, *Papers of William Penn,* 1:113, 115–17.
4. Ibid., 2:659, 484, 3:647; Billopp, *Thomas and Anne Billopp Farmar,* p. 11; James Claypoole, "Extracts from the Letter-book of James Claypoole," *Pennsylvania Magazine of History and Biography* 10 (1886): 403. Lewis D. Cook, "Farmar of Ardavaleine, County Tipperary, Ireland, and of Whitemarsh, Philadelphia County, Pennsylvania," *Pennsylvania Genealogical Magazine* 21 (1956): 101.
5. Penn to Thomas Lloyd, August 6, 1685, Penn Papers, 5:249, Pennsylvania Historical Society, Philadelphia.
6. Major Farmar's will was proved January 2, 1686 (N.S.), and letters of administration issued for the estate of Jasper, Jr., on January 19, 1686 (N.S.): "A Partial List of the Families Who Arrived at Philadelphia between 1682 and 1687," *Pennsylvania Magazine of History and Biography* 8 (1884): 336–37.
7. "A Letter from Doctor More," *Pennsylvania Magazine of History and Biography* 4 (1880): 451–52; Penn Papers, 5:609; Penn, *Papers of William Penn,* 3:131.
8. Penn, *Papers of William Penn,* 2:485; Charles P. Keith, *Chronicles of Pennsylvania* (Philadelphia, 1917), pp. 143, 415, 419, 446, 504–5, 560; Gregory B. Keen, "The Descendants of Joran Kyn, the Founder of Upland," *Pennsylvania Magazine of History and Biography* 4 (1880): 354n.; Howard M. Jenkins, "The Family of William Penn," *Pennsylvania Magazine of History and Biography* 21 (1897): 335–36.
9. Penn Papers, 6:729.
10. Penn to Thomas Farmar, June 20, 1700, Penn Papers, 8:493. Penn, *Papers of William Penn,* 3:594, 628n. See also William H. Benedict, "Thomas Farmar, First Mayor of New Brunswick, N.J.," *Proceedings of the New Jersey Historical Society* 13

(1926): 45–51. Gary B. Nash, *Quakers and Politics: Pennsylvania, 1681–1726* (Princeton, N.J., 1968), p. 233n.

11. Penn to Evans, August 9, 1703, Penn Papers, 10:1077.

12. Keith, *Chronicles of Pennsylvania,* p. 442; Benedict, "Thomas Farmar," p. 46.

13. Billopp, *Thomas and Anne Billopp Farmar,* pp. 33–39; Cook, "Farmar of Ardavaleine," pp. 115–17; Orra E. Monette, *First Settlers of ye Plantations of Piscataway and Woodbridge Olde East New Jersey, 1664–1714* (Los Angeles, 1930), pp. 91, 94, 114–15, 339, 446; John P. Wall, *The Chronicles of New Brunswick, New Jersey, 1667–1931* (New Brunswick, N.J., 1931), pp. 19–23; Ira K. Morris, *Morris's Memorial History of Staten Island, New York* (New York, 1898), 1:137; John E. Pomfret, *Colonial New Jersey* (Princeton, N.J., 1973), pp. 136, 150; Eugene R. Sheridan, *Lewis Morris* (Syracuse, N.Y., 1981), p. 74; William H. Benedict, *New Brunswick in History* (New Brunswick, N.J., 1925), pp. 21–22, 27, 30–32, 48; Donald L. Kemmerer, *Path to Freedom: The Struggle for Colonial Self-Government in New Jersey, 1703–1776* (Princeton, N.J., 1940), pp. 87, 92, 94, 102–4, 359–61. Thomas L. Purvis, "'High-Born, Long-Recorded Families': Social Origins of New Jersey Assemblymen, 1703 to 1776," *William and Mary Quarterly* 37 (1980): 592–615. The most recent analyses of colonial New Jersey politics, Thomas L. Purvis, *Proprietors, Patronage, and Paper Money* (New Brunswick, N.J., 1986), and Michael C. Batinski, *The New Jersey Assembly, 1738–1775* (Lanham, Md., 1987), confirm Thomas Farmar's tendency to side with the governors' parties. Batinski, p. 264, adds, "Evidence suggests that he died insane."

14. Benedict, *New Brunswick,* pp. 30–32; Morris, *Memorial History,* 1:138–42.

15. G.E.C., *The Complete Peerage* (London, 1945), 10:573–74; Billopp, *Thomas and Anne Billopp Farmar,* pp. 8, 101; *Dictionary of National Biography,* s.v. "Fermor."

16. New Jersey, *Documents Relating to the Colonial History of New Jersey* (Trenton, N.J., 1891), 15:84ff.

17. On the expedition in general see Herbert W. Richmond, *The Navy in the War of 1739–48* (Cambridge, England, 1920), 1:33–35, 102–23; John W. Fortescue, *A History of the British Army* (London, 1910), 2:57–79; William Laird Clowes, *The Royal Navy* (London, 1898), 3:68–80; John Creswell, *Generals and Admirals: The Story of Amphibious Command* (Westport, Conn., 1976), pp. 38–54; Joseph A. Devine, "The British North American Colonies in the War of 1739–1748," Ph.D. dissertation, University of Virginia, 1968.

18. New Jersey, *Documents Relating to the Colonial History of New Jersey* (Trenton, N.J., 1891), 15:112–17; W. Y. Baldry and A. S. White, "Gooch's American Regiment of Foot, 1739–1742," *Journal of the Society for Army Historical Research* 16 (1937): 235–39.

19. Pennsylvania, *Minutes of the Provincial Council of Pennsylvania* (Harrisburg, Pa., 1851), 4:440.

20. New Jersey, *Documents,* 6:99–101; 15:133–35, 169, 183; New Jersey, *Archives of the State of New Jersey,* 1st ser. (Paterson, N.J., 1895), 12:35–46; Lewis Morris, *The Papers of Lewis Morris,* ed. William A. Whitehead, Collections of the New Jersey Historical Society (Newark, 1852), 4:116, 148; Edgar J. Fisher, *New Jersey as a Royal Province, 1738 to 1776* (New York, 1911), pp. 320–22; Kemmerer, *Path to Freedom,* pp. 160–62; Devine, "British North American Colonies," pp. 30–41, 52.

21. New Jersey, *Documents,* 15:129–33; Morris, *Papers,* pp. 102–3, 105, 107, 148.

22. Morris, *Papers*, pp. 108, 114–17; Devine, "British North American Colonies," pp. 61–64; Albert Harkness, Jr., "Americanism and Jenkins' Ear," *Mississippi Valley Historical Review* 37 (1950): 71.
23. Commission Book, 1744–46, W.O. 25/21.
24. Estimate for H.M. Regiment of Foot raised in America, October 6, 1741, W.O. 24/199; *An Account of the Expedition to Carthagena* (London, 1743), pp. 38, 55; Baldry and White, "Gooch's American Regiment," p. 237.
25. Tobias Smollett, "An Account of the Expedition against Carthagena," in *The Works of Tobias Smollett* (New York, 1901), 12:212.
26. *Account of the Expedition*, p. 38.
27. Smollett, *Works*, 12:215.
28. *Gentleman's Magazine* 11 (July 1741): 385.
29. *Gentleman's Magazine* 14 (April 1744): 209.
30. *Account of the Expedition*, pp. 55–56; *Gentleman's Magazine* 13 (April 1743): 207. Admiral Vernon had advised General Wentworth, "The men you keep most in action will have best health and best courage, by preserving their bodies and spirits from the rust of idleness." Edward Vernon, *The Vernon Papers*, ed. E. M. Ranft, Navy Records Society Publications, no. 99 (London, 1958), p. 109. It is surprising to encounter contemporary derogatory judgments repeated by Sir John Fortescue: "The twelve hundred Americans who still survived . . . were in fact little better than an encumbrance." But then Sir John was also made nervous by the "Irish papists." Fortescue, *British Army*, 2:72, 78.
31. *A Journal of the Expedition to Carthagena . . . in answer to . . . An Account of the Expedition* (London, 1744), pp. 38, 55.
32. Smollett, *Works*, 12:216.
33. Devine, "British North American Colonies," p. 91.
34. *Boston Weekly News-letter*, June 25–July 2, 1742, no. 1,945; New Jersey, *Archives*, 1st ser., 12:96–97.
35. Devine, "British North American Colonies," p. 92; Harkness, "Americanism and Jenkins' Ear," p. 80 n. 92.
36. Devine, "British North American Colonies," pp. 93–95. Estimates of survivors of the American regiment range from about three hundred to seven hundred. Total casualties for the expedition came to 70 percent, mostly caused by yellow fever. John R. McNeill, "The Ecological Basis of Warfare in the Caribbean, 1700–1804," in *Adapting to Conditions*, ed. Ultee, p. 35.
37. Harkness, "Americanism and Jenkins' Ear," p. 84; Morris, *Papers*, pp. 148–49, 157.
38. New Jersey, *Documents*, 15:237–38; Kemmerer, *Path to Freedom*, pp. 163–64.
39. Morris, *Papers*, pp. 148–49, 157; Harkness, "Americanism and Jenkins' Ear," p. 84; E. Alfred Jones, "The American Regiment in the Carthagena Expedition," *Virginia Magazine of History and Biography* 30 (1922): 14; William A. Foote, "The Pennsylvania Men of the American Regiment," *Pennsylvania Magazine of History and Biography* 87 (1963): 34; John Farmar's date of rank is given as August 27, in W.O. 25/20:306; August 25 in W.O. 25/21.
40. Proceedings General Officers, Horse Guards, May 11–12, 16, 1743; May 1, 1744: W.O. 71/7; Devine, "British North American Colonies," pp. 99–100.

41. Commission Books 1744–46: W.O. 25/21; W.O. 25/91. In addition to Farmar, in 1744 the 19th recruited from Gooch's regiment Ensign William Ogilvie, Ensign William Murray, and Lieutenant William Brown (who was broken late in 1746). George Daniel took half-pay in South Carolina until 1748, returned to England, and joined the 19th as captain in 1756. Rowland Phillips, a British officer of the 40th Foot who joined Gooch's regiment in 1741, became major of the 19th in 1756. M. L. Ferrar, *Officers of the Green Howards* (London, 1920), pp. 39–40.

Douglas E. Leach, "The Cartagena Expedition, 1740–42, and Anglo-American Relations," in *Adapting to Conditions*, ed. Ultee, pp. 43–55, and *Roots of Conflict: British Armed Forces and Colonial Americans, 1677–1763* (Chapel Hill, N.C., 1986), argues forcefully the growing distrust between Englishmen and Americans, their "mutually unfavorable perceptions," at this date; he fails to consider the significant exceptions to his conclusion noted above.

42. W.O. 64/10; *Army Lists*; F. Brodigan, *Historical Records of the Twenty-eighth North Gloucestershire Regiment* (London, 1884), pp. 12–22; Richard Cannon, *Historical Records of the Twenty–second, the Cheshire Regiment of Foot* (London, 1849), pp. 8–11.

II. King George's Wars

1. A *List of the General and Field-Officers* (London, 1754–), hereafter cited as *Army List*.

2. The standard regimental histories are Richard Cannon, *Historical Record of the Nineteenth Regiment of Foot* (London, 1848); M. L. Ferrar, *Historical Record of the Green Howards* (London, 1911); Geoffrey Powell, *The Green Howards* (London, 1968). See also John Pine, A *Representation of the Cloathing of His Majesty's Household, and of All the Forces upon the Establishments of Great Britain and Ireland* (London, 1742), a very rare hand-colored folio, War Office Library, London. The Green Howards' Regimental Museum, Richmond, Yorkshire, contains many relics but few records for this period.

3. "The Battle of Fontenoy," *Journal of the Society for Army Historical Research* 6 (1927): 95.

4. Fortescue, *British Army*, 2:111–21; Powell, *The Green Howards*, p. 29; Rex Whitworth, *Field Marshal Lord Ligonier* (Oxford, 1958), pp. 99–103; Evan Charteris, *William Augustus Duke of Cumberland: His Early Life and Times* (London, 1913), pp. 178–91 and 365 (where Howard's regiment is improperly identified).

5. C. T. Atkinson, "Jenkins' Ear, the Austrian Succession War, and the 'Forty-five," *Journal of the Society for Army Historical Research* 22 (1943–44): 291–92, 294–96; S.P. 41/17.

6. Fortescue, *British Army*, 2:153–55; Whitworth, *Field Marshal Lord Ligonier*, 135–42; Powell, *The Green Howards*, 30–31.

7. Charles Colville, "Military Memoirs of Lieut.-General the Hon. Charles Colville," *Journal of the Society for Army Historical Research* 27 (1949): 103.

8. *Gentleman's Magazine* 17 (July 1747): 308, 317–18; Fortescue, *British Army*, 2:158–63; Whitworth, *Field Marshal Lord Ligonier*, 150–55; Charteris, *Cumberland*, 311–18; Powell, *The Green Howards*, p. 31; Colville, "Memoirs," pp. 103–4, 145–49.

9. Colville, "Memoirs," p. 81; Whitworth, *Field Marshal Lord Ligonier,* p. 163; Powell, *The Green Howards,* p. 15; Ferrar, *Officers of the Green Howards,* p. 42.
10. Fortescue, *British Army,* 2:613; Atkinson, "Jenkins' Ear," p. 298.
11. *Green Howards' Gazette* 42 (1934): 84; W.O. 27/1, 27/2, 71/51:152.
12. Manuscript Letterbook of Lord George Beauclerk, National Library of Scotland, microfilm copy National Army Museum, London. Returns of the 19th Regiment W.O. 17/21, 17/121; Beauclerk to War Office, April 19, May 7, 1757, W.O. 613/107. Extracts from the "Newcastle Journal," *Green Howards' Gazette* 42 (1934): 84, 102–3.
13. W.O. 27/6. On army routines see J. A. Houlding, *Fit for Service: The Training of the British Army, 1715–1795* (Oxford, 1981).
14. Typescript letters of Nicholas Delacherois, December 16 and 22, 1757, National Army Museum, London.
15. Beauclerk to Holdernesse, September 12, 1758, May 26, 1759, and generally between October 1759 and February 1760, Beauclerk Letterbook.
16. Beauclerk to Barrington, August 14, 1760, Beauclerk Letterbook.
17. Beauclerk to Treasury, July 28, 1759, Beauclerk Letterbook.
18. Beauclerk to Ligonier, August 21, 1759, Beauclerk Letterbook.
19. Beauclerk to Barrington, December 29, 1757, March 28, 1758, Beauclerk Letterbook; Whitworth, *Field Marshal Lord Ligonier,* p. 238. Rickson's formal notification, with rank of lieutenant colonel, was not issued until January 15, 1760: Beauclerk to Barrington, January 22, 1760, Beauclerk Letterbook; W.O. 1/614:275.
20. Beauclerk to Barrington, March 23, April 8, April 22, 1758, Beauclerk Letterbook. Farmar's memorial does not appear here or in the War Office correspondence. Douglas secured his appointment; the 2nd Battalion 19th became the 66th Regiment.
21. Beauclerk to Barrington and Ligonier, August 16, 1759, Beauclerk Letterbook.
22. Farmar to Beauclerk, October 23, 1760, W.O. 1/614.
23. Beauclerk to Barrington, October 23, 1760 and Barrington's endorsement, W.O. 1/614.
24. Lumisden to Beauclerk, October 18, 1760, W.O. 1/614; W.O. 2/33.
25. Beauclerk to Townshend, March 31, 1761, W.O. 1/615.
26. Beauclerk to Townshend, July 2, 1761, citing Townshend's letter of June 26, W.O. 1/615.
27. Townshend to Farmar, May 28, 1761, W.O. 4/64. Farmar took rank in the regiment from June 2, 1761, *Army List;* W.O. 25/112.
28. Townshend to Lieutenant Colonel John Reed, October 26, 1761, W.O. 4/66.
29. Douglas Sutherland, *Tried and Valiant: The History of the Border Regiment* (London, 1972), pp. 15–34. See also George Noakes, *A Historical Account of the Services of the 34th and 55th Regiments* (Carlisle, 1875).
30. "Uniforms of the Thirty-fourth Regiment of Foot from 1702 to 1914," *Border Magazine* 2 (1951): 79–82.
31. W.O. 27/6.
32. Fortescue, *British Army,* 2:530–31; Powell, *The Green Howards,* pp. 33–34; Lieutenant Hamilton, "A Brief Journal of the Reduction of Belleisle, Anno 1761," manuscript notebook, National Army Museum, London. F. J. Hebbert, "The Belle-Ile Expedition of 1761," *Journal of the Society for Army Historical Research,* 64 (1986): 81–93.

33. Hamilton, "Brief Journal"; Muster rolls, 34th Regiment, W.O. 17/143. In the curious way of the small eighteenth-century British army, two other future Mobilians saw action at Belle Isle: Elias Durnford, a newly fledged engineer, and John Lorimer, surgeon of the 97th Foot and subsequently surgeon to the garrison. S.P. 41/24:267.
34. Robert Beatson, *Naval and Military Memoirs of Great Britain from 1728 to 1783* (London, 1804), 3:395; David Syrett, *The Siege and Capture of Havana, 1762*, Navy Records Society Publications, no. 114 (London, 1970), pp. 53–54. Farmar was officially the commanding officer of the 34th Regiment after October 24, 1762, when Lieutenant Colonel Reed was detached by Lord Albemarle. W.O. 17/143.
35. John Entick, *The General History of the Late War* (London, 1764), 5:375–78, draws upon the journal of an officer evidently familiar with this action and signing himself "G.C." (Carleton?); he credits Farmar with the direction of the defense of the batteries. Sonia Keppel, *Three Brothers at Havana* (Salisbury, England, 1981), p. 70, drawing upon family papers and Thomas Mante's *History of the Late War* (London, 1772), gives Farmar credit for repulsing the attack after Carleton was wounded. Beatson, *Naval and Military Memoirs*, 2:557, cites Patrick McKellar's diary (as does Syrett, *Siege and Capture*, pp. xxxi, 258–59) and gives the credit to Carleton, who was indeed wounded while pursuing the enemy. It would appear that Chief Engineer McKellar's knowledge was limited to another part of the field.
36. Henry Miller Lydenberg, ed., *Archibald Robertson, Lieutenant-General Royal Engineers: His Diaries and Sketches in America* (New York, 1930), p. 62. Syrett, using Spanish sources and following McKellar, sets the attacking force at 1,300, of whom 32 were killed and "an infinite number wounded," British casualties at about 50 (*Siege and Capture*, p. xxxi).
37. Syrett, *Siege and Capture*, pp. xxii–xxxiii; see also Francis Russell Hart, *The Siege of Havana, 1762* (Boston, 1931); Tom Pocock, "The Capture of Havana, 1762," *History Today* 12 (1962): 580–86.
38. W.O. 34/55.
39. S. G. P. Ward, "The Letters of Captain Nicholas Delacherois, 9th Regiment," *Journal of the Society for Army Historical Research* 51 (1973): 8–9; Hart, *Siege of Havana*, p. 48.
40. Albemarle-Amherst correspondence, W.O. 34/55. The considerable ill feeling engendered by Albemarle's share of the prize money, £122,697.10.6, has clouded his reputation; a rather better picture of the man emerges from his correspondence. McNeill, "Ecological Basis of Warfare," p. 36, concludes that 40 percent of the 14,000 British troops in the Havana expedition lost their lives, mostly to disease.
41. Albert C. Bates, ed., *The Two Putnams: Israel and Rufus in the Havana Expedition, 1762, and in the Mississippi River Exploration, 1772–73* (Hartford, Conn., 1931), pp. 101, 106.
42. Beatson, *Naval and Military Memoirs*, 3:407.

III. Mobile, 1763–1765

1. W.O. 2/33; Secretary at War to Keppel, May 10, 1763, W.O. 4/72; Egremont to Commanding Officer, May 21, 1763, in *Mississippi Provincial Archives, 1763–1766*,

English Dominion, vol. 1, ed. Dunbar Rowland (Nashville, Tenn., 1911), pp. 131–32 (cited hereafter as *M.P.A.*).

2. Keppel to Amherst, July 18, 1763, W.O. 34/55; Keppel to Farmar, July 19, 1763 *M.P.A.*, pp. 128–29; Farmar to Ellis, August 31, 1763, Mississippi Provincial Archives English Dominion (transcripts), 1:247 (cited hereafter as M.P.A.E.D.); Journal of Colonel Christopher French, Library of Congress, Washington, D.C. The limited documentation available to Clinton N. Howard, "The Military Occupation of British West Florida, 1763," *Florida Historical Quarterly* 17 (1938–39): 181–99, detracts from its utility; Robert L. Gold, *Borderland Empires in Transition: The Triple-Nation Transfer of Florida* (Carbondale, Ill., 1969), pp. 106–13, is better. It is amusing to find a regimental historian, Douglas Sutherland (*Tried and Valiant,* pp. 36–37), declaring that the 34th was "extremely lucky" to go to Florida in 1763—"they were stationed for four years in the pleasant and fertile land of West Florida."

3. Farmar to Ellis, Kingston, August 31, 1763; Lieutenant Colonel David Erskine to Ellis, August 10, 1763, M.P.A.E.D., 1:247, 236. Farmar to Amherst, December 9, 1763, Jeffrey Amherst Papers, William L. Clements Library, University of Michigan, Ann Arbor, is his earliest version of the occupation of Mobile; it is much the same as Farmar to Secretary at War, January 24, 1764, W.O. 1/49, printed in *M.P.A.*, pp. 7–17, which is cited hereafter for the reader's convenience. Charles L. Price and Claude C. Sturgill, "The Role of the British Navy in the Landing in West Florida in 1763 as Revealed in the Letters of Captain William Bayne," *Alabama Review* 30 (1977): 54–55, adds new information. In contrast to Farmar's financial situation, Prevost, who was ordered to Pensacola before Keppel left Havana, was provided with £3,000 for expenses. Howard, "Military Occupation," p. 183. On Farmar's proclamation see D. C. McMurtrie, ed., *A Broadside Issued at Mobile* (privately printed, 1939).

4. Log, *Stag,* ADM 51/498; Prevost to Amherst, August 31, 1763, Amherst Papers; Price and Sturgill, "Role of the Navy," pp. 59–61; Carl A. Brasseaux, *A Comparative View of French Louisiana, 1699 and 1762* (Lafayette, La., 1979), p. 102.

5. Log, *Stag,* ADM 51/498; Farmar to DeVelle, October 2, 1763, *M.P.A.*, pp. 58–59; Price and Sturgill, "Role of the Navy," pp. 59–61.

6. Farmar to Amherst, December 9, 1763, Amherst Papers; Log, *Stag,* ADM 51/498; Kerlérec to Farmar, October 2, 1763, *M.P.A.*, pp. 54–58; D'Abbadie to Farmar, October 4, 1763, *M.P.A.*, pp. 34–35; DeVelle to Farmar, October 14, 1763, *M.P.A.*, p. 34; Farmar to Secretary of War, January 24, 1764, *M.P.A.*, pp. 9–11; Marc de Villiers du Terrage, *The Last Years of French Louisiana,* ed. Hosea Phillips, Carl A. Brasseaux, and Glenn R. Conrad (Lafayette, La., 1982), p. 185 n. 28. Price and Sturgill, "Role of the Navy," p. 57, term Farmar's complaint against DeVelle "grossly unfair," and rightly attribute delay in occupying Mobile to "the naval obstacles to the landing." Of the latter there can be no doubt, but neither, in view of the evidence he had in hand, can Farmar's natural distrust of French men and motives be faulted; he had every reason to get his men ashore as soon as he could. Peter J. Hamilton's romantic portrayal of Highlanders with bagpipes occupying Mobile, led by James Robertson, is entirely imaginary: see *Colonial Mobile* (rpt. ed., University, Ala., 1976), p. 217.

7. Report of the State of Fort Charlotte, November 30, 1763, *M.P.A.*, pp. 19–20. Robertson's Report, March 8, 1764, C.O. 5/83.

8. Kerlérec to Farmar, October 2, 1763, *M.P.A.*, p. 56; Farmar to Secretary at War, January 24, 1764, *M.P.A.*, p. 15.
9. *M.P.A.*, p. 32.
10. See D'Abbadie's Journal in Brasseaux, *Comparative View*, pp. 102–3.
11. Robert R. Rea, "Lieutenant Colonel James Robertson's Mission to the Floridas, 1763," *Florida Historical Quarterly* 53 (1974): 33–43. Robertson remarked of the Indians, "French manners are in vogue . . . a Chief bows like a dancing Master, kisses both your cheeks and makes you a french compliment." C.O. 5/83.
12. D'Abbadie to Farmar, October 4, 1763, *M.P.A.*, pp. 34–35.
13. Farmar to Secretary at War, January 24, 1764, *M.P.A.*, pp. 9–10; Rea, "Robertson's Mission," p. 44.
14. Farmar to D'Abbadie, November 9, 1763, *M.P.A.*, p. 36; Villiers du Terrage, *Last Years*, p. 198; A Counsel held with the Chacta Nation (with seals), Gage Papers, American Ser., 137, William L. Clements Library, University of Michigan, Ann Arbor; Robertson to Amherst, November 15, 1763, Amherst Papers; *M.P.A.*, pp. 83–91; D'Abbadie to Kerlérec, November 6, 1763, quoted in Daniel H. Thomas, "Fort Toulouse," *Alabama Historical Quarterly* 22 (1960): 204–5.
15. Farmar to Secretary at War, January 24, 1764, *M.P.A.*, pp. 10–12.
16. Robert R. Rea, "The Trouble at Tombeckby," *Alabama Review* 21 (1968): 21.
17. Thomas, "Fort Toulouse," pp. 204–6; Rea, "Robertson's Mission," pp. 45–46; Farmar to Ellis, January 24, 1764, W.O. 1/49.
18. Farmar to Ellis, January 24, 1764, W.O. 1/49 and *M.P.A.*, p. 9; Robert R. Rea, "A New Letter from Mobile, 1763," *Alabama Review* 22 (1969): 230–37.
19. Robert R. Rea, "Assault on the Mississippi: The Loftus Expedition, 1764," *Alabama Review* 26 (1973): 174–77; Rea, "Robertson's Mission," pp. 46–47.
20. Farmar to Secretary at War, January 24, 1764, *M.P.A.*, p. 16.
21. Cecil Johnson, *British West Florida, 1763–1783* (New Haven, Conn., 1943), pp. 6–7, 14–23.
22. Robin F. A. Fabel, *Bombast and Broadsides: The Lives of George Johnstone* (Tuscaloosa, Ala., 1987); Alden, *General Gage in America*; Robert R. Rea, "Outpost of Empire: David Wedderburn at Mobile," *Alabama Review* 7 (1954): 217–18.
23. Rea, "New Letter," p. 236.
24. *M.P.A.*, p. 31.
25. Farmar to Secretary at War, April 7, August 1, October 2, 1764, *M.P.A.*, pp. 116–22; Farmar to Gage, May 7, 1764, Gage Papers. Milo B. Howard, Jr., and Robert R. Rea, *The Memoir Justificatif of the Chevalier Montault de Monberaut* (University, Ala., 1965), pp. 15–22.
26. D'Abbadie to Gage, December 24, 1763, Gage Papers; Halifax to Johnstone, May 12, 1764, *M.P.A.*, pp. 147–49; Gold, *Borderland Empires*, p. 63.
27. Richard J. Hooker, ed., *The Carolina Backcountry on the Eve of the Revolution: The Journal . . . of Charles Woodmason, Anglican Itinerant* (Chapel Hill, N.C., 1953), p. 82.
28. The Case of Richard Jones in Johnstone to Gage, January 2, 1765, Gage Papers. Farmar to Secretary at War, December 29, 1764. State Papers Military, 41/25.
29. The Case of Charles Conner, January 2, 1764, in Johnstone to Gage, January 2, 1765, Gage Papers.

30. Farmar to Gage, February 14, 1764, Gage Papers; Farmar to Secretary at War, December 29, 1764, S.P. 41/25; An Impartial Relation of the Behaviour of Major Robert Farmar . . . with regards to Daniel Ward, Merchant, in Johnstone to Gage, January 2, 1765, Gage Papers.
31. Amherst to Commanding Officer, August 24, 1763, Amherst Papers; Gage to Farmar, May 7, 1764, Gage Papers.
32. Gage to D'Abbadie, March 20, 1764; Gage to Farmar, March 31, 1764 Gage Papers; Farmar to Amherst, November 17, 1763, Amherst Papers.
33. J. Farmar to Gage, February 14, 1764; Gage to Farmar, March 31, May 7, 1764; Gage to J. Farmar, May 7, 1764, Gage Papers. War Office to ______, June 9, 1764, S.P. 41/25.
34. Farmar to Secretary at War, April 7, 1764, *M.P.A.*, pp. 116–17; Farmar to Gage, April 17, May 7, 1764, Gage Papers.
35. Farmar to Secretary at War, March 2, April 7, 1764, *M.P.A.*, pp. 115–16; Farmar to Gage, March 29, 1764, Gage Papers.
36. Farmar to Gage, August 7, 1764, Gage Papers; Farmar to Secretary at War, August 1, September 15, October 2, 1764, *M.P.A.*, pp. 119–20. See also Robert R. Rea, "Graveyard for Britons: West Florida, 1763–81," *Florida Historical Quarterly* 47 (1969). Johnstone described the "disorder" at Mobile as "something in effect like a Plague." Three officers from Pensacola who visited Mobile died of the fever; all who went to Mobile caught it. *M.P.A.*, p. 169.
37. Loftus to Gage, April 19, 1764; Farmar to Gage, April 3, 1764, Gage Papers; Rea, "Assault on the Mississippi," pp. 173–93.
38. Farmar to Gage, April 17, 1764; Gage to Farmar, June 14, 21, 1764; Gage to Stuart, June 19, 1764, Gage Papers; Rea, "Assault on the Mississippi," pp. 189–92.
39. Farmar to Stuart, March 5, 1764; Stuart to Gage, May 20, 1764; Loftus to Gage, May 20, August 17, 1764; Farmar to Gage, August 20, 1764, Gage Papers.
40. Campbell to Gage, August 20, December 10, 1764; Campbell to Farmar, October 29, 1764; Farmar to Gage, August 7, 1764; Farmar to The Mortar, etc., August 18, 1764, Gage Papers.
41. Stuart to Gage, October 12, November 19, 1764; Stuart to Farmar, October 31, 1764, Gage Papers.
42. Stuart to Gage, November 19, 1764; Stuart to Farmar, November 1, 3, 1764; Charles Stuart to John Stuart, November 10, 16, 17, 19, 1764; Gage to Farmar and Loftus, August 1, 1764, Gage Papers.
43. Johnstone to Farmar, October 25, November 2, 1764, Gage Papers.
44. Farmar to Johnstone, November 9, 1764, Gage Papers.
45. Farmar to Gage, December 21, 1764, Gage Papers.
46. Ibid.
47. Johnstone to Farmar, November 15, 1764; Farmar to Johnstone, n.d. [November, 1764], Gage Papers.
48. Johnstone to Farmar, November 29, 1764, Gage Papers.
49. Minutes of Council, December 14, 1764, Gage papers. There seems no reason to doubt the tenor of this report, although Loftus and Lind refused to attest to its ac-

curacy. Johnstone to Loftus and Lind, and their replies December 22, 1764, Gage Papers.

50. Farmar to Gage, December 21, 1764, and enclosures, Gage Papers.

51. Farmar to Gage, December 24 and 27, 1764; Johnstone to Farmar, December 23, 1764, Gage Papers.

52. Johnstone to Farmar, December 26, 1764, Gage Papers.

53. Loftus to Gage, April 10, 1765; Johnstone to Gage, January 2, April 12, 1765, Gage Papers.

54. Johnstone to Gage, January 2, 1765, Gage Papers.

55. Farmar to Gage, January 5, 1765, Gage Papers; W.O. 1/6:118.

56. Johnstone to Conway, October 24, 1765, M.P.A.E.D., 1:293.

57. Campbell to Gage, December 31, 1764, Pittman to Gage, January 6 and 8, 1765; Johnstone to Gage, January 2, 1765, Macpherson to Johnstone, n.d.; Johnstone's departure dated by Farmar to Gage, February 10, 1765, Gage Papers.

58. Farmar to Gage, December 24, 1764, Gage Papers.

59. Johnstone to Lindsay, December 10, 1765; Minutes of a meeting, January 7, 1765; Johnstone to Farmar, January 22, 1765, Gage Papers.

60. Brasseaux, *French Louisiana*, pp. 131–35; Villiers du Terrage, *Last Years*, pp. 228–30.

61. Farmar to Gage, December 21, 1764, Gage Papers.

62. Farmar to Gage, January 17, 1765; Stuart to Gage, March 19, 1765, Gage Papers. Stuart considered D'Abbadie's death a blessing.

63. Farmar to Gage, December 24, 1764, January 17, February 10, 1765; Campbell to Gage, February 2, 1765, Gage Papers.

64. Johnstone to Farmar, January 7, 1765; Farmar to Johnstone, January 13, 1765, Gage Papers.

65. Gage to Farmar, September 26, November 26, 1764, Gage Papers.

66. Farmar to Gage, December 21, 1764, Gage Papers.

67. Gage to Farmar, February 16, 1765, Gage Papers.

68. Gage to Farmar, February 17, 18, 1765; Gage to Johnstone, February 19, 1765; Gage to Loftus, February 19, 1765, Gage Papers; Gage to Secretary at War, February 23, 1765, W.O. 1/6:120.

69. Farmar to Gage, March 2, 1765, Gage Papers.

70. Johnstone to Gage, April 10, 1765, Gage Papers.

71. Farmar to Wegg, April 14, 1765; Wegg to Hillsborough, September 27, 1770, M.P.A.E.D., 4:493–98, 503–4; Farmar to Gage, March 11, 1765, W.O. 1/6:191. Johnstone soon removed Wegg as attorney general.

72. Farmar to Gage, March 11, 1765; Wedderburn to Wainwright, March 2, 7, 1765; Macpherson-Farmar correspondence, March 7–9, 1765, Gage Papers.

73. Johnstone to Gage, April 10, 1765, Gage Papers; Rea, "Outpost of Empire," pp. 217–32.

74. Wedderburn to Alexander Wedderburn, April 14, 1765, Wedderburn Papers, William L. Clements Library, University of Michigan, Ann Arbor; Rea, "Outpost of Empire," p. 223.

75. Farmar to Wedderburn, March 2, 1765; Wainwright's affidavit, March 7, 1765; Wedderburn to Gage, April 9, 1765, with enclosures, Gage Papers.
76. Farmar to Gage, March 21, 1765, Gage Papers.
77. Ross to Farmar, February 21, 1765; Pittman to Farmar, March 8, 1765; Farmar to Gage, March 24, 1765, Gage Papers.
78. Johnstone to Farmar, March 20, 1765; Farmar to Johnstone, March 21, 1765; Stuart to Farmar, March 22, 1765, Gage Papers.
79. Farmar to Gage, March 2, March 30, 1765; J. Farmar to Gage, April 8, 1765; Blackwell to Gage, April 21, 1765, Gage Papers. Blackwell complained that both Farmar and Wedderburn threatened him because he withheld funds from the regiments.
80. Johnstone to Farmar, March 20, 1765; Stuart to Gage, April 11, 1765, Gage Papers. Proceedings of the Congress, *M.P.A.*, pp. 215–55.
81. Gauterais to Farmar, March 19, 1765; Sinnott to Farmar, March 2, 19, 1765; Farmar to Gage, April 29, 1765; St. Ange to ______, April 28, 1765, Gage Papers.
82. Farmar to Gage, April 13, 25, 29, 1765; contracts, April 20, 1765, Gage Papers.
83. Farmar to Gage, April 10, 13, 1765; Answers made by Major Farmar, Gage Papers.
84. Gage to Johnstone, April 18, 1765, Gage to Bouquet, May 15, 23, 1765; Gage to Farmar, May 23, 1765, Gage Papers.

IV. Up the Mississippi to the Illinois

1. Wedderburn to Gage, May 7, 1765; Farmar to Gage, May 16, 1765; Farmar to Stuart, May 31, 1765, Gage Papers. Farmar paid £215.11.9 for *Alexander* and £280.14.9½ for *Polly*, Treasury Papers, T.1/440:110–11, Public Record Office, London.
2. Farmar to Stuart, May 31, 1765; Aubry to Pittman, May 15, 1765, Gage Papers.
3. Farmar to Gage, May 16, June 1, 1765, Gage Papers. Farmar memorial and Aubry's reply, May 23, 26, 1765, in *The Critical Period, 1763–1765*, ed. Clarence W. Alvord and Clarence W. Carter, Illinois Historical Collections, vol. 10 (Springfield, Ill., 1915), pp. 498–99, 512–13. Robert R. Rea, "Military Deserters from British West Florida," *Louisiana History* 9 (1968): 124–27.
4. Farmar to Gage, June 1, 1765; Wedderburn to Gage, July 15, 1765, Gage Papers; Accounts, Treasury Papers, T.1/448:276; Rea, "Military Deserters," p. 127. Muster rolls of the 34th Regiment record twenty-four more desertions between New Orleans and Natchez. W.O. 17/143.
5. Farmar to Gage, June 21, 1765, Gage Papers. Fraser to Gage, June 17, 1765, in *Critical Period*, ed. Alvord and Carter, p. 519. If Farmar's statement that he had "a passage of five months and five days" is precisely accurate (Farmar to Treasury, December 16, 1765), he left New Orleans on June 28 or, as reported by a New Orleans merchant, on June 29 (Wedderburn to Gage, July 15, 1765, Gage Papers).
6. "Journal of the Proceedings of His Majesty's 22nd Regiment up the River Mississippi," Library of Congress; see also Gerald O. Haffner, "Major Arthur Loftus' Journal of

the Proceedings of His Majesty's Twenty-second Regiment up the River Mississippi in 1764," *Louisiana History* 20 (1979): 325–34.

7. Philip Pittman, The *Present State of the European Settlements on the Missisippi,* ed. Robert R. Rea (Gainesville, Fla., 1973), p. 5.

8. Robertson to Gage, September 2, 1765, Gage Papers. At the end of August, hostile Alabama and Houma Indians plundered Robertson's camp at the Iberville and forced him to flee to New Orleans.

9. Campbell to Gage, June 20, 1765; Farmar to Gage, July 21, 1765; Pittman to Gage, July 22, 1765, Gage Papers.

10. Farmar to J. Stuart, December 16, 1765, C.O. 5/67:33–35.

11. Robertson to Bouquet, September 4, 1765, Gage Papers; Accounts, Treasury Papers, T.1/448:263; Pittman, *Present State,* p. 35.

12. Farmar to Gage, August 12, 1765; Pittman to Gage, August 17, 1765, Gage Papers. Farmar to Ellis, August 12, 1765; Farmar to Gage, August 12, 1765, W.O. 1/6:531, 265; Pittman, *Present State,* pp. 37–39.

13. Proceedings of a Regimental Court Martial, August 4, 1765, Gage Papers.

14. Farmar to Ellis, August 12, 1765; Farmar to Gage, August 12, 1765, W.O. 1/6:265, 531.

15. Campbell to Gage, August 16, 1765, Gage Papers.

16. Ibid.

17. Lt. Ford's Remarks and Journal in Stuart to Gage, March 14, 1766, Gage Papers; *Newport Mercury,* January 13, 1766.

18. Pittman, *Present State,* pp. 37–38.

19. Memorial of Lieutenants Henry, Sedgwick, Ford, and Ensign Robinson, January 10, 1766, Gage Papers.

20. Pittman, *Present State,* pp. 40–41; Accounts, September 27, 1765, Treasury Papers, T.1/448:264. Sobym may have been hired from the convoy that passed Farmar at the Arkansas. Farmar to Gage, March 18, 1766. Gage Papers. On Morris's unsuccessful expedition see Howard H. Peckham, *Pontiac and the Indian Uprising* (Princeton, N.J.: 1947), pp. 256–60.

21. Stirling to Gage, October 18, 1765; Stirling to Gage, December 15, 1765, Gage Papers. Farmar to Stuart, December 16, 1765, in *The New Regime, 1765–1767,* ed. Clarence W. Alvord and C. E. Carter, Illinois Historical Collections, vol. 11 (Springfield, Ill., 1916), pp. 127–29.

22. Farmar to Treasury, December 16, 1765, Treasury Papers, T.1/437:370–72; Gage to Stuart, March 11, 1766, Gage Papers.

23. Farmar to Treasury, December 16, 1765, Treasury Papers, T.1/437:370–72.

24. Ibid.; Accounts, Treasury Papers, T.1/448:226; Farmar to Stuart, December 16, 1765, C.O. 5/67:33–35.

25. Farmar to Treasury, December 16, 1765, Treasury Papers, T.1/437:370–72; Aubry to Minister, March 12, 1766, in *New Regime,* ed. Alvord and Carter, p. 186; Farmar to Gage, December 16, 1765, Gage Papers.

26. Stirling to Gage, December 15, 1765, Gage Papers. Stirling was a few leagues north of New Orleans shortly after January 1, 1766: Capt. James Chisholm to Gage, Fort Bute, March 13, 1766, Gage Papers.

27. Harry Gordon, "Considerations on the Military and Political Situations," November 20, 1767, Sir Henry Clinton Papers, 4:32, William L. Clements Library, University of Michigan, Ann Arbor.
28. Pittman, *Present State,* pp. 42–50; Natalie Maree Belting, "The French Villages of the Illinois Country," *Canadian Historical Review* 24 (1943): 14–23; Jack M. Sosin, "The French Settlements in British Policy for the North American Interior, 1760–1774," *Canadian Historical Review* 39 (1958): 185–208; Villiers du Terrage, *Last Years,* p. 175.
29. Lieutenant James Eidingtown to ______, October 17, 1765, Chatham Papers, PRO 30/8, vol. 97, Public Record Office, London; Stirling to Gage, October 18, 1765, and Farmar to Gage, December 16, 1765, Gage Papers; Farmar to Treasury, December 16, 1765, Treasury Papers, T.1/437:370–72; Pittman, *Present State,* p. 45; Cession of Fort de Chartres, in *New Regime,* ed. Alvord and Carter, pp. 91–100.
30. Farmar to Gage, December 16, 1765; Lieutenant Alexander Fraser to Gage, December 16, 1765, Gage Papers.
31. Farmar to Gage, December 16, 1765; Pittman to Gage, December 17, 1765, Gage Papers; Accounts, Treasury Papers, T.1/437:373.
32. Farmar to Gage, December 19, 1765, Gage Papers.
33. Memorial to Gage, January 10, 1766, Gage Papers.
34. Gage to Farmar, March 12, March 14, 1766, Gage Papers. Farmar's expenditures even attracted the attention of the southern secretary, the earl of Shelburne, when they were reported to have reached £30,000. Benjamin Franklin to William Franklin, October 11, 1766, in *New Regime,* ed. Alvord and Carter, p. 400.
35. Farmar to Gage, March 18, 1766, Gage Papers. Proclamation, February 13, 1766, in *New Regime,* ed. Alvord and Carter, pp. 153–54.
36. Farmar to Gage, March 28, 1766, Gage Papers.
37. Jennings' Journal, in *New Regime,* ed. Alvord and Carter, p. 177; Meurin to Bishop Briand, March 23, 1767, ibid., p. 524.
38. Farmar to Gage, March 18, March 28, April 8, April 24, May 9, 1766, Gage Papers. Farmar to Stuart, December 16, 1765, C.O. 5/67:33–35; Farmar to Barrington, March 28, 1766, S.P. 41/25.
39. See my introduction to Pittman, *Present State,* xxix–xxxii; Farmar to Gage, March 18, 1766; Pittman to Gage, March 20, 1766, Gage Papers.
40. James Chisholm to Gage, March 13, 1766; Farmar to Gage, March 18, April 24, May 9, May 24, 1766, Gage Papers. On Reed see Shy, *Toward Lexington,* pp. 356–57.
41. Proceedings of the Court Martial in Reed to Gage, June 9, 1766; Pittman to Gage, June 18, 1766; Farmar to Gage, May 24, 1766, Gage Papers.
42. Pittman to Gage, June 18, 1766; Reed to Gage, June 19, 1766, Gage Papers.

V. Court Martial at Pensacola

1. The same might be said with regard to the more famous Major Robert Rogers. Shy, *Toward Lexington,* is more sensitive to the realities of the army in North America than Leach, *Roots of Conflict.*

2. Gage to Secretary at War, February 23, 1765, W.O. 1/6:120.

3. Bouquet to Gage, April 17, 1765, Bouquet Papers, Additional MSS 21637, British Library, London; Gage to Bouquet, May 15, 1765; May 23, 1765, Gage Papers.

4. Gage to Farmar, May 23, 1765; Bouquet to Farmar, May 23, 1765; Farmar to Gage, May 24, 1766, Gage Papers.

5. Bouquet to Gage, June 4, 1765, June 13, 1765, Bouquet Papers.

6. Simpson to Gage, August 25, 1765; Pilot to Gage, September 2, 1765; John Campbell to Gage, September 7, 1765; Johnstone to Gage, September 21, 1765; Wedderburn to Gage, n.d. (September 1765); Gage to Wedderburn, October 23, 1765, Gage Papers.

7. Gage to Reed, October 30, 1765, Gage Papers. Gage to Secretary at War, November 8, 1765, W.O. 1/6:299. Gage to Tayler, November 16, 17, 19, 1765, and January 3, 1766, Gage Papers. Gage to Secretary at War, December 21, 1765, W.O. 1/6:333.

8. Reed to Gage, June 19, 1766; Gage to Reed, September 15, 1766; Gage to Tayler, September 29, 1766; Gage to Reed and Gage to Pittman, October 6, 1766, Gage Papers.

9. Johnstone to Tayler, December 13, 1766 (two letters), Frederick Haldimand Papers, British Library, London.

10. M.P.A., pp. 405–9; Clarence E. Carter, ed., *The Correspondence of General Thomas Gage* (New Haven, Conn., 1931), 1:88, 2:342.

11. Fabel, *Bombast and Broadsides*, pp. 54, 56.

12. Tayler to Gage, September 25, 1766; Tayler to Gage, December 13, 1766; Haldimand to Gage, June 16, 1767, Gage Papers. Johnstone to Tayler, December 13, 1766, Haldimand Papers.

13. "The Accusations of Major Robert Farmar . . . against Lieutenant Alexander Maclellan," and Farmar to Tayler, February 4, 1767, Gage Papers.

14. Maclellan to Tayler, February 21, March 10, 1767, Gage Papers. Tayler to Maclellan, March 9, 1767, Haldimand Papers.

15. Pittman, *Present State*, p. xxiv; Haldimand to Gage, April 31 [*sic*], 1767, Gage Papers.

16. Robert R. Rea, "Brigadier Frederick Haldimand: The Florida Years," *Florida Historical Quarterly* 54 (1976): 512–19.

17. Haldimand's memorandum (*c.* March 28, 1767), Haldimand Papers. Haldimand to Gage, April 6, 1767, Gage Papers.

18. Haldimand to Gage, June 16, 1767, Haldimand Papers.

19. Farmar to Hutcheson, June 18, 1767, Haldimand Papers.

20. Gage to Haldimand, May 1, 1767; Gage to Pittman, May 31, 1767, Gage Papers.

21. Farmar to Hutcheson, June 18, 1767; Haldimand to Gage, June 16, June 17, 1767, Gage Papers. Gage to Haldimand, May 1, 1767, Haldimand Papers.

22. Farmar to Haldimand, June 30, 1767, Gage Papers.

23. Haldimand to Gage, June 30, 1767, Gage Papers.

24. Farmar to Haldimand, July 1, 1767; Browne to Haldimand, July 6, 1767, Haldimand Papers.

25. Gage to Haldimand, June 13 and September 5, 1767, Gage Papers. Gage to Barrington, August 31, 1767, in *Correspondence of Gage,* ed. Carter, 2:433.
26. Haldimand to Gage, September 1 and October 30, 1767; Marsh to Haldimand, November 19, 1767, Gage Papers. Pittman, *Present State,* p. xxxvi.
27. Haldimand to Gage, November 28, 1767, Gage Papers.
28. Sutherland to James Grant, October 1, 1767, Grant Papers, bundle 243, Ballindalloch Castle, Scotland. My thanks to Robin F. A. Fabel for this citation. Haldimand to Gage, December 21, 1767, Gage Papers.
29. Returns of deceased, July 25, 1765 to July 10, 1767, Haldimand Papers.
30. Farmar to Gage, November 28, 1767; Gage to Farmar, February 16, 1768, Gage Papers.
31. Gage to Barrington, January 23, 1768, in *Correspondence of Gage,* ed. Carter, 2:448. Gage to Haldimand, February 9, 1768, Gage Papers.
32. Haldimand to Gage, December 5, 1767, January 28, February 2, 1768; Haldimand to Tayler, September 15, 1767; Tayler to Haldimand, August 6, 1767, Haldimand Papers. Gage to Jenkins, May 5, 1767, Gage to Fuser, May 5, 1767, Gage to Haldimand, October 19, 1767, February 9, 1768; Phillips to Gage, June 15, *c.* July 14, December 7, 1767; Tayler to Gage, August 11, 1767; Hodgson to Gage, December 4, 1767; Haldimand to Gage, February 27, 1768; James Grant to Gage, July 30, 1767, Gage Papers.
33. Haldimand to Gage, April 29, 1768, Gage Papers.
34. Unless otherwise noted, all information regarding the trial is derived from the "Proceedings," W.O. 71/51:58–232.
35. Fort York was evacuated October 15, 1764, reoccupied 1766–67. See Rea, "The Trouble at Tombeckby."
36. Phynn to Sir William Johnson, April 15, 1768, *Mobile Register and Journal* 1, no. 13 (December 15, 1841): 2.
37. Accounts, Haldimand Papers, Additional MSS 21682/94:113, 154. Phillips to Gage, August 28, 1768, Gage Papers.
38. Haldimand to Gage, April 20, April 29, 1768, Gage Papers. Haldimand to Gage, September 28, 1768, Haldimand Papers. As the 15th Regiment was relieved of duty in North America in the summer of 1768, Gage ordered Pittman to report to New York as soon as the court martial was concluded, but there is no evidence that he did so. The 21st and 31st regiments were withdrawn from Pensacola to St. Augustine later in 1768, and Pittman probably returned directly to England from West or East Florida. Gage to Haldimand, April 29, June 27, 1768, Gage Papers. Pittman, *Present State,* p. xxxix.
39. Farmar to Haldimand, April 28, 1768, Gage Papers.
40. Haldimand to Farmar, August 21, 1768, in *Report on Canadian Archives, 1885,* ed. Douglas Brymner (Ottawa, 1886), p. 147. Farmar to Haldimand, August 30, 1768, Haldimand Papers.
41. Gage to Barrington, June 16, 1768, in *Correspondence of Gage,* ed. Carter, 2:475. Hutcheson to Farmar, August 24, 1768, Haldimand Papers. Charles Gould to Gage, August 10, 1768, W.O. 71/51 and Gage Papers.

42. Gage to Farmar, December 3, 1768, Gage Papers. Gage to Barrington, October 30, 1768, in *Correspondence of Gage*, ed. Carter, 2:498.
43. Gage to Barrington, February 4, 1769, Gage Papers and W.O. 1/8.
44. Farmar to Gage, April 14, 1769, Gage Papers.
45. Durnford to Haldimand, May 16, 1769, Haldimand Papers.
46. As evidenced by Durnford to Hillsborough, London, July 22, 1769, C.O. 5/114:325.
47. Gage to Bradshaw, May 12, 1769, in *Correspondence of Gage*, ed. Carter, 2:508. Ogle's date of rank was November 23, 1768: Barrington to Hillsborough, November 24, 1768, W.O. 25/143, and *Army Lists*. He was succeeded by Captain John Lind in 1771.
48. "The Memorial of Robert Farmar Late Major of His Majesty's 34 Regiment," C.O. 5/114:285–86. The memorial is undated but must have been written after December 1769, probably before March 1770. Farmar's statement that the court martial's decision was not public at the time of writing is ambiguous, for it was approved in London in 1768 and circulated in North America early in 1769. Farmar may simply have been protesting that it had not attracted any attention.

Captain John Eliot, R.N., was appointed governor in succession to Johnstone in March 1767, but he did not come to Pensacola until April 2, 1769; he committed suicide on May 2, 1769, so Farmar's application for the vacancy was not untimely. See Robert R. Rea, "John Eliot, Second Governor of British West Florida," *Alabama Review* 30 (1977): 243–65; Rea, "The Naval Career of John Eliot, Governor of West Florida," *Florida Historical Quarterly* 57 (1979): 451–67.
49. *Journal of the Commissioners for Trade and Plantations, 1768–1775* (London, 1920–38), p. 189.
50. The multiple complexities of Major Farmar's official financial transactions may be suggested by the entries in Treasury Papers, T.1/437 and T.1/440. Warrants in his name for £25,560 were submitted for payment between 1764 and 1768. R. C. Simmons and P. D. G. Thomas, eds., *Proceedings and Debates of the British Parliaments Respecting North America, 1754–1783* (New York, 1983), 1:469; 2:6, 256, 259, 416, 420, 531.
51. Gage to Bradshaw, May 12, 1769; Gage to Grey Cooper, November 10, 1770, in *Correspondence of Gage*, ed. Carter, 2:508, 562–63. Cooper to Gage, August 17, 1770, Gage Papers.
52. *London Magazine* 40 (February 1771): 104.
53. *Monthly Review* 44 (January 1771): 77; *Gentleman's Magazine* 41 (February 1771): 85; *Critical Review* 31 (January 1771): 80. No copy of the pamphlet is known to exist.
54. Pittman, *Present State*, pp. xl–xlvi. Like Farmar, Lieutenant Colonel Ralph Walsh and Philip Pittman, after withdrawing from West Florida, vainly sought colonial governorships. In 1770 Pittman resigned his commission in the 15th Regiment and sailed to India as a captain in the East India Company army. He died in India in 1775. Pittman's petition for the lieutenant governorship of Tobago, C.O. 5/114:185–86; Walsh's petition for the governorship of West Florida, C.O. 5/114:145–46.
55. Farmar's presence in Mobile is established by Fitz: Connor to Haldimand, February 19, 1771, Haldimand Papers.

VI. Planter and Politician

1. See Gold, *Borderland Empires.*
2. Farmar to Ellis, January 24, 1764, W.O. 1/49; certificate, November 29, 1768 Haldimand Papers; Add. MSS 21677, ff. 24–29, 108.
3. Haldimand to Farmar, January 23, 1769; Farmar to Haldimand, January 23, 1769; Haldimand to Nugent, February 10, 1769, Haldimand Papers.
4. Farmar to Wedderburn, April 19, 1765, and Contingent Account, Haldimand Papers.
5. Johnstone to Board of Trade, April 1, 1766, M.P.A., p. 456.
6. Jacqueline Olivier Vidrine, *Love's Legacy: The Mobile Marriages . . . 1724–1786* (Lafayette, La., 1985), p. 325 n. 2. *American State Papers, Class VIII, Public Lands* (Washington, D.C., 1832), 1:839.
7. Clinton N. Howard, *British Development of West Florida 1763–1769* (Berkeley, Calif., 1947), pp. 32, 52.
8. Council Minutes, April 2, 1765, M.P.A.E.D., 3:417; C.O. 5/602:437.
9. *Journal of the Committee for Trade and Plantations, 1764–1767,* May 8, 1764, p. 49. M. Browne to Board of Trade, February 1, 1768, M.P.A.E.D., 3:47.
10. Council Minutes, February 2, 1765, M.P.A.E.D., 3:411; Howard, *British Development of West Florida,* p. 56.
11. Council Minutes, February 6, April 12, 1765, M.P.A.E.D., 3:415, 417–18; Howard, *British Development of West Florida,* pp. 56, 63, 69; C.O. 5/605:276, 290.
12. Farmar to Haldimand, June 30, 1767, Haldimand Papers.
13. Robert R. Rea and Milo B. Howard, Jr., eds., *The Minutes, Journals, and Acts of the General Assembly of British West Florida* (University, Ala., 1979), pp. 3–5.
14. Johnstone to Board of Trade, October 22, 1766, M.P.A.E.D., 3:577–78.
15. Rea and Howard, *Minutes,* pp. 71–73.
16. Ibid., p. 142.
17. Ibid., pp. 159–73. In fact, this assembly did not meet again.
18. Ibid., p. 174; Rea, "John Eliot"; Rea, "The Naval Career of John Eliot, Governor of West Florida."
19. Depositions of Hartley and Kimbe, June 12, 1769, C.O. 5/577:357–74; M.P.A.E.D., 3:403–10.
20. Westropp to Browne, May 12, 1769, M.P.A.E.D., 3:389.
21. Browne to Hillsborough, June 14, 1769, M.P.A.E.D., 3:401.
22. Trial record, M.P.A.E.D., 3:431–39.
23. Browne to Hillsborough, July 26, 1769, M.P.A.E.D., 3:427–29; C.O. 5/586:257.
24. Petition of May 12, 1769, M.P.A.E.D., 3:372–76. Not surprisingly, Richard Hartley and William Kimbe signed a letter in support of Browne about the same time. M.P.A.E.D., 3:385–86.
25. The minutes of the fourth assembly do not list attendance, but in view of Farmar's prominence in the third general assembly, the absence of his name in the proceedings of its successor is strongly suggestive. Rea and Howard, *Minutes,* pp. 174–76.
26. M.P.A.E.D., 10:1637–40, 1645.
27. C.O. 5/577:197–98.

28. *Journal of the Commissioners for Trade and Plantations, 1768–1775*, p. 189; W.O. 64/10, 17/124.
29. Inventory, British West Florida Papers, General Land Grant Office, Record Group 49, Division D, National Archives, Washington, D.C. Council Minutes, April 24, 1769, in "Minutes of the Council of West Florida," ed. James A. Padgett, *Louisiana Historical Quarterly* 23 (1940): 366–67. C.O. 5/606:60.
30. C.O. 5/608:114–15; M.P.A.E.D., 10:160; Mrs. Dunbar [Eron] Rowland, "Mississippi's Colonial Population and Land Grants," Mississippi Historical Society *Publications*, Centenary Ser., no. 1 (1916), p. 413. On this region and Amos Ogden see Robin Fabel, "The Letters of R: The Lower Mississippi in the Early 1770s," *Louisiana History* 24 (1983): 402–27.
31. C.O. 5/608:260. Complications regarding this property may be traced in Council Minutes of August 28, 1777, and September 16, 1777, C.O. 5/631, and October 1, 1777, C.O. 5/635:26.
32. Farmar to Philip Livingston, January 2, 1778, British West Florida Papers, Land Grant Office.
33. Winston De Ville, ed., *English Land Grants in West Florida* (Ville Platte, La., 1986), pp. 5, 15, 30.
34. Durnford to Gage, January 20, 1770, Gage Papers.
35. Haldimand to Gage, June 27, 1770, December 28, 1771, Gage Papers.
36. Haldimand to Gage, June 12, 1771, Gage Papers.
37. Haldimand to Gage, August 4, 1771, Gage Papers.
38. Mrs. Dunbar [Eron] Rowland, "Peter Chester," Mississippi Historical Society *Publications*, no. 5 (1925), p. 135.
39. Rea and Howard, *Minutes*, pp. 244–46, 257.
40. Ibid., pp. 259, 264–71.
41. Ibid., pp. 272–73.
42. C.O. 5/608:433–34.
43. Audit Office Papers, 13/590–92, Public Record Office, London.
44. Farmar to Livingston, January 2, 1778, British West Florida Papers, Land Grant Office.
45. British West Florida Papers, General Land Grant Office, Record Group 49, Division D. Some names and locations in this document are illegible.
46. *Mobile Advertiser*, no. 211 (June 9, 1836), p. 1.
47. Council Minutes, May 16, 1774, C.O. 5/634:206; October 3, 1777, C.O. 5/635:30.
48. See J. Barton Starr, *Tories, Dons, and Rebels: The American Revolution in British West Florida* (Gainesville, Fla., 1976).
49. Council Minutes, March 10, 1778, C.O. 5/635:98–99.
50. Rea and Howard, *Minutes*, pp. 274–75.
51. Farmar Papers, Alabama Department of Archives and History, Montgomery.
52. Rea and Howard, *Minutes*, pp. 297–300, 314.
53. M.P.A.E.D., 8:245–58. Lucille Griffith, "Peter Chester and the End of British Empire in West Florida," *Alabama Review* 30 (1977): 14–33, offers a less sympathetic view of the opposition to the governor.

VII. Old Soldier at Home

1. James Adair, *Adair's History of the American Indians*, ed. Samuel Cole Williams (1775; reprint ed., New York, 1973), p. 308.
2. Fabel, *Bombast and Broadsides*, p. 33.
3. So with Adair's editor, S. C. Williams, *supra*, and with the oft-cited references to Peter J. Hamilton, *Colonial Mobile*, pp. 253–54. Dunbar Rowland, M.P.A., 1:7–8n, at least had doubts. Aubry, who is cited as the source of confusion, was quite clear: see Marc de Villiers du Terrage, *Les Dernièrs Années de la Louisiane Française* (Paris, 1904), p. 215, and *Last Years*, p. 247.
4. On the delicacy of service relationships see A. N. Gilbert, "Law and Honour among Eighteenth-Century British Army Officers," *Historical Journal* 19 (1976): 75–87.
5. Farmar to [Christopher Miller], April 22, 1768, Farmar Papers.
6. Embarkation orders, February 2, 1769, Haldimand Papers.
7. Miller to Ellis, February 21, 1766, Ellis MSS, Library of the Linnean Society, London; see also Jeremy Black and Robert R. Rea, eds., "Alabama in 1776," *Gulf Coast Historical Review* 3 (1987): 112–14.
8. See Robin F. A. Fabel, *The Economy of British West Florida, 1763–1783* (Tuscaloosa, Ala., 1988), p. 138. A year later, Miller was in London soliciting Ellis's support of his application for a land grant of 20,000 acres. He remarked that he had left fourteen Negroes working on his plantation in West Florida and that it was "the first rice plantation attempted by a natural born [British] subject in that province." Miller to Ellis, April 16, 1767, Ellis MSS.
9. See William S. Coker and Thomas D. Watson, *Indian Traders of the Southeastern Spanish Borderlands: Panton, Leslie and Company and John Forbes and Company, 1783–1847* (Pensacola, Fla., 1986).
10. Farmar to [Christopher Miller], April 22, 1768, Farmar Papers.
11. Inventory, British West Florida Papers, General Land Grant Office; Mary Farmar's claim, February 12, 1783, Audit Office Papers, 12/99:20; Peter J. Hamilton, *Colonial Mobile* (University, Ala., 1976), p. 254.
12. The marriage date of 1766 given in Billopp, *Thomas and Anne Billopp Farmar*, p. 102, is obviously in error; perhaps 1756? Ford to Farmar, December 10, 1764, Gage Papers, does not refer specifically to the son's birth, but only such an event or the family's very recent arrival would justify Ford's comment.
13. Farmar Papers; Billopp, *Thomas and Anne Billopp Farmar*, p. 80, incorrectly calls the second daughter Mary Elizabeth.
14. "A Register of Births and Christenings from 26th of June 1768 to the 10th of June 1770 in the Town and Garrison of Pensacola," M.P.A.E.D., 4:352.
15. Padgett, "Minutes," pp. 366–67; Council Minutes, November 5, 1776, C.O. 5/631.
16. See "Field Survey of the Riber Mobile . . . with the different settlements and lands marked thereon," in *Crown Collection of Photographs of American Maps*, ed. Archer E. Hulbert, ser. 3, nos. 91–95. The grant is dated September 14, 1769. The site is near the modern town of Stockton, Alabama.

17. All information regarding Farm Hall derives from the Inventory completed May 19, 1780, British West Florida Papers, unless otherwise noted.
18. John Stuart, in Stuart to Haldimand, May 15, 1771, Haldimand Papers, notes the paucity of settlement beyond Farmar's place.
19. Farmar to Mrs. Davis, February 22, 1776, C.O. 5/40:436-38.
20. On slavery in the colony see the fine chapter on the subject in Fabel, *Economy of British West Florida*, pp. 22–48.
21. Council Minutes, November 5, 1776, C.O. 5/631.
22. Farmar's slave Drummer was convicted of burglary and felony, August 24, 1770. Sentenced to be executed, he was pardoned by Governor Chester and ordered removed from the colony. Fabel, *Economy of British West Florida*, pp. 26–27; for other references to Farmar's slaves, see pp. 214, 226.
23. See Robert R. Rea, "Planters and Plantations in British West Florida," *Alabama Review* 29 (1976): 220–35.
24. Inventory, British West Florida Papers, General Land Grant Office.
25. Farmar to Major John Lind, February 21, 1776, C.O. 5/40:432–34.
26. Farmar to Mrs. Davis, February 22, 1776, C.O. 5/40:436.
27. Drummond and Cox to Barrington, May 1, 1769, W.O. 1/9; Colonel Frederick Cavendish to Messrs. Cox and Drummond, c. July 18, 1769, Miscellaneous War Office In-letters, W.O. 1/990. Like Gage, Cavendish was generous toward Farmar because West Florida was, financially, a hardship duty post.
28. Fabel, *Economy of British West Florida*, p. 157.
29. Farmar to Hillsborough, n.d. 1769, C.O. 5/114:285–86; Barrington to Colonial Office, November 23, 1768, W.O. 25/143.
30. Audit Office Papers, 12/99:20.
31. Vidrine, *Love's Legacy*, p. 377.
32. William Bartram, *The Travels of William Bartram*, ed. Francis Harper (New Haven, Conn., 1958), pp. 255–57, 278, 410.
33. Farmar to Lind, February 21, 1776, C.O. 5/40:432–34.
34. Ibid.
35. Farmar to Mrs. Davis, February 22, 1776, C.O. 5/40:436–38.

VIII. Farewell to British West Florida

1. Rea, "Brigadier Frederick Haldimand," pp. 528–29.
2. Farmar to Lind, February 21, 1776, C.O. 5/40:432–34.
3. Farmar to Mrs. Davis, February 22, 1776, C.O. 5/40:436–38.
4. For the war in West Florida see Robin F. A. Fabel, "West Florida and British Strategy in the American Revolution," in *Eighteenth-Century Florida and the Revolutionary South*, ed. Samuel Proctor (Gainesville, Fla., 1978), pp. 49–67; and Starr, *Tories, Dons, and Rebels*.
5. Francisco de Borja Medina Rojas, *José de Ezpeleta, Gobernador de la Mobila* (Seville, 1980), pp. 140 n. 6, 190.
6. Ibid., p. 141.

7. British West Florida Papers, General Land Grant Office. Gordon and McGillivray were among the few British Mobilians who actively cooperated with Ezpeleta at this time: Borja, *José de Ezpeleta,* pp. 160, 168.
8. Borja, *José de Ezpeleta,* pp. 159–60.
9. Ibid., pp. 162, 184ff.
10. Ibid., pp. 187–88 n. 100; Billopp, *Thomas and Anne Billopp Farmar,* pp. 80–81, 102–5; William S. Coker and Hazel P. Coker, *The Siege of Mobile, 1780, in Maps* (Pensacola, Fla., 1982), p. 107. Barde is reported to have been Swiss by birth, to have attended the Royal Military College at Woolwich, and to have been commissioned in 1774.
11. Borja, *José de Ezpeleta,* p. 429.
12. John W. Caughey, *Bernardo de Gálvez in Louisiana, 1776–1783* (1934; reprinted, Gretna, La., 1972), p. 206.
13. Billopp, *Thomas and Anne Billopp Farmar,* pp. 103–4.
14. January 8, 1781, in the *Army List;* variously January 18 and January 24, 1781, in W.O. 12/6998.
15. *Army List;* W.O. 25/16. Byrd (Bird) also had property in West Florida.
16. W.O. 12/6999.
17. *Army List,* 1792; Nesbitt W. Wallace, *A Regimental Chronicle and List of Officers of the 60th or the King's Royal Rifle Corps* (London, 1879); Billopp, *Thomas and Anne Billopp Farmar,* pp. 81, 90, where he is said to have retired from the army in 1789.
18. Billopp, *Thomas and Anne Billopp Farmar,* pp. 104–5.
19. Ibid., pp. 91–93.
20. Ibid., p. 80; William Panton to Elizabeth M. Farmar, May 31, 1800, John Forbes Papers, Mobile Public Library, Mobile, Alabama.
21. February 12, 1783, Audit Office Papers, 12/99:20.
22. Farmar Papers.
23. Panton to Elizabeth M. Farmar, May 31, 1800, Forbes Papers. Evidence of Elizabeth and Catherine's efforts in 1799–1800 in the Farmar Papers.
24. *American State Papers, Class VIII, Public Lands* (Washington, D.C., 1832), 1:601, 605, 741–42, 781–82, 839, 851. Alan V. Briceland, "Land, Law, and Politics on the Tombigbee Frontier, 1804," *Alabama Review* 33 (1980): 101–2. May W. McBee, ed., *The Natchez Court Records, 1767–1805* (Greenwood, Miss., 1953), p. 449.
25. Billopp, *Thomas and Anne Billopp Farmar,* pp. 80–81. Evidence of the efforts of the Vauberceys and other descendants to recover something of Major Farmar's estate in 1820–21 may be found in the Farmar file, Museum of the City of Mobile, Mobile, Alabama.
26. *U.S. Statutes at Large,* 6:761 (25th Cong., 3rd sess., chap. 105).

Bibliography

Manuscripts

Public Record Office, London

Admiralty Papers
Audit Office Papers
Chatham Papers
Colonial Office Papers
State Papers
Treasury Papers
War Office Papers

British Library, London

Henry Bouquet Papers
Frederick Haldimand Papers (copies in the Public Archives of Canada, Ottawa)

National Army Museum, London

Lord George Beauclerk Letterbook (original in the National Library of Scotland, Edinburgh)
Nicholas Delacherois Letters (typescript)
Hamilton, "A Brief Journal of the Reduction of Belleisle"

Library of the Linnean Society, London

John Ellis Papers

William L. Clements Library, University of Michigan, Ann Arbor

Jeffery Amherst Papers
Henry Clinton Papers
Thomas Gage Papers
David Wedderburn Papers

Alabama Department of Archives and History, Montgomery

Farmar Papers and memorabilia

Mississippi Department of Archives and History, Jackson

Mississippi Provincial Archives, English Dominion

Mobile Public Library, Mobile, Alabama

John Forbes Papers

Museum of the City of Mobile, Mobile, Alabama

Farmar file

Pennsylvania Historical Society, Philadelphia

William Penn Papers

Library of Congress, Washington, D.C.

Arthur Loftus Journal (with the Journal of Colonel Christopher French)

National Archives, Washington, D.C.

British West Florida Papers, General Land Grant Office

Primary Sources in Print

Periodicals and Newspapers

Boston Weekly News-letter
Critical Review
Gentleman's Magazine
London Magazine
Monthly Review
Newport Mercury

Books and Articles

Family and Early Life

Claypoole, James. "Extracts from the Letter-book of James Claypoole." *Pennsylvania Magazine of History and Biography* 10 (1886).

"A Letter from Doctor More." *Pennsylvania Magazine of History and Biography* 4 (1880).

Morris, Lewis. *The Papers of Lewis Morris.* Edited by William A. Whitehead. Collections of the New Jersey Historical Society, vol. 4. Newark, 1852.

New Jersey. *Archives of the State of New Jersey,* 1st ser. Paterson, N.J. 1895.

______. *Documents Relating to the Colonial History of New Jersey.* Trenton, N.J. 1891.

"A Partial List of the Families Who Arrived at Philadelphia between 1682 and 1687." *Pennsylvania Magazine of History and Biography* 8 (1884).

Penn, William. *The Papers of William Penn.* Edited by Richard Dunn and Mary Dunn. Philadelphia, 1981–.

Pennsylvania. *Minutes of the Provincial Council of Pennsylvania.* Harrisburg, Pa., 1851.

Military Career to 1763

An Account of the Expedition to Carthagena. London, 1743.

"The Battle of Fontenoy." *Journal of the Society for Army Historical Research* 6 (1927).

Colville, Charles. "Military Memoirs of Lieut.-General the Hon. Charles Colville." *Journal of the Society for Army Historical Research* 27 (1949).

Delacherois, Nicholas. "The Letters of Captain Nicholas Delacherois, 9th Regiment." Edited by S. G. P. Ward. *Journal of the Society for Army Historical Research* 51 (1973).

Entick, John. *The General History of the Late War.* London, 1764.

A Journal of the Expedition to Carthagena . . . in answer to . . . An Account of the Expedition. London, 1744.

A List of the General and Field Officers. London, 1754–93.

Pine, John. *A Representation of the Cloathing of His Majesty's Household, and of All the Forces upon the Establishments of Great Britain and Ireland.* London, 1742.
Smollett, Tobias. *The Works of Tobias Smollett.* New York, 1901.
Syrett, David, ed. *The Siege and Capture of Havana, 1762.* Navy Records Society Publications, no. 114. London, 1970.
Vernon, Edward. *The Vernon Papers.* Edited by E. M. Ranft. Navy Records Society Publications, no. 99. London, 1958.

West Florida and the Illinois

Adair, James. *Adair's History of the American Indians.* Edited by Samuel Cole Williams. New York, 1973.
Alvord, Clarence W., and Clarence E. Carter, eds. *The Critical Period, 1763–1765.* Illinois Historical Collections, vol. 10. Springfield, Ill., 1915.
———. *The New Regime, 1765–1767.* Illinois Historical Collections, vol. 11. Springfield, Ill., 1916.
American State Papers, Class VIII, Public Lands. Washington, D.C., 1832.
Bartram, William. *The Travels of William Bartram.* Edited by Francis Harper. New Haven, Conn., 1958.
Black, Jeremy, and Robert R. Rea, eds. "Alabama in 1766." *Gulf Coast Historical Review* 3 (1987).
Brasseaux, Carl A., ed. *A Comparative View of French Louisiana, 1699 and 1762.* Lafayette, La., 1979.
Brymner, Douglas, ed. *Report on Canadian Archives, 1885.* Ottawa, 1886.
Carter, Clarence E., ed. *The Correspondence of General Thomas Gage.* New Haven, Conn., 1931.
De Ville, Winston, ed. *English Land Grants in West Florida.* Ville Platte, La., 1986.
Hooker, Richard J., ed. *The Carolina Backcountry on the Eve of the Revolution: The Journal . . . of Charles Woodmason, Anglican Itinerant.* Chapel Hill, N.C., 1953.
Howard, Milo B., Jr., and Robert R. Rea. *The Memoir Justificatif of the Chevalier Montault de Monberaut.* University, Ala., 1965.
Journal of the Commissioners for Trade and Plantations. London, 1920–38.
McBee, May W., ed. *The Natchez Court Records 1767–1805.* Greenwood, Miss., 1953.
McMurtrie, Douglas C., ed. *A Broadside Issued at Mobile.* Privately printed, 1939.
Padgett, James A., ed. "Minutes of the Council of West Florida." *Louisiana Historical Quarterly* 23 (1940).
Pittman, Philip. *The Present State of the European Settlements on the Missisippi.* Edited by Robert R. Rea. Gainesville, Fla., 1973.
Rea, Robert R. "A New Letter from Mobile, 1763." *Alabama Review* 22 (1969).
Rea, Robert R., and Milo B. Howard, eds. *The Minutes, Journals, and Acts of the General Assembly of British West Florida.* University, Ala., 1979.
Rowland, Dunbar, ed. *Mississippi Provincial Archives, 1763–1766.* Vol. 1, *English Dominion.* Nashville, Tenn., 1911.

U.S. Statutes at Large.

Vidrine, Jacqueline O., ed. *Love's Legacy: The Mobile Marriages Recorded in French Transcribed, with Annotated Abstracts in English, 1724–1786.* Lafayette, La., 1985.

Secondary Works

Family and Early Life

Batinski, Michael C. *The New Jersey Assembly, 1738–1775.* Lanham, Md., 1987.

Benedict, William H. *New Brunswick in History.* New Brunswick, N.J., 1925.

______. "Thomas Farmar, First Mayor of New Brunswick, N.J." *Proceedings of the New Jersey Historical Society* 13 (1926).

Billopp, Charles Farmar. *A History of Thomas and Anne Billopp Farmar.* New York, 1907.

C., G. E. *The Complete Peerage.* London, 1945.

Cook, Lewis D. "Farmar of Ardavaleine, County Tipperary, Ireland, and of Whitemarsh, Philadelphia County, Pennsylvania." *Pennsylvania Genealogical Magazine* 21 (1956).

Fisher, Edgar J. *New Jersey as a Royal Province, 1738 to 1776.* New York, 1911.

Jenkins, Howard M. "The Family of William Penn." *Pennsylvania Magazine of History and Biography* 21 (1897).

Keen, Gregory B. "The Descendants of Joran Kyn, the Founder of Upland." *Pennsylvania Magazine of History and Biography* 4 (1880).

Keith, Charles P. *Chronicles of Pennsylvania.* Philadelphia, 1917.

Kemmerer, Donald L. *Path to Freedom: The Struggle for Colonial Self-Government in New Jersey, 1703–1776.* Princeton, N.J., 1940.

Monnette, Ora E. *First Settlers of ye Plantations of Piscataway and Woodbridge Olde East New Jersey, 1664–1714.* Los Angeles, 1930.

Morris, Ira K. *Morris's Memorial History of Staten Island, New York.* New York, 1898.

Nash, Gary B. *Quakers and Politics: Pennsylvania, 1681–1726.* Princeton, N.J., 1968.

Pomfret, John E. *Colonial New Jersey.* Princeton, N.J., 1973.

Purvis, Thomas L. "'High-Born, Long-Recorded Families': Social Origins of New Jersey Assemblymen, 1703 to 1776." *William and Mary Quarterly* 37 (1980).

______. *Proprietors, Patronage, and Paper Money.* New Brunswick, N.J., 1986.

Sheridan, Eugene R. *Lewis Morris.* Syracuse, N.Y., 1981.

Stephen, Leslie, and Sidney Lee, eds. *Dictionary of National Biography.* London, 1885–1901.

Wall, John P. *The Chronicles of New Brunswick, New Jersey, 1667–1931.* New Brunswick, N.J., 1931.

Military Career to 1763

Atkinson, C. T. "Jenkins' Ear, the Austrian Succession War, and the 'Forty-five.'" *Journal of the Society for Army Historical Research* 22 (1943–44).

Baldry, W. Y., and A. S. White. "Gooch's American Regiment of Foot, 1739–1742." *Journal of the Society for Army Historical Research* 16 (1937).

Bates, Albert C., ed. *The Two Putnams: Israel and Rufus in the Havana Expedition, 1762, and in the Mississippi River Exploration, 1772–73.* Hartford, Conn., 1931.

Beatson, Robert. *Naval and Military Memoirs of Great Britain from 1728 to 1783.* London, 1804.

Brodigan, F. *Historical Records of the Twenty-eighth North Gloucestershire Regiment.* London, 1884.

Cannon, Richard. *Historical Record of the Nineteenth Regiment of Foot.* London, 1848.

———. *Historical Records of the Twenty-second, the Cheshire Regiment of Foot.* London, 1849.

Charteris, Evan. *William Augustus Duke of Cumberland: His Early Life and Times.* London, 1913.

Clowes, William Laird. *The Royal Navy.* London, 1898.

Creswell, John. *Generals and Admirals: The Story of Amphibious Command.* Westport, Conn., 1976.

Devine, Joseph A. "The British North American Colonies in the War of 1739–1748." Ph.D. dissertation, University of Virginia, 1968.

Ferrar, M. L. *Historical Record of the Green Howards.* London, 1911.

———. *Officers of the Green Howards.* London, 1920.

Foote, William A. "The Pennsylvania Men of the American Regiment." *Pennsylvania Magazine of History and Biography* 87 (1963).

Fortescue, John. *A History of the British Army.* London, 1910.

Gilbert, A. N. "Law and Honour among Eighteenth-Century British Army Officers." *Historical Journal* 19 (1976).

Green Howards' Gazette.

Harkness, Albert. "Americanism and Jenkins' Ear." *Mississippi Valley Historical Review* 37 (1950).

Hart, Francis Russell. *The Siege of Havana, 1762.* Boston, 1931.

Hebbert, F. J. "The Belle-Ile Expedition of 1761." *Journal of the Society for Army Historical Research* 64 (1986).

Houlding, J. A. *Fit for Service: The Training of the British Army, 1715–1795.* Oxford, 1981.

Jones, Alfred. "The American Regiment in the Carthagena Expedition." *Virginia Magazine of History and Biography* 30 (1922).

Keppel, Sonia. *Three Brothers at Havana, 1762.* Salisbury, England, 1981.

Leach, Douglas E. *Arms for Empire: A Military History of the British Colonies in North America, 1607–1763.* New York, 1973.

———. "The Cartagena Expedition, 1740–42, and Anglo-American Relations." In *Adapting to Conditions: War and Society in the Eighteenth Century,* edited by Maarten Ultee. Tuscaloosa, Ala., 1986.

———. *Roots of Conflict: British Armed Forces and Colonial Americans, 1677–1763.* Chapel Hill, N.C., 1986.

Lydenberg, Henry M. *Archibald Robertson, Lieutenant-General Royal Engineers: His Diaries and Sketches in America.* New York, 1930.

McNeill, John R. "The Ecological Basis of Warfare in the Caribbean, 1700–1804," In *Adapting to Conditions: War and Society in the Eighteenth Century,* edited by Maarten Ultee. Tuscaloosa, Ala., 1986.

Noakes, George. *A Historical Account of the Services of the 34th and 55th Regiments.* Carlisle, England, 1875.

Pocock, Tom. "The Capture of Havana, 1762." *History Today* 12 (1962).

Powell, Geoffrey. *The Green Howards.* London, 1968.

Richmond, Herbert W. *The Navy in the War of 1739–1748.* Cambridge, England, 1920.

Sutherland, David. *Tried and Valiant: The History of the Border Regiment.* London, 1972.

Syrett, David. "The British Landing at Havana: An Example of an Eighteenth-Century Combined Operation." *Mariner's Mirror* 55 (1967).

"Uniforms of the Thirty-fourth Regiment of Foot from 1702 to 1914." *Border Magazine* 2 (1951).

Whitworth, Rex. *Field Marshal Lord Ligonier.* Oxford, 1958.

Woodfine, P. L. "The War of Jenkins' Ear: A New Voice in the Wentworth-Vernon Debate." *Journal of the Society for Army Historical Research* 65 (1987).

West Florida and the Illinois

Alden, John R. *General Gage in America.* Baton Rouge, La., 1948.

______. *John Stuart and the Southern Colonial Frontier.* Ann Arbor, Mich., 1944.

Belting, Natalie Maree. "The French Villages of the Illinois Country." *Canadian Historical Review* 24 (1943).

Borja, Francisco de Medina Rojas. *José de Ezpeleta, Gobernador de la Mobila.* Seville, 1980.

Briceland, Alan V. "Land, Law, and Politics on the Tombigbee Frontier, 1804." *Alabama Review* 33 (1980).

Caughey, John W. *Bernardo de Gálvez in Louisiana, 1776–1783.* 1934. Reprint. Gretna, La., 1972.

Coker, William S., and Hazel P. Coker. *The Siege of Mobile, 1780, in Maps.* Pensacola, Fla., 1982.

Coker, William S., and Thomas D. Watson. *Indian Traders of the Southeast Spanish Borderlands: Panton, Leslie and Company and John Forbes and Company, 1783–1847.* Pensacola, Fla., 1986.

Fabel, Robin F. A. *Bombast and Broadsides: The Lives of George Johnstone.* Tuscaloosa, Ala., 1987.

______. *The Economy of British West Florida, 1763–1783.* Tuscaloosa, Ala., 1988.

______. "The Letters of R: The Lower Mississippi in the Early 1770s." *Louisiana History* 24 (1983).

______. "West Florida and British Strategy in the American Revolution." In *Eighteenth-Century Florida and the Revolutionary South,* edited by Samuel Proctor. Gainesville, Fla., 1978.

Gold, Robert L. *Borderland Empires in Transition: The Triple-Nation Transfer of Florida.* Carbondale, Ill., 1969.

Griffith, Lucille. "Peter Chester and the End of British Empire in West Florida." *Alabama Review* 30 (1977).

Haffner, Gerald O. "Major Arthur Loftus' Journal of the Proceedings of His Majesty's Twenty-second Regiment up the River Mississippi in 1764." *Louisiana History* 20 (1979).

Hamilton, Peter J. *Colonial Mobile.* Reprint. University, Ala., 1976.

Howard, Clinton N. *The British Development of West Florida, 1763–1769.* Berkeley, Calif., 1947.

———. "The Military Occupation of British West Florida, 1763." *Florida Historical Quarterly* 17 (1938–39).

Johnson, Cecil. *British West Florida, 1763–1783.* New Haven, Conn., 1943.

Peckham, Howard H. *Pontiac and the Indian Uprising.* Princeton, N.J., 1947.

Price, Charles L., and Claude C. Sturgill. "The Role of the British Navy in the Landing in West Florida in 1763 as Revealed in the Letters of Captain William Bayne." *Alabama Review* 30 (1977).

Rea, Robert R. "Assault on the Mississippi: The Loftus Expedition, 1764." *Alabama Review* 26 (1973).

———. "Brigadier Frederick Haldimand: The Florida Years." *Florida Historical Quarterly* 54 (1976).

———. "Graveyard for Britons: West Florida, 1763–81." *Florida Historical Quarterly* 47 (1969).

———. "Lieutenant Colonel James Robertson's Mission to the Floridas, 1763." *Florida Historical Quarterly* 53 (1974).

———. "John Eliot, Second Governor of British West Florida." *Alabama Review* 30 (1977).

———. "Military Deserters from British West Florida." *Louisiana History* 9 (1968).

———. "The Naval Career of John Eliot, Governor of West Florida." *Florida Historical Quarterly* 57 (1979).

———. "Planters and Plantations in British West Florida." *Alabama Review* 29 (1976).

———. "Outpost of Empire: David Wedderburn at Mobile." *Alabama Review* 7 (1954).

———. "The Trouble at Tombeckby." *Alabama Review* 21 (1968).

Rowland, Mrs. Dunbar [Eron]. "Mississippi's Colonial Population and Land Grants." Mississippi Historical Society *Publications,* Centenary Ser., no. 1 (1916).

———. "Peter Chester . . . 1770–1781." Mississippi Historical Society *Publications,* no. 5 (1925).

Shy, John. *Toward Lexington: The Role of the British Army in the Coming of the American Revolution.* Princeton, N.J., 1965.

Sosin, Jack M. "The French Settlements in British Policy for the North American Interior, 1760–1774." *Canadian Historical Review* 39 (1958).

Starr, J. Barton. *Tories, Dons, and Rebels: The American Revolution in British West Florida.* Gainesville, Fla., 1976.

Thomas, Daniel H. "Fort Toulouse." *Alabama Historical Quarterly* 22 (1960).
Villiers du Terrage, Marc de. *Les Dernièrs Années de la Louisiane Française.* Paris, 1904.
______. *The Last Years of French Louisiana.* Edited by Hosea Phillips, Carl A. Brasseaux, and Glenn R. Conrad. Lafayette, La., 1982.
Wallace, Nesbitt W. *A Regimental Chronicle and List of Officers of the 60th or the King's Royal Rifle Corps.* London, 1879.

Index